LOVE
ACROSS
BORDERS

LOVE
ACROSS
BORDERS

Passports, Papers, and Romance in a Divided World

ANNA LEKAS MILLER

ALGONQUIN BOOKS OF CHAPEL HILL 2023

Published by

ALGONQUIN BOOKS OF CHAPEL HILL
Post Office Box 2225
Chapel Hill, North Carolina 27515-2225

an imprint of Workman Publishing Co., Inc.
a subsidiary of Hachette Book Group, Inc.
1290 Avenue of the Americas
New York, New York 10104

Printed in the United States of America.
Design by Steve Godwin.

The publisher is not responsible for websites (or their content) that are not owned
by the publisher.

Library of Congress Cataloging-in-Publication Data

Names: Lekas Miller, Anna, 1990- author.
Title: Love across borders : passports, papers, and romance in a divided world /
    Anna Lekas Miller.
Description: First Edition. | Chapel Hill, North Carolina : Algonquin Books of Chapel
    Hill, 2023. | Includes bibliographical references. | Summary: "Love Across Borders
    takes readers through contentious frontiers around the world to reveal the widespread
    prejudicial laws intent on dividing us. Anna Lekas Miller tells her own gripping story of
    meeting Salem Rizk in Istanbul, where they were reporting on the Syrian civil war. But
    when Turkey started cracking down on refugees, Salem, who is Syrian, wasn't allowed
    to stay there, nor could he safely return to Syria. In this look at the global immigration
    crisis, Lekas Miller interweaves love stories similar to her own with a study of the history
    of passports, the legacy of colonialism, and the discriminatory laws shaping how people
    move through the world every day"—Provided by publisher.
Identifiers: LCCN 2022061160 | ISBN 9781643752334 (Hardcover) |
    ISBN 9781643755229 (eBook)
Subjects: LCSH: Border security—Case studies. | Love—Political aspects. |
    International travel regulations. | Passports—Political aspects. | Statelessness. |
    Xenophobia. Classification: LCC JV6225 .L45 2023 |
    DDC 323.6/709—dc23/eng/20230118
LC record available at https://lccn.loc.gov/2022061160

10 9 8 7 6 5 4 3 2 1
First Edition

To everyone who has ever fought or is currently fighting borders to be with the people they love.

CONTENTS

LOVE ACROSS BORDERS

PROLOGUE: AN INDECENT PROPOSAL

I had only known Salem for one week before I accidentally proposed to him.

"You know," I said, flirtatiously perching myself on the edge of his sofa, an IKEA foldout couch with a quintessential bachelor pad aroma of cigarette smoke and spilled alcohol, "I wouldn't mind marrying someone so that they could have a US passport."

In my defense, we had hit it off. A friend had put us in touch when I told her that I was travelling to Istanbul and wanted to meet other journalists. According to her, Salem was "the guy" for all things Syria, a confirmed badass known for filming nail-biting footage of the front lines of the war and for smooth-talking jihadists whenever another journalist ran into a problem. He was a staple of the freelance journalism community, a motley crew of rogue brothers and sisters that drank like sailors and had each other's backs as they dipped in and out of conflict zones. As a young reporter, I was captivated by their courage and camaraderie.

Growing up in the United States at a time when the Middle East was thought of as a universal enemy, I knew how important it was to capture the realities of war and show it to the world. Forever wars were justified as patriotism and then forgotten about, as if invading Iraq and Afghanistan didn't inevitably kill hundreds of thousands of innocent people who had nothing to do with the so-called War on Terror. I took it personally. I am Lebanese-American on my mother's side, and always felt a little bit closer to the people who were living under the bombs than the people who were dropping them. I started writing because I wanted people to know that these wars weren't over, and that both American intervention and indifference were killing people. I wanted people to give a fuck.

Eventually I became a journalist. It felt like the best way to fuse my writing with my desire to inform and see the world. The minute that I decided that was what I was going to do, I couldn't imagine doing anything else. Now, I had just turned twenty-five and had come to Istanbul to meet Syrian activists who still believed in the revolution and refugees who had recently escaped conflict zones. I wanted to talk to Turkish anarchists trying to change politics, artists who were inspired by the political changes happening around them, and anyone else who would take the time to have a coffee with me and tell me their stories. Salem was exactly the kind of person that I needed to know.

"Let's we meet in Taksim," he said, suggesting that we enjoy the city's nightlife. He was calling me from Şanlıurfa, a small city near the Syrian border, better known for grooming hardline Islamists than free-flowing alcohol and all-night parties. He had been researching a story about women who had escaped ISIS-held territories only to find themselves pregnant with the fighters' children. Needless to say, he was eager to blow off some steam.

At first sight, Salem seemed to ooze machismo almost too effortlessly, with slicked-back black hair and a fitted leather jacket even though the late summer air hung thick with humidity. He flicked a cigarette into the street as he told me he had a bar in mind, casually mentioning that he had recently almost been kidnapped in Syria. I was annoyed. War correspondents seem to always think that their frontline stories would make young journalists want to sleep with them, and while I'm sure it often works, something about war as a seduction tactic made me uncomfortable. But the more we talked, the more I felt drawn to him, the tough guy façade falling away as he told me stories of his favorite reporting trips and his chosen family of journalists in Istanbul. He affectionately called them "the fuckers."

"You have got to meet the fuckers," he said, enthusiastically slamming his glass on the table. "My fucker Javier? He taught me how to use a camera," he whooped. "My fucker Andrea? That fucker is my wife! We shared a room in Syria together for more than a year. What a fucker."

I couldn't help laughing at the way he talked about his friends. He was both loving and irreverent, praising them for everything from being the world's best wingmen to watching out for him when he took long trips back to Syria. Before long, it felt as if we had always known each other, stumbling over ourselves laughing through Istanbul's back alleys, popping into nightclubs to dance to cheesy pop songs on sticky floors, taking breaks to suck on cigarettes outside, babbling about our hopes and dreams with drunken enthusiasm.

"When I was eight years old, I wanted to be an international thief," I told him, blowing cigarette smoke into the humid summer air, eager to show him that I was capable of being an international woman of mystery. "Mostly I just wanted a life of interesting travel."

His eyes glistened with the mischievous delight of discovering a long-lost partner in crime.

"You're fucking crazy and I love it," he said, pulling me toward him. He tasted like nicotine and a promise of adventure.

Our judgment might have been clouded by tequila and pheromones, but it was clear from the start that we were cut from the same cloth, two adrenaline junkies who wanted to see the world and be the ones to witness and document history. We both had an endless list of stories that we wanted to cover and places that we wanted to see, driven by a sense of urgency that these stories mattered. There was only one difference. I had a US passport and could travel as I pleased. Salem was from Syria and, largely for that reason, was stuck in the Middle East.

So, one week later, when the accidental proposal fell out of my mouth, his response caught me off guard.

"No, I will not be do this," he said, in his imperfect but determined English. He suddenly became serious for the first time since we met.

"I will not marry with you until my passport gives me the same rights as your passport."

I was mortified. I had not intended to propose to *him*—we had only just met. We were still lounging around his apartment late into the morning, ignoring our deadlines and responsibilities in favor of long, meandering conversations and bouts of more raucous activities. It was the short but delicious window of the classic fling, where every moment spent together is a moment suspended in time, lighthearted and untethered to the realities of the world, in part because of the mutual understanding that it is only temporary.

It was too early for any kind of commitment. It was definitely too early to suggest marriage fraud.

Also, in what world did he imagine this happening? As a US citizen, I could breeze through the passport control gates of airports around the world with barely a glance at my documents. As a Syrian, Salem could go to a grand total of twenty-nine countries without a visa—a list that was getting smaller as more and more people fled the war, and more and more countries closed their doors to refugees. If Salem—or any Syrian passport holder for that matter—wants to expand their world even by one country, they have to fill out numerous forms, promising not to overstay their welcome, and pay hundreds of dollars to consular officers and visa processing centers. The refusal rate is high and there are no refunds.

It was the reason that Syrians—and others from similarly war-torn countries—were starting to gather in Istanbul, meeting smugglers who claimed that they could get them to Europe for a price. While it is safe to say that most of them would prefer to travel legally—it is less deadly and significantly cheaper than paying a smuggler—countries like Germany and the United Kingdom rarely gave visas to anyone who couldn't prove that they wouldn't stay, and people fleeing a war typically don't have time to wait around to see if they will be the exception. So, more and more people had started taking matters into their own hands, purchasing bright orange lifejackets from sporting supply shops, using Google Maps to navigate the stretch of sea that separates the westernmost point of the Turkish coastline from the nearest Greek island.

But taking matters into your own hands could have deadly consequences. Just a few days before I met Salem, photojournalist Nilüfer Demir captured the moment that three-year-old Aylan Kurdi's lifeless body washed ashore on a Turkish beach, showing the world exactly what fleeing a war looks like today. It was easy to imagine Kurdi's mother dressing him in a red sweater and little blue shoes, taking him in her arms as they boarded a rickety fishing boat, hoping to reach the Greek island of Kos and start a new life. Now his sweater was matted against his body with salt water. If Kurdi's family had been allowed to board a plane, he would probably still be alive today.

For me, the logic was simple. Marrying someone for a passport was a way to balance out a fundamentally unbalanced world.

For Salem, it meant accepting that the world had to be this way in the first place.

––––––––

I could not have known when I first met Salem that our story would take me on a journey into the lives of other people who were fighting to be together in a world divided by passports and papers. As I traveled around Turkey—first to the Syrian border, where I met people who had left the war behind mere days before, and then to the coastal city of Izmir, where I spent time with others who were waiting to hear from smugglers when they, too, would board rickety boats across the sea—I was often struck by how much we had in common. On my first trip to Gaziantep, a mid-sized Turkish city about an hour's drive away from the Syrian border, a friend of a friend generously invited me for dinner. When he told me that he was making fasooliyeh, a Syrian stew of green beans and meat bathed in tomato sauce flavored with garlic and coriander, I immediately felt nostalgic. It was almost identical to the recipe that my Lebanese family in the United States made—and had been my favorite when I was a child.

"I can't believe you're making fasooliyeh," I said, smiling. I always enjoyed making small talk about food before interviews—a ritual that, in the Middle East, can go on for hours.

"You know, us Syrians and Lebanese—we have pretty much the same food," he said, spooning a heaping portion onto my plate. We both associated the same flavors with home—and yet, he was a refugee and I was the Western journalist interviewing him, simply because my family had left the Middle East several generations ago and his had not. It felt so random and unfair, that his friends were selling all their belongings to pay a smuggler to take them to Greece, while most of mine had the entire world open to them.

"I'm considering going to Europe," he said, suddenly. "Do you think I should?"

I never knew how to answer these kinds of questions. Journalists are told not to get involved in the lives of people that they interview, but sometimes an interview is a conversation, and a conversation is a connection. It is difficult to not feel as if you are suddenly involved in their story as well. Newscasters were fretting over the fact that more and more people were making the journey, wringing their hands over the so-called "refugee crisis," all the while missing the point that the crisis was not caused by the refugees, but by the borders that made them into refugees in the first place. Meanwhile more and more people were packing their bags, casually asking one another "When do you travel?" as if they were going on a short trip and would be back the following week.

As I gathered the stories for this book, I traced these journeys in other parts of the world, as well. I started in the Middle East, with places that were familiar to me—such as Syria, Lebanon, and Palestine—but quickly noticed that this theme of passports and papers, the worlds they open and the worlds they close, was playing out everywhere. It was a common topic—even a source of gallows humor in the Middle East—but it was also the reason that more and more people were fleeing countries like Honduras and Guatemala and taking harrowing trips through Mexico to reach the United States, or being smuggled across Africa through the Sahara Desert in hopes of reaching peace and prosperity in Europe. Meanwhile, immigrant communities in the United States and Europe also were carrying the burden of borders, long after they had crossed them. Pieces of paper could make the difference between a family staying together or being torn apart.

At first, I was interested in passports—the way that the documents we are born with can determine whether we are considered an expat or an immigrant, a migrant or a refugee. But the more I fell in love with Salem, the more I grew curious about how these documents shape our love stories. What does it mean to fall in love in a world that is divided by passports and papers? When I was feeling romantic, I thought about the love stories that are set in motion by someone moving to another part of the world—two people who would have never met one another had they not been displaced, or who grew closer as they followed one another into the unknown. Other times, I ruminated on what happens when borders get in the way.

———

In Istanbul, it was easy to pretend that the world had no borders. Salem and I got to know each other over long, meandering walks along the Bosphorus, marveling at the way its sparkling emerald waters swirled together, one continent bleeding into another without so much as a signpost or border guard to delineate where one ended and the other began. Often, Istanbul is a victim of tired clichés about what happens when the East meets the West, but its geography truly creates a meeting place unlike any other. Visitors are known for gawking at the way religious women swoosh through conservative neighborhoods in black abayas while girls in crop tops sip cocktails just up the street, but the city's mix of cultures and exchange of ideas goes far beyond what women choose to wear and who does and doesn't drink alcohol. It is a place where Islamic scholars can discuss the merits of political Islam in mosques designed by the Ottomans and secular activists can debate the future of democracy in cafes once frequented by James Baldwin and Leon Trotsky. It is a prestigious international capital, attracting everyone from Vladimir Putin to Beyoncé. It is a melting pot of political exiles and refugees, the singsong notes of Syrian Arabic and Farsi blending with the rich baritones of Kurdish and Urdu.

For Salem and me, it gave us a place to meet—and fall in love. As two journalists fascinated by each other's worlds, it was the perfect place to exchange ideas, unencumbered by the fact that I was an expat, while he was a refugee. I told him about what it felt like to be Arab-American after the September 11 attacks. He told me stories of living through the US invasion of Iraq and witnessing the beginnings of the Syrian revolution.

"When I was twelve, I wrote a letter to George Bush, begging him not to go to war in Iraq," I told him, eager to show him that not all Americans were war-mongering bigots who wanted to bulldoze the Middle East. He smiled at the image of a twelve-year-old American girl fervently believing that one letter from a middle schooler could stop a war.

"I was arrested by the Americans," he said, as casually as if he had been sharing that he had once been caught shoplifting as a teenager.

I quickly learned that Salem was no stranger to state violence. He is Syrian, but grew up in Baghdad, living through the US invasion of Iraq and the brutal sectarian war that followed. As if living through one civil war was not enough, he moved to Syria a few years later only to be arrested again, this time by the Syrian regime. For two years, he disappeared into Syrian president Bashar al-Assad's jails, cut off from everyone he knew apart from his childhood best friend, Musab. They were bound, shackled, and then shuttled between prisons whose names alone evoked stories of men and women being tortured with boiling water and zaps of electricity, or raped. Sometimes he was held in cells that were so overcrowded that the men had to sleep physically on top of one another. Other times he was held by himself in a cell so small that he could barely move.

Still, he somehow managed to conjure up funny stories from this time—something I later realized was a survival skill as much as it was a coping mechanism. One of his favorites to tell was of him and Musab, blindfolded, forced to the ground and certain that they would be lashed by prison guards at any minute. Salem, sensing that Musab was next to him, whispered: "Hey—What do you think Paris Hilton is doing right now?"

Most people would have been eager to leave these traumas in the past, but Salem was not most people. Instead, he spun them into stories, using his experiences to shed light on why Syrians were continuing to fight for freedom in spite of the regime that tried to keep them silent. He knew smugglers and dissidents, revolutionaries and jihadists. He had an encyclopedic knowledge of the history of the Middle East and could talk for hours on the minutiae of the battles that had shaped the region.

It was all incredibly hot.

When Salem and I first met late in 2015, it felt as if Istanbul was insulated from the types of violence that people in other parts of the region were fleeing. As time went on, more and more of these stories crept closer and closer to the city that I was starting to call home. A suicide bomber exploded himself in Sultanahmet, shocking tourists visiting the Hagia Sophia and the Blue Mosque. While Turks are unfortunately no strangers to sporadic suicide attacks, largely from Leftist political groups targeting police officers, ISIS claimed responsibility for this attack—leaving many wondering if the extremist group would stake its claim in Turkey. Next, there was an attempted coup—an insurrection meant to unseat the

Turkish government and throw the country into chaos in a violent night of whirring military helicopters and sporadic shooting. Ultimately, the coup failed—but the city changed for good. Everyone was suspect, and almost everyone I had ever interviewed there—from a university professor who frequently spoke out against the government's authoritarian tendencies to a fortune teller who had predicted the coup from a soldier's tea leaves—was called in for questioning. Every night, there was a rally in Taksim Square, nationalists and frightened citizens alike waving Turkish flags and chanting—the display of loyalty for Prime Minister Recep Tayyip Erdoğan and the Turkish state was an Orwellian performance of nationalism for the sake of survival.

It became more and more difficult to be a journalist by the day. Turkish journalists who didn't work for the government-aligned papers were called in for questioning, scrutinized, and surveilled for even a hint of disloyalty. Sources would only speak on the condition of anonymity, paranoid that their words could be twisted into support for the coup's plotters. Even foreign correspondents—accustomed to a privileged position above the fray of the conflicts that they observed—found themselves the objects of suspicion, accused of being spies with foreign agendas. Frustrated with how nearly impossible it was to report on the country with any accuracy, many packed up their bags and left.

Many of our Syrian friends wanted to leave, too—but unlike the journalists, most did not have the freedom to pack up and fly to a new country of their choosing. Long before the attempted coup, many had started slowly saving up the thousands of dollars needed to pay a smuggler for a spot on a flimsy raft or rickety boat to Greece, fully aware of the risks that it entailed. Rumors were circulating that the Turkish coast guard was going to start cracking down on the smuggling route, leaving them stuck in a country that might also descend into a civil war. I had interviewed dozens of people preparing to make the trip before, but seeing my friends contemplate such a dangerous journey made me feel uniquely helpless. All I could do was press money into their hands to make sure they bought a high-quality lifejacket and ask them to call me the minute they arrived.

Nevertheless, Salem and I had no plans to leave—largely because we had nowhere else to go. Salem had no interest in being a refugee, and I had no interest in living anywhere without him. Istanbul was our home, the place that allowed us to fall in love without caring who we were, or where we were from. Everything might be crumbling around us, but we would always be at home arm in arm, looking out over the turquoise waters of the Bosphorus, marveling at the way the water swirled together, where his world met mine in the only city on Earth where our love story was possible.

The city was ours. Until the day it wasn't.

————

"I'm being banned from Turkey," Salem's voice came in flat, without so much as a greeting.

I was in my friend's living room when I got the call. Salem had just spent the past two weeks in Iraq filming the US-backed military offensive to take back Mosul from ISIS, and I was eagerly awaiting his return after a particularly tumultuous time apart. We were used to communicating frequently whenever we were away from one another, but Salem rarely had cell phone reception on the front lines of Mosul. I distracted myself from imagining how an ISIS car bomb could swallow a convoy of journalists by spending long hours with friends, cooking elaborate meals and playing board games with them while we waited out a snowstorm together. We thought it would be a quiet beginning to the new year.

Instead, an ISIS shooter dressed as Santa Claus stormed an Istanbul nightclub on New Year's Eve, starting 2017 by opening fire on more than 700 people whose only options to survive were to play dead or leap into the freezing Bosphorus. Even though I was far away from the nightclub, Salem assumed the worst and chased a signal through the abandoned streets of Eastern Mosul until he could get ahold of me. Neither of us imagined then that the danger that would change our lives would be lurking at passport control, a few days later.

"What are they going to do?" I rationalized, energetically pacing around my friend's apartment. It felt as if we were surrounded by disasters, first a war, next a terrorist attack that happened too close for comfort, now Salem was being told that he couldn't come home. "Kick out a Syrian refugee that has nowhere to go?"

Salem was not the first journalist to be kicked out of Turkey. Dozens of other foreign correspondents had recently been either detained or denied entry, typically after reporting from the Kurdish areas in the Eastern part of the country. But while other journalists wore their deportations with a badge of honor—a sign that they had committed crimes of journalism worthy of exile—their definition of exile was setting themselves up in a comfortable city like Athens or Berlin and continuing their work as usual.

Meanwhile Salem was already living in exile—and had no way of escaping to a safer city in Europe or North America, as some of our friends did. Worse yet, if some bureaucrat decided that he should be sent back to Syria, he would certainly be killed. It was dangerous for anyone. But with Salem's track record of being wanted by the regime and making films critical of ISIS along with numerous other jihadist groups, he wouldn't stand a chance.

I leaned out of the window and uncharacteristically lit a cigarette, a habit I previously had only indulged in socially. Istanbul was supposed to be our romantic sanctuary, where it didn't matter that I was an expat while he was a refugee. An Iranian-Canadian friend once joked that Istanbul's Atatürk Airport was the only place in the world where it didn't matter which of her two passports she presented. Now, it felt like everything was changing; I didn't see how our love story could survive without the city that had brought us together.

As our world began to fissure and fracture, I realized how quickly borders could stop a love story in its tracks. How can two people navigate a world that won't allow them to be together? As a journalist, I had witnessed the way that the Syrian civil war had uprooted its people, scattering them to Lebanon and Turkey, and later Europe, sometimes sending loved ones fleeing in opposite directions. But this was happening in other parts of the world, as well. I had a US passport and could at least travel and see if a long-distance relationship could work. What about people who did not?

I set out to write this book to chronicle the stories of people who love one another in spite of borders. It is the story of Syrian lovers who fell for each other despite being separated by the Mediterranean Sea, and of a Honduran queer couple who fled street gangs and death threats to be together, only to be separated by ICE agents once they crossed into the US. It is about US citizens who were separated from their partners, some by Obama's deportation policies and others by Trump's Muslim ban, showing that borders continue to stand in the way of people trying to be with their loved ones, regardless of which party holds political power.

Many parts of this book have a naturally American orientation. I am an American journalist who came of age during the war on terror and started gathering these stories at a time when Donald Trump was bellowing about building a wall at the US–Mexico border and ordering a total and complete shutdown of Muslims entering the United States. But this xenophobia is not limited to US borders, and neither are these stories. This book also tells the stories of people who came to the United Kingdom as subjects of the British Empire, only to be unlawfully stripped of their citizenship in a national scandal that left thousands of families stranded between the Caribbean and the United Kingdom. It is the stories of young men from West Africa who dreamed of opportunities in Europe only to encounter the rise of xenophobia and neofascism after leaving their loved ones behind.

A book about borders must also reckon with the question of citizenship and statelessness. For this reason, I have also included stories of Palestinians who were born stateless in refugee camps, and people who fell through the bureaucratic cracks when the victors of war drew the borders of new countries, erasing people's homelands from the map. What happens when you belong to a country that no longer exists? Papers are not just the flimsy pages of a passport or the brittle plastic of a residency permit. They are identity documents, grounding us in a society, granting us the right to live, work, and vote. Sometimes, we can extend these privileges to the people that we love. Other times, we cannot. Inevitably, it affects the way that we move through the world and fall in love.

At times, this book is my story. As Salem and I found ourselves navigating a world that opened its doors for my passport and put up its walls for his, I became obsessed with the ways that arbitrary laws and invented boundaries were shaping our ability to be together. Some of these questions were practical. Where could we live in a world that felt as if it had no room for our relationship? As we wrestled with the fallout of the Syrian civil war and the Muslim ban, we got to know each other in a strange kind of exile, where our love—and my passport—were the only things that held us together. What if our anger at the situation turned into anger at one another? I was afraid of the way these rules could limit our love, and of the jealousy I felt toward couples who could love without restrictions.

Who could we be if these laws did not exist?

I recognize that my story is unique in that both my US passport and my job as a journalist granted me a degree of freedom that is not afforded to most people who find themselves divided by borders. For this reason, I often slip into the background as a narrator, and only emerge to connect others' stories with my own where I see the need. Nevertheless, I found that we all shared an understanding of the way that policies and immigration had shaped our stories, and a fear of the arbitrary rules and invisible lines that we knew could break our hearts.

I also felt compelled to dig into the histories and rationales for borders themselves. Why is it that refugees fleeing wars in Syria, Iraq, and Afghanistan are forced to take dangerous journeys across the sea to seek asylum in Europe, while citizens of the European Union can fly wherever they please? How come so many Mexican families in the United States are living in the shadows while US citizens are slamming tequila shots during spring break in Cabo San Lucas? I brought my questions to historians and scholars, who helped me piece together the ways that white supremacist ideology and colonial legacies have shaped borders into the global maze that they are today.

Ironically, I started writing this book at a time when COVID-19 had shut down the world, and travel, for the first time in my lifetime, was limited for everyone. Some interviews that I hoped to conduct in person were instead gathered over the course of many Zoom calls, Facebook chats, and WhatsApp voice memos. At first, I worried that this technique might cause me to lose essential details, the "color" that we depend on as journalists. Later, I realized that our long conversations and glimpses into one another's lives through a computer screen mirrored the way that loved ones connect when they have been separated by borders for much longer.

Borders have not always been this way. Syrian passengers were once on board the Titanic. Mexican communities continuously inhabited the present-day United States longer than the Anglo-Americans who drove them off their lands. Passports were once little more than identity documents. Rights have not always been tied to citizenship. But we have let borders conquer and divide us into a broken and unequal world. What would it mean to break free?

Above all else, this book is a journey into the hearts of people fighting an unjust system to be together. While it is impossible to include, or even attempt to represent every story of love and borders around the world, I hope it offers a snapshot into the myriad ways that borders shape our lives and impact our ability to be with the people we love. As you read this book, I invite you to imagine a world where borders do not exist. It is not as far-fetched as you might think. Most borders are mind-bogglingly new, and many of these stories would look quite different if history had unfolded differently. Mine would probably look different as well.

We are told that love conquers all. What happens if you do not have the right passport?

1 | *Be Brave*

The fishing boat was bigger than Wala'a imagined it would be, though it still looked somehow defunct. As she watched it bob in the water from the rocky shore of the Turkish beach, she wondered if it had been resurrected from a trash heap for its final voyage. If it were daylight, she might have seen the Greek islands dancing on the horizon, just ten kilometers away from where she was standing. If it were daylight, she might have forgotten about her fear of the sea, and instead thought about what it might be like on the other side.

But smugglers' boats don't sail during daylight hours. Instead, it was pitch black—the sound of the sea smacking against the shore reminding her that it would only take one wave to send her and everyone else on board tumbling into its dark and unforgiving depths. She shivered as the wind cut through her clothes, reminding her that she was about to step into the unknown.

"I was absolutely terrified," she told me, her enormous brown eyes becoming even wider as she remembered the moments before she boarded the boat and left behind everything that she had ever known.

I first met Wala'a at the Melissa Centre in Athens, Greece—a community center, named after the Greek word for "honeybee," that brings together migrant women from around the world. When I introduced myself as a writer looking for stories of love and borders, Wala'a immediately shot me a mischievous glance. "If it weren't for the war in Syria,

I would have never met the love of my life," she told me, revealing a dark and slightly twisted sense of humor. Naturally, I immediately felt drawn to her. She is about my age—that is to say, twenty-seven or twenty-eight—and she is not only beautiful, but perfectly styled, with a floral-print headscarf that matches her top and turquoise eyeliner flicked into little wings that make her look like a sparkly cat.

It is difficult to imagine her shrouded in dark colors, hiding from the prying lights of police officers. It is even more difficult to fathom that she is one of many. During 2016 alone, more than 350,000 people made the same journey, on unseaworthy vessels that looked as if they could capsize at any moment, transforming the rocky inlets of the Turkish coastline into transit points, challenging the notion of borders as God-like arbiters of where certain people can and cannot go. Most that year, like Wala'a, were Syrian, fleeing the brutal civil war that was destroying their country—but many were also Iraqi and Afghan, and some came from as far away as Bangladesh and Cameroon. Many were trying to reunite with family members who had already made the dangerous voyage—family members who had been hopeful that their relatives could join them later by a safer route. But when family reunification policies took too long, they took to the sea, as well.

And Wala'a? Wala'a was taking a chance on love. His name was Ahmed.

"I kept hearing his voice tell me, 'Be brave, habibti,'" she told me, bringing me back to the moment that she was getting ready to board a tiny fishing boat, just before it would be optimistically pushed toward Greece.

For days, she had thought only about the swirling sea, the way it could swallow anyone whole. But in that moment, she let herself close her eyes and imagine what it would be like to see Ahmed for the first time.

As of that moment, she had never laid eyes on him—at least, not in person. Even though they had both grown up in the same city in Syria, the war was enough to ensure that they never crossed paths at home.

Once the fighting engulfed her city, Wala'a fled across the mountains to Lebanon, hoping that the war would end and she would one day be able to return home.

But the fighting did not stop—instead it dragged on, spreading throughout the country, transforming ordinary cities into front lines. Meanwhile, Syrians in Lebanon were beginning to weigh their options— they could either continue to wait out the war or take their chances on one of the smugglers' boats and try to reach Europe. It was dangerous— during 2015 alone, more than 4,000 people drowned or disappeared on the ten-kilometer trip between the Turkish coast and the nearest Greek island, and this does not count the number of people who were held up at gunpoint by smugglers or turned around by the Turkish coast guard.

"I think you should come with me," Wala'a's aunt—whom she affectionately calls Khalto Lamia—told her one night, in the apartment they shared together just outside the northern city of Tripoli. "You need to leave Lebanon if you are going to have a life worth living."

First, Khalto Lamia would fly to Istanbul and meet a smuggler who would arrange their journey for a price. Fifteen hundred dollars was the going rate at the time for a spot on a rubber boat, but there were discounts for children and anyone who dared to travel during the winter months, when the seas were higher and boats had a greater chance of capsizing. Just imagining the trip turned Wala'a's stomach into knots.

"I don't want to cross the sea," she argued, unable to get the images of families clinging to one another in the water out of her mind. It felt reckless and desperate, as if she were accepting that her life was disposable. Besides, she had a job in Lebanon—teaching English to Syrian children whose education had been cut short by the war. It made her feel like she was doing something useful. It made her feel like she would someday be able to go home.

"A new life doesn't just come to you," her aunt told her, lovingly but sternly. "You have to seize it."

So, Khalto Lamia went ahead—and left Wala'a behind in Lebanon, as she wished. At first, it seemed as if she really was seizing a new life. As soon as she arrived in Greece, she assured Wala'a that the sea was calm, and she had nothing to worry about. But now, it was far more difficult to move on to Germany. Ever since hundreds of thousands of people had walked across the open borders of the European Union to Germany in 2015, many governments had cracked down on their allegedly open borders, building walls and setting up checkpoints to ensure that refugees wouldn't move through their countries. Now, most people without EU citizenship needed to hire smugglers to get from Hungary to Germany, or even from Greece to Macedonia.

Khalto Lamia had made it safely to Greece, but, for now, she was stuck there.

Most afternoons, she would go for long, aimless walks and stop to drink coffees and smoke cigarettes with anyone who cared to chat. It was during one of these long, lazy, yet somehow also anxious afternoons that she met a young man whose eyes twinkled mischievously as he introduced himself as "Ahmed, from Aleppo." She took a liking to him when he offered her a cigarette to calm her nerves.

"So, Ahmed from Aleppo," she asked, lighting the Gauloise Blond and blowing smoke out the side of her mouth. "Are you married?"

Wala'a never wanted an arranged marriage. She always imagined herself free-falling in love, an act of fate that struck when the stars aligned and everything fell into place. But Khalto Lamia had other plans, and if she had to align the stars herself, she would. Wala'a should not have been surprised when she called her, gushing into the phone. "I've found someone for you."

"You must speak to him right now." Wala'a shook her head in mock exasperation, realizing that it was impossible to escape an ambush.

"Hello?" Ahmed said, shyly—even though he was very interested in meeting Wala'a, he hadn't expected it to happen quite this quickly.

"I see you have met my dearest aunt," she laughed, and it is easy to imagine Ahmed relaxing the moment that she did—her laugh is whimsical, like wind chimes on a summer breeze, enough to make anyone fall in love the moment they hear it for the first time.

Wala'a was surprised, too. Ahmed's voice was soft and familiar, more like the cadence of an old friend than a stranger coming in over a crackling phone line. "We had this warm feeling between us from the very beginning," she said, remembering how that first phone call turned into two, and two turned into three, and soon she found herself giddily skipping around her apartment with the phone pressed against her face for hours, talking about everything from their favorite places in Syria to the places that he hoped to someday show her in Greece.

"I thought he was so worldly and open minded," she remembered. "He was so different than anyone I had ever met before." Still, as their flirtation blossomed into a romance, he started to express that he wouldn't be able to continue like this forever. "I hate all of this technology," he told her. "I want you here, with me."

Wala'a wanted to be with him, too—but she didn't want to cross the sea. "If you are going to be with me, it has to be like this," Wala'a responded, trying to convince herself that she was able to fall in love over a pixelated Skype connection, that she could feel connected to another person through a crackling WhatsApp call.

Day by day, Ahmed grew accustomed to the long phone calls. Wala'a became more curious about what it might be like to meet him in real life. "I loved talking to him, but it was starting to feel like there was a barrier between us," she confessed. "There are so many emotions that you cannot read, so much room for miscommunication."

Falling in love with Ahmed made her realize that she no longer felt attached to living in Lebanon. At first, it felt familiar, a place that shared both a border and a language with Syria, allowing her to fantasize about someday being able to go back. But as time wore on, it became more and more difficult to be a Syrian in Lebanon, a reminder that she would never be quite at home there. At first, it had been easy for Syrians to come to Lebanon. Around the time that Wala'a left Syria, in 2012, the border was open, and Syrians could stay in Lebanon for up to six months. But as the war dragged on, the Lebanese government started cracking down on refugees—first limiting entry, and then requiring visas, which essentially closed the border altogether. I remember living in Lebanon when Lebanese landlords started refusing to rent to Syrians and my Syrian friends started changing their accents when taxi drivers asked where they were from. Some lost their jobs, and others had trouble getting hired in the first place. Often, children tried to sell roses in the street, begging for money to support their families who had no other options.

Many of those who have been lucky enough to have never been in the position of fleeing a war do not understand why someone who has already fled to a "safe" country needs to flee further. Why should someone from Syria who has fled the war at home flee further than neighboring countries, like Lebanon or Turkey? But the sense of refuge is often fleeting, and protections can be stripped away as quickly as they are granted, making life all but unlivable. Hostility and prejudice can chip away at someone's humanity just as easily as barrel bombs and artillery fire can. Who can be blamed for longing for a life worth living?

Wala'a often found herself wondering what would have happened if she had traveled to Europe with her aunt. Maybe she would have met Ahmed there—then again, maybe they would have passed one another in the street as strangers, never knowing what could exist between them. Perhaps they were only brought together by the borders keeping them apart, and were never meant to be more than an idea, a possibility. Or maybe not; maybe Khalto Lamia was right, and she had to seize the life she wanted.

"It is getting more and more difficult to be in Lebanon," Wala'a confessed to Ahmed one evening, as she prepared dinner—a ritual that made her feel particularly lonely, especially when she remembered cooking elaborate meals, sharing them with the people that she loved.

"I eat alone, I pray alone," she continued, not sure if she was having a conversation with Ahmed, or an argument with herself. "What is the point if I'm always alone?"

Wala'a felt doors closing. Ahmed sensed an opening.

"If I asked you to be my wife, would you come to Greece?"

And that is how she found herself making her way to the rickety fishing boat as it bobbed in the dark sea, wondering what it would be like to marry a man she was in love with but had never met. As she put one foot in front of the other, she realized that she was stepping into the unknown in so many ways. *Be brave,* she told herself, slipping the life jacket over her head.

It would only take one wave to end her journey, but if she didn't face that possibility, she would never discover the life that could be waiting for her on the other side. If she didn't push through her fear, she might never learn the meaning of true courage—or for that matter, true love. If she didn't challenge the borders meant to keep her in one place, she might never know what it feels like to break free.

The boat lurched forward as she stepped on board. There was no turning back.

————

Sometimes, Wala'a wonders what it would have been like to meet Ahmed in Syria.

"We both grew up in Aleppo," she laughed, shrugging her shoulders. For a moment, I imagine another world, one where her country hadn't been transformed into a battlefield and her love story could have played out on the narrow, winding streets of the old city that now only existed in her memories.

Maybe they would have met at university. Wala'a studied English literature, poring over every novel she could find, translating each page until it came alive with meaning. She loved to play with new words, turning them around in her mouth until their foreignness became familiarity, imagining the new worlds that they could unlock. Ahmed might have listened to her, as she gushed about the books she adored, and plotted how he could see her outside of the university's walls. Maybe he would sneak out at night to surprise her at her bedroom window, smiling at her as she tried to shoo him away, her heart racing at the thought of being caught by a nosey neighbor.

Maybe, just for a moment, she wouldn't care.

Who would they be if it weren't for the revolution that turned the country upside down? It started as hushed whispers. Everyone was talking about the news coming out of Egypt and Tunisia, where dictators like Hosni Mubarak and Zine el Abidine Ben Ali who had held power for decades were toppled by protestors in a matter of days. Many wondered if Syria could be next—it was almost impossible to imagine the country without the steely blue eyes of President Bashar al-Assad gazing down from the billboards, without the feeling that "the walls had ears," which was confirmed every time the security forces snatched up someone for daring to express their opinion. Many disappeared into prisons as Salem once had, though most were not lucky enough to come out alive.

Knowing this, it is even more awe-inspiring that a group of Syrian teenagers scrawled "Your turn, Doctor" on a wall in the southern province of Daraa, just a few weeks after Egypt's Hosni Mubarak had relinquished power. It was a subtly coded message—Bashar al-Assad had trained as an optometrist.

At first, the protests were euphoric. Wala'a remembers the way that people danced in the streets, shouting in one soaring voice: "The People! We want / an end to the regime!"

It did not take long for peaceful protests to become a bloodbath. Assad's security forces unleashed reams of bullets over the protestors, killing them indiscriminately. Some grew tired of facing the regime's violence without fighting back. So they put down their banners and picked up guns, vowing to liberate their country, one neighborhood at a time. City streets became front lines as the regime snipers occupied the rooftops. Soon, the army responded with barrel bombs, shrapnel-filled fuel tanks falling from the sky. Explosions became a part of the soundscape and Aleppo disappeared under a mushroom cloud of flying rubble and black smoke, its skyline, once thought to be eternal, reduced to smoking craters. It was a heartbreak of its own—a heartbreak that Wala'a didn't want to experience again.

———

One crash. Then another. The rhythm of the waves was quickening, the incessant snare drum of mother nature escalating into a deadly crescendo. Wala'a gripped the edge of the boat, her knuckles turning white as she cursed herself for imagining this trip could end in anything other than death. With every crash, more water rushed into the wooded slats, soaking everyone onboard in freezing salt water. "I saw so much fear in their faces," she said, remembering the moment she saw her feelings reflected in the people around her. "We were absolutely facing death."

By now, the waves were smacking against the sides of the boat with relentless force. At times they were so high that they crashed over the entire boat, baptizing everyone on board in brine. Someone started to pray. Another started to vomit, as wafts of bile mixed with the smell of gasoline that had started slowly leaking into the sea.

"Everything will be alright"? Bullshit, she thought. We are going to die here.

Wala'a pulled out her phone. Miraculously, she still had a signal.

"If this boat sinks and I die, I will haunt you for the rest of your life," she hissed into the microphone to Ahmed, certain that she wouldn't live to see his response.

Just like that, the boat snapped in half.

—————

One of the most nauseating aspects of this story is that, every day, a passenger ferry sails from the Turkish city of Ayvalik to the Greek port of Mytilene. For just twenty-five euro, a passenger who has the kind of passport that unlocks the world—from the US, Canada, Germany, or anywhere else in the so-called "Global North"—can sit on the top deck, gazing out over the horizon as one territory bleeds into another in the gently rippling Aegean's blue.

For everyone else, this invisible line is a reminder of a life just out of reach. If you are standing on a beach in Turkey, Greece is only ten kilometers away, but it may as well be a different world. Even though everyone has the right to apply for asylum once they are on European soil, for refugees, there is no legal way to physically get there. The ferry that shuttles tourists back and forth would never let them board without a visa, a visa that is nearly impossible to obtain. The low-cost airlines that fly the same route multiple times a day would likely turn them away before they even reached passport control.

But it hasn't always been this way. Listening to Wala'a's story, I found myself wondering what it would have been like if the Syrian civil war had happened one hundred years ago. Perhaps it would have scattered people across the world the way it did with Wala'a and Ahmed, but I wanted to know when it became dangerous to cross borders. Once, people moved through the world freely, unencumbered by visas and border controls, because visas and border controls did not exist. It was not that long ago that this was the case for emigrants from the Middle East, as well.

"People were not immigrating from Syria, but rather from villages and towns that made up the Ottoman empire," Akram Khater told me, reminding me that at the turn of the twentieth century, Syria and Lebanon had no border between them at all. A Lebanese-American historian and the founder of the Moise A. Khayrallah Center for Lebanese Diaspora Studies at North Carolina State University, Dr. Khater combs through old records from the Ottoman Empire to better understand these histories and how they compare and contrast with the experiences of diasporas from the Middle East today.

"Immigration was seen as an investment," he continued, explaining that in the late 1800s and early 1900s, many people in Greater Syria, like those in Italy, Ireland, and other countries, saw immigration an escape from poverty. There wasn't a war to flee the way that there is today, but the silk industry that had once been the backbone of the economy in what is now Syria and Lebanon was collapsing, leaving families stripped of their livelihoods. When steamship tickets became more affordable, immigration became a way to imagine, and build, a new—and presumably, better—life.

"If you want to draw a contrast, you could say that they were voluntary immigrants rather than refugees," Dr. Khater continued, playfully alluding to politicians who argue that some people are more deserving of protection than others. A refugee, according to this line of thinking, is fleeing war or political persecution. Meanwhile, migrants are evil opportunists, committing the cardinal sin of trying to improve their lives.

"But economic hardships, or even the scare of going into poverty, drove people to migrate," he continued, reminding me that the line between a refugee and an "economic migrant" has always been blurred. It is something that I thought about frequently, as more and more people that I knew prepared to flee to Europe, despite the risks it entailed. Maybe they were safe from the war in a country like Turkey or Lebanon, but they also needed to secure their future, which was increasingly impossible as both governments cracked down on refugees. Around the world, people have always migrated for better work opportunities, or to be closer to family. But whether this is legal or illegal, celebrated or looked down upon, depends on the passport that one holds, and the options that come with it.

For the generation of emigrants who left the Middle East during the late 1880s, it was perfectly legal to travel wherever they wanted and stay for as long as they liked. As long as they could wrestle together sixty dollars to purchase a ticket on a steamship, there were no visa requirements, and few immigration controls. It was so common to travel this way that there were even Syrian passengers on the Titanic, though you would never know it from popular representations of the ship. Most of them were poor farmers and could only afford a ticket in steerage. Historians speculate they either never heard the evacuation instructions or didn't understand them; the announcement was in English, and the Syrians on board likely only spoke Arabic.

It breaks my heart to imagine these early émigrés, confused and horrified as icy waters filled the hold of the supposedly unsinkable ship, trying to make sense of panicked instructions in a language that they didn't understand—or worse, being forgotten about completely. Now refugee shipwrecks have become so commonplace that they barely make the news, much less our history books. We have replaced the steamships that once chugged across the sea with jet planes that zip through the sky, and yet the list of who can buy a ticket is far more exclusive. Our technology has advanced to a point that two people can meet and fall in love over WhatsApp, and yet, depending on where they are from, they possibly cannot meet without risking their lives, disappearing into the sea before they have a chance to fall into one another's arms.

What happened?

Was it passports? Often, I blame these flimsy booklets for allowing some people to move freely, while keeping others firmly in their place. Without passports, there would be no means to distinguish and rank citizens based on their nationality, no debate over who is worthy of protection and who is not. Salem and I would not be worried about being kicked out of Turkey, and Wala'a would be able to be with Ahmed without risking her life for love.

Passports were originally little more than identity documents. Citizenship as a concept emerged in Ancient Greece, but the Romans were the first to use documents to prove their identity, distinguishing themselves from those who were enslaved. Chinese traders had bronze coins to identify themselves, which later evolved into paper documents to facilitate travel and commerce, while in Japan these kinds of permissions were printed onto wooden tablets. Meanwhile in West Africa, "passport masks"—little tokens with intricately carved faces often sewn into fabric and worn around the neck—were used to identify tribes and facilitate trade before colonial times.

But the word *passport* likely comes from "laissez passer," a document used to control movement in Europe, initially required in order to pass through the gates, or, in French, portes of city walls during medieval times. Mostly, these documents were meant to keep vagrants and vagabonds from the French countryside from coming into the cities, protecting the elite from those they saw as riffraff and peasants. Even then, it was the internal movement of poor people, not the international movement of foreigners, that passports sought to control. Everyone else moved freely.

French revolutionaries were the first to protest the way that passport controls were being used to control freedom of movement. "To allow a man to travel is to allow him to do something that no one has the right to deny: it is a social injustice," a commentator who went by the penname Peuchet wrote in 1790 in the widely circulated *Le Moniteur Universel*, going on to argue that passports were a form of slavery, characterizing the French ancien régime as "slave masters" exerting control over the lower classes. But when King Louis XIV fled the country, the national assembly sealed the border to prevent other members of the monarchy from absconding.

After the revolution, the French went back and forth on the need for passport controls—a balancing act between the desire for freedom and the need for national security. Meanwhile, the British saw them as an instrument for controlling the economy. Even though the Magna Carta enshrined the right to free movement both within Britain and for those traveling across its borders in peacetime, the Alien Restriction Act of 1836 required ship captains to declare the name, rank, occupation, and description of any "aliens" on board. While there was no war to speak of at the time, John C. Toprey, in *The Invention of the Passport*, points out that there were bad harvests in Scotland and the breakup of traditional agriculture in Ireland, which pushed England to think more about regulating the movement of foreigners to protect its unstable economies.

During the 1880s, the United States became the first country to use passports to discriminate against foreigners based on nationality. Labor unions in California were becoming suspicious of Chinese immigrants, who were making money building railroads, posing competition for other workers. The unions lobbied Congress to pass the Chinese Exclusion Act in 1882, which effectively banned all immigration from China. Ironically, this led to the first "illegal" immigration: Chinese laborers would travel to Mexico and cross the US–Mexico border, then an open frontier. Up until that moment, passports had been used to restrict how certain social classes could cross borders, or move freely throughout a given land. Now, they were being politicized to exclude immigrants based on their nationality, foreshadowing the way that ethnic prejudice would later determine who was a desirable immigrant, and who was not.

Soon, the US followed Europe's example, experimenting with laws restricting entry of anarchists, radicals, and sex workers, creating new rules to prioritize some immigrants over others. World War I pushed countries across Europe and around the world to systemize passport control as a temporary national security measure, putting an end to the days of being able to charm one's way across a border. But national security was not the only justification for passports. Passports were used to control emigration as well, particularly from Germany and Italy, whose draft dodgers often escaped to the United States.

Still, there was a moment that might have turned the tide. After the Paris Peace Conference, the newly formed League of Nations organized a meeting in 1920 to determine the future of the passport. Passport controls had proliferated around the world during the war, but many policymakers were still in favor of abolishing borders—their words, not mine—and met to discuss whether it might be possible to ease travel restrictions, and restore freedom of movement, no documents required.

It is surreal to imagine a meeting with the future of freedom of movement hanging in the balance. It is even stranger to imagine a room full of decision-makers debating the merits of open borders as a way to pave the way forward for lasting peace. What if this happened in the halls of the US Congress or the EU parliament today? At the time, it was not a radical argument, but a practical one. Passports created a sense of distrust between nations and could create long and cumbersome lines at border crossings. It would delay reconstruction, slowing the movement of fuel and building materials across borders. They also mentioned that it could interfere with personal relationships, though they did not specify which kinds.

Ultimately, the committee decided that it was too early to abolish passports. They agreed to revisit the idea in the future, but in reality it was already too late. During the war, eugenic pseudoscience gained popularity across the United States, pushing the idea that humans could selectively breed to stamp out undesirable traits—which, for them, included dark skin, textured hair, and mental illness or disability. Previously, proponents of these ideas had been a small minority—but, as prominent eugenicists such as Harry Laughlin started to build relationships with US Congress members, lobbying began for legislation that would criminalize mixed-race relationships and restrict immigration, paving the way for laws that would shape both love and borders for years to come.

"I think we now have sufficient population in our country for us to shut the door and to breed up a pure, unadulterated American citizenship," said Senator Ellison DuRant Smith of South Carolina, pushing for immigration restrictions. With his support, the Immigration Act of 1924 was born—and with it, the world's first sweeping immigration quotas. It was carefully crafted to allow immigration from Western European nations to remain largely unaffected, while curbing immigration from Eastern and Southern Europe and almost eliminating immigration from Asia, Africa, and the Middle East. It solidified white supremacy as the cornerstone of the so-called American race.

"America must remain American," said President Calvin Coolidge, as he signed the bill into law.

Immigrants might be restricted by these borders, but ideas were not. It did not take long before the new legislation caused a ripple effect around the world, inspiring others to manipulate immigration and citizenship laws to reflect their prejudice. A young Adolf Hitler watched the unfolding policies with great interest, noting the way that lawmakers first successfully relegated Black and Native Americans to second-class citizens, while fantasizing about applying this to minority groups in Germany. As he writes in *Mein Kampf*, " . . . there is currently one state in which one can observe at least the beginnings of better conception. This, of course, is not Germany, but the American Union. The American Union categorically refuses the immigration of physically unhealthy elements and simply excludes immigrants of certain races."

It is chilling to see how these early ideas went on to shape the Nuremberg Laws, infamously stripping Jews of their citizenship. Suddenly citizens of nowhere, Jews fleeing the Holocaust faced an unwelcoming world as more and more countries closed their doors to refugees. One of the most striking examples of this is the SS *St. Louis*, a ship bound for Cuba carrying more than 900 refugees fleeing the Holocaust, who were hoping to claim asylum in the United States once their visas were approved. Cuba was a sort of transit zone, easy enough to get a visa, close enough to the United States to wait, and far enough from Nazi Germany to feel safe.

However, when the Cuban government didn't allow the ship to dock, the passengers remained unmoored at sea for weeks, terrified that they would be sent back. One man drank poison in his cabin. Another threw himself off the side of the boat. Even though the ship's captain sent a desperate telegram to President Franklin D. Roosevelt, pleading with him to allow the ship to dock, it was ignored. Later, the State Department responded, saying that the passengers aboard were subject to immigration restrictions and must wait their turn. But the refugees aboard the SS. *St. Louis* didn't have time to wait, and the ship had already turned around and was sailing back to Nazi Germany. As it sailed past Miami, the US Coast Guard trailed it, just to make sure it would not dock without permission.

Eventually, the ship was allowed to sail to Belgium, where Belgium, France, the Netherlands, and Great Britain each agreed to admit one-fourth of the refugees on board, a mere 200-some people per nation. Many of these same people still tragically died in the Holocaust as the Nazis went on to occupy swaths of French and Dutch territory, deporting people who had already fled the Nazi occupation to concentration camps. Seventy-three years later, in 2012, the United States State Department formally apologized to the survivors of the SS *St. Louis*. "We who did not live it can never understand the experience of those 937 Jews who boarded the SS *St. Louis* in the spring of 1939," said Deputy Secretary of State William Burns, addressing fourteen survivors of the voyage at a ceremony held in their honor.

"Our government did not live up to its ideals," he continued. "We were wrong. And so, we made a commitment that the next time the world confronts us with another SS *St. Louis*—whether the warning signs are refugees in flight or ancient hatreds resurfacing—we will have learned the lessons of the SS *St. Louis* and be ready to rise to the occasion." Now, his words ring hollow. Even though we have progressed to a point that jet planes zip through the sky, and hundreds of thousands of people hold biometric passports that can be identified with machines, 330,000 people still had no better option than to board inflatable rafts and practically defunct fishing boats to escape their war-torn homelands in 2016, alone. What started as a national security measure during World War I has now ballooned into an insurmountable fortress that drove more than one million people to brave the crossing between Turkey and Greece between 2015 and 2022, all because of a world that has been constructed around the idea that some people are more worthy of freedom of movement than others.

At least twenty thousand died trying.

———————

Despite her fears, nothing could have prepared Wala'a for the sudden crack of the wood, the shock of tumbling into the sea. Freezing water rushed into her ears as her heart pounded against her lungs, punching against her skin. It felt like her headscarf was choking her as her lungs screamed for air. She thrashed her arms in panic, not sure if it would bring her closer to the surface or push her to the bottom of the sea.

Wala'a broke the surface to the sound of screaming. Hysterical cries pierced the night sky, one overlapping the other as she tried to make out what they were saying. "It was so dark, I couldn't see anyone," she said, remembering the moments that she spent fighting for her life. "There was only crying. It was horrible."

She jolted as a piece of the boat hit her arm.

"I knew it was my only chance," she told me, recalling when she realized the driftwood could save her life. At first, she tried to hoist her body onto it, groaning as she attempted to lift as much of her body out of the water as possible. Icy wind sliced through her skin, and she slid back into the water, shivering.

"I was like Rose in *Titanic*, except I was completely alone," she continued, placing her hand to her forehead for dramatic effect. I couldn't believe she was able to laugh about something so obviously traumatic. "My hijab was gone, my glasses were gone," she continued, flicking her hand in the air each time she said "gone." "One shoe was on my foot, the other sailed away."

As she clung to the piece of the boat, she wondered how Ahmed could have convinced her that she had nothing to fear. *Be brave*, he told her, knowing that she might be swallowed by the sea, while he was sitting comfortably in his apartment in Athens. He had left Syria long before the war started and had moved to Greece before it became a major transit point for refugees. He might love Wala'a and truly want to give her the strength to face her fears. But really, he didn't know anything about what she had just been through.

"I did not feel like I could ever forgive him," she said. "I told him I was afraid, but he convinced me to go anyway."

It was not only the sea. What if Ahmed was not the person that she imagined him to be? It is easy to create a fantasy together; it is much more difficult to bring that dream into reality. What would it be like when she could no longer tell him what she thought he wanted to hear, but had to navigate the turbulent waters of an actual relationship, as wild and unpredictable as the sea itself? Their love could vanish just as quickly as it had arrived in her life. She would be left unmoored and alone, with no one to save her but herself.

"Be brave," she whispered.

———

Flashing lights.

"I wasn't sure if it was a boat or I was starting to see things," she said, remembering the surreal image of red and white lights on the horizon.

She squinted into the distance. If it was a boat, it might be the Turkish coast guard. "I couldn't bear the thought of going back to Turkey," she remembered. "It would have been better to just die there." But if it was the Greek coast guard, they would take her to Greece. If it was the Greek coast guard, she still had a chance.

"Help me!" she shouted, mustering strength she did not know that she still had. "I'm still alive."

As the ship came closer, the lights illuminated the water around her. A tousle-haired boy was treading water, staring at her, smiling a gap-toothed smile. He looked as if he was drooling at her.

"My love," he said in halting English. She couldn't believe she was clinging to a piece of driftwood, on the brink of death, and still being harassed. "Your hair," he said, continuing to fixate on her. "Very beautiful."

Panicking, she reached to see if her headscarf was still in place and nearly lost her grip. "I wanted to shout at him," she tells me, remembering the surreal moment. "But I realized he could get angry and shove me under. So I just glared at him instead."

The ship was getting closer.

"Take this," a voice shouted as a piece of rope fell into the water next to her. She grabbed on to it, steadying herself as the man that the voice belonged to helped her aboard.

Stunned, she looked around her.

"You're one of the only ones who survived," the man told her, handing her a blanket. "I'm not sure how you did it."

———

"Are you Wala'a?"

She blearily rubbed her eyes and saw a man standing over her—but it wasn't Ahmed.

It felt like last night was a dream. The snap of the boat breaking. The cold shock of freezing water filling her ears. The piece of driftwood that saved her life. Her embarrassment at being seen without her headscarf, replaced almost immediately with her fear that the man harassing her would hurt her if she didn't respond. "I remembered that we sailed for about half an hour, rescuing other people," she told me later, piecing together how she got to the island. "There were some men, and one other woman from Syria. But so many people had died—there were children, floating on the surface of the water."

Once she reached the island, she was greeted by two Greek volunteers. "They were fantastic ladies," she said, smiling. "They helped me change my clothes and gave me warm tea." At that moment her body failed her. Suddenly the world went from blurry to black as she collapsed, the prolonged shock of the freezing water knocking her unconscious.

One of the women took her to a hospital, where a doctor gave her an injection, and then to a hotel, where she fell into a deep slumber. When she woke up, a strange man was standing over her, but Ahmed was nowhere to be seen.

"Who are you?" she asked quizzically. "I want to see my husband— you are not my husband."

"It is you," the man said, his eyes lighting up. "Ahmed asked me to make sure you were okay."

She felt as if she had been tricked. Why couldn't Ahmed come himself? She knew that he had received her message, that he knew that her body might be no more her body than a nameless corpse. Perhaps he assumed she was dead. "Where is my husband?" she asked again, her strength suddenly returning to her as anger.

"The waves are very high, I don't think he will be able to come today," the man continued. "He will come tomorrow, after the storm passes." The storm. The storm that had nearly taken her life as she clung to a piece of driftwood, her teeth chattering as she told herself to be brave. The storm that forced her to face death as she fought for her life, all to take a chance on love. She felt foolish for thinking it would be any different.

Now she was alone on an island where she didn't know anyone, where she didn't speak the language, and had nothing to her name. Her body might fail her again at any moment, with no one to catch her should she fall. "What will I do now?" she exclaimed, indignantly. "I want to go back to Lebanon."

Just then, she turned—and that is when she saw him. Unmistakably, Ahmed was leaning in the door frame, one curl falling over his forehead, a mischievous smile across his face as he waited for her to notice him. "Ahmed!" she screamed, cupping her hand over her mouth.

"My love!" he exclaimed, running toward her. "Thank God you are here." For the first time, there were no barriers. No blurry, crackled connections, no distance between them. A few months later, they got married in Athens and honeymooned at the Olympos Hotel, the same place where they laid eyes on one another for the first time. While Wala'a is still terrified of the sea, every time they walk near Piraeus Port in Athens, Ahmed grips her hand a little bit tighter, and she feels safe with him.

"Every day I become a little bit less scared," she told me. "He really did teach me to be brave."

Once, she taught English to Syrian children whose education had been interrupted by the war. Now, she is teaching Arabic to children whose mothers are worried that living in a new country will make them lose their language, their connection to their culture and their family members who are still in Syria. Teaching the Arabic alphabet and playing traditional songs makes her feel like she can take a little bit of Syria with her wherever she goes, and know that not all is lost.

But her proudest accomplishment is her daughter, Asil. "She is truly the love of my life," she said, showing me a picture of a rosy-cheeked baby girl with huge dark eyes that look exactly like hers.

"Everything was worth it for her."

2 | *Penguins and Birds*

It took two days for a Turkish border guard to put Salem on a one-way flight to Erbil, Iraq.

"Have a nice deportation," I said, desperately trying to lighten the mood. At the time, most Syrians couldn't even go to Iraq, but a high-level politician in the Kurdish regional government whom Salem had once interviewed had agreed to fix him a temporary visa so that he could fly back to Erbil. Even so, he couldn't go to all of Iraq—just the Kurdish-controlled areas, which were contested territory, Iraqi if you asked some, Kurdish if you asked others.

"Thank you!" he said, indulging my attempt at humor. We had both been awake for nearly all the forty-eight hours that he was detained. At this point, all we could do was try to make each other laugh.

I didn't know what else to do besides follow him. If there was ever a time to use the accidental privilege of a US passport, it felt like the time was now. A few days later, I boarded a flight to Erbil, and as the plane cut through the clouds, I stared down at the jagged mountains below, zigzagging an invisible line between Turkey and Syria, then Syria and Iraq. It looked breathtaking from the sky, one country effortlessly bleeding into the other. It made me remember a time when I was still living in Beirut, a few months before, and a Syrian-Palestinian friend of mine had shown me a painting that he made of a penguin staring longingly at a flock of birds in the air.

"The penguin, he is a refugee," my friend explained. As a descendent of Palestinian refugees who had fled the Nakba, the violent beginnings of the state of Israel that displaced at least 700,000 Palestinians, and then had to flee the war in Syria himself, he was all too familiar with what it felt like to be a penguin.

"He is thinking, 'I'm a bird just like them. Why can't I fly, too?'"

I didn't know what to expect when I landed in Erbil. I had grown up with images of Iraq as a war zone, military tanks rolling through the streets of Baghdad, protestors knocking down statues of Saddam Hussein as onlookers cheered. My mom brought me to rallies against the US invasion and fiercely cursed George W. Bush with colorful streams of expletives at every opportunity—which I thought was hilarious, because I was twelve. Still, it gave me a political consciousness at a young age, a deep understanding that even though the war was taking place on the other side of the world, it might just as easily be me or my family living under the rain of bombs.

But everything I had heard about Erbil challenged my anti-imperialist upbringing. While Salem had told me countless stories of running from the US soldiers in Baghdad who were ruthlessly targeting and rounding up Sunni Muslims that they saw as loyal to Saddam Hussein, the view from Erbil was different. For the majority Kurdish population in the region, the US invasion actually *was* a liberation from decades of discrimination and systemic human rights abuses endured under Saddam Hussein. These culminated in the Anfal massacre in 1988, the unleashing of pure mustard gas on dozens of Kurdish villages, killing at least 50,000 ethnically Kurdish people. The event was more commonly known as Saddam "gassing the Kurds."

Now, Erbil was the de facto capital of Iraqi Kurdistan and supposedly they adored the Americans—both for their role in toppling their former oppressor, and the US government's more recent support of their fight against the so-called Islamic State. Perhaps this affinity explains why the Erbil International Airport felt more like a military base in Western Texas than a Middle Eastern capital, complete with watch towers and security guards in army fatigues with rifles slung across their chests. Nevertheless, there was a war weariness in their appearance—the soldiers appeared to be wearing hand-me-downs, and most of them looked no older than eighteen or nineteen.

It hadn't struck me before that most of the soldiers putting their lives on the line to fight ISIS were probably younger than me.

Still, they had managed to secure the airport with a complicated maze of security checks designed to thwart would-be suicide bombers and other terrorist attacks, making it almost impossible to greet someone at Arrivals. But Salem managed to sweet-talk—or more likely, bribe—his way past the security guards. He was the only one in the empty Arrivals area, waiting for me, smiling. I melted into his arms, letting his warmth envelop me.

"Baby, this is Erbil," he whispered in my ear, squeezing me, gently reminding me that I shouldn't be so openly affectionate with a man in public. I had completely forgotten—this wasn't Turkey or Lebanon, where it was normal to openly hug or kiss, at least in the major cities. Here, even a sleeveless top or mid-length skirt could earn a woman unwanted attention. Public displays of affection were strictly off-limits. I jumped backward.

He smiled, taking my suitcase.

"Let's go on a trip."

I loved the idea. A spontaneous trip somewhere in Iraq felt exactly like the kind of thing we would do together. It felt subversive to make his deportation into our romantic getaway, a middle finger to the Turkish border guard who had tried to keep us apart. A friend recommended a small hotel tucked away in the Kurdish mountains, far away from the fighting and the front lines. It felt like the perfect place to reconnect and plan our future together. Besides, I had only ever read about Iraq in the context of war and occupation. I wanted to see the ways that it was beautiful.

As the scenery changed from the sprawling desert plains that I associated with Iraq to the foothills of the mountains that I did not, the markings of war—both past and present—were everywhere. Peshmerga soldiers, the Kurdish military force, stood at checkpoints, stopping every car to make sure that there weren't weapons or explosives stashed in the trunk. Salem and I were routinely taken to separate rooms so that I could be searched by a female soldier, who would pat me down to make sure that I didn't have a suicide bomb wrapped around my chest. It felt strange to experience how ordinary it was to check and be checked for explosives, a routine that was built into everyday life.

When we arrived at the hotel, the fresh mountain air whipped our faces as children ran around in the white powder snow. A funicular—the only funicular in Iraq, the operator proudly told me—carried visitors farther up the mountain, letting us take in breathtaking views of jagged peaks that seemed to puncture the stratosphere before dropping off into the abyss. It was hard to imagine that only two hours away ISIS snipers were shooting at Peshmerga soldiers in desert towns.

As soon as we got to our room, we jumped on each other. It was easy to pretend that we had never been separated, that we were just an ordinary couple that wanted to ravage one another in a hotel room.

"What are we going to do," I groaned, trying to steer our conversation toward our dilemma. As good as it felt to have his body wrapped around mine, I knew that we needed to talk. I had so many questions. Should I pack up our apartment in Istanbul and move to Erbil? I wasn't ready to give up our life there, even though I knew that the decision was out of my control. Was there any chance that he could come back? It was a long shot—with no information about why he had been banned, it would be hard to argue why the ban should be reversed. Could we do long distance?

"You can work here," he responded, shrugging as if it were as simple as finding work in a coffee shop. Instead, he was suggesting that I start covering the war on ISIS, a prospect that terrified me as much as it intrigued me. Documenting war was natural for Salem, but I had never covered a front line before. I deeply admired the journalists who drove straight into danger, but the thought of regularly facing bullets, bombs, and kidnapping threats as occupational hazards terrified me. I covered the peripheries of conflict—stories of refugees and displacement, the way that political decisions shaped ordinary people's lives. I longed to be fearless enough to document the wars themselves, but the thought of narrowly escaping sniper fire one day only to run back toward it the next felt insane.

I looked at Salem. "Do they even make flak jackets in my size?"

One of the few activities at the hotel was a small paintball court, where children donned discarded peshmerga fatigues and shot each other with alarmingly realistic-looking guns. Salem suggested that we take a break from talking and join them, imagining that running around in the snow would lighten our mood. But with war on my mind, even the innocuous click of the paintball gun and its harmless colorful pellets filled my eyes with tears.

"I'm not sure I can do this," I choked, the wet snow creeping into my shoes, feeling ridiculous for over-analyzing the symbolism of being shot with a paintball pellet in the Kurdish mountains.

"It's up to you," Salem muttered. He didn't have a choice.

I stayed up late that night. I couldn't stop thinking about how the future of our relationship was in my hands. I could visit Erbil, and maybe even move there. I could learn to dodge bullets and duck for cover from car bombs. What about the dangers that I couldn't see? It wouldn't be easy to build a life together when the only place on earth that we could physically be together was a narrow sliver of contested territory that always seemed to be on the wrong side of a war or a political dispute.

Eventually the politics that shaped this land could catch up with us, just as they had in Istanbul.

I could also catch the next plane out and never look back. After all, the passport in my pocket meant that ISIS and border controls did not need to be my problems. I could sip champagne and stare down at borders from a cushioned seat in the sky, pretending that I was unaffected by the conflicts that I covered and the people that I met. I knew plenty of foreign correspondents who seemed to live their lives this way, letting their translators absorb the trauma of their interviews as they barricaded themselves in upscale neighborhoods and received awards for their fearless reporting. I understood their need for boundaries, and the slippery concept of journalistic integrity, the idea that we need to maintain distance from the stories that we cover in order to remain objective. But there was no way to understand why a journalist like me could build a career from such tragedy while a journalist like Salem was forced to live it.

A world where both of our passports had the same rights had never felt so far away.

As the snow settled outside, I wondered if love was enough to transcend these barriers. Over the years, I had watched enough girlfriends prioritize a boyfriend's ambitions over their own to know that following a man was my worst nightmare. For a journalist, it could mean giving up on a story that you had spent years following and starting over from scratch. I didn't know if my editors who called me for stories from Turkey would want stories from Iraq, or even think of asking me to write them. I felt embarrassed to tell them that I had moved for personal reasons.

But this felt bigger than the stories I covered from day to day, or even the question of choosing a relationship over a career. It was a symptom of the unequal world that we lived in, one where I inevitably had the upper hand. It felt more nauseating than liberating, and while I frequently wrote about these kinds of inequalities, I didn't know what to do when I was faced with them in my personal life.

I thought about the glossy magazines that I sometimes wrote for, and more often devoured out of guilty pleasure. As a college student, I had learned more about sexual pleasure and gained the courage to date from the pages of magazines like *Cosmopolitan* and *Marie Claire,* eagerly lapping up advice about unusual sex positions and contemplating the politics of birth control. Sometimes I grew annoyed that there weren't more women that looked like me in their pages, or articles that connected sexual politics to the wider world. But most of the time, I found their advice empowering—or at least, interesting.

Suddenly these magazines felt irrelevant. Where was the romantic advice on what to do if your boyfriend is suddenly deported? There were no listicles on what to do in the event of separation, no top ten romantic destinations for when your sweetheart has a passport that isn't worth the paper that it's printed on. Most of the advice in these so-called women's magazines targeted comfortable, middle-class couples, offering sex and dating tips for heterosexual women who saw marriage as an aspiration for reasons beyond fixing someone's immigration status. It ignored people who are navigating a country that is trying to lock up or kick out their loved ones. Structural inequality was neither sexy nor romantic.

I wished someone could give me an answer to my question: What do you do when you are a bird falling in love with a penguin?

Was it time to break up? I could save myself now from the heartache and pain that felt inevitable. It would be difficult to feel like equals again, the way that we had in Istanbul. What if resentment grew between us? I would understand if he suddenly hated me for being able to travel wherever I wanted; I hated myself a little bit for this unearned freedom. I could also grow tired of being cooped up in the same country, worried that it would somehow limit the career that I had fought so hard to build for myself. I couldn't even bring him to meet my family. What if the well was already poisoned?

But I didn't want to break up. Salem was unlike anyone else I had ever met—funny, smart, adventurous. He loved the things about me that previous partners had merely put up with. He was excited by the fact that I was curious about the world and didn't want to have a traditional life. It was an accident of birth that I had a US passport in the first place. How could I give up on our relationship when I had the one tool to make it work?

A passport is meaningless if it is not used to expand your world beyond the borders of your imagination. I could fly between Istanbul and Erbil, covering stories in both places until I was ready to relocate. I could see it as an opportunity to become the fearless war correspondent I had always dreamed of becoming and embark on an entirely new adventure with Salem. It might not be what we had envisioned, but I knew that it would be anything but ordinary.

Maybe there was no blueprint for how to build a relationship in this shifting and unpredictable world, but we could write our own rules together. We might learn to navigate the inevitable highs and lows of being in a new, strange place, not knowing what our future would hold. We might fail miserably. Maybe we would fall out of love, but if we did, we would know that it was our decision, and not the decision of a border guard.

What is love if not the courage to step into the unknown?

3 | *Your Relationship or Your Country?*

A few days after I got back to Istanbul, Trump announced the Muslim ban.

It felt like a punch in the gut. I was already heartbroken, sitting alone in our old apartment, shell-shocked by how empty it felt when there were not at least three journalists crashing on the sofa or an elaborate meal simmering away in our tiny kitchen. Our house was never just our home, it was a family home, ready to welcome anyone passing through with a cup of coffee or a hot meal. Sometimes a cup of coffee would turn into a glass of wine, which would turn into a bottle, which could turn into long, gushing conversations about the world around us, which sometimes lead to dancing on the furniture. Salem's hospitality was unmatched, though a bit unconventional. My personal favorite example of his hosting is when a friend asked if he could have another beer. Salem slapped him forcefully on the back, yelling, "This is your house! You can take a shit in my living room!"

This was the living room in which Salem had concocted an elaborate plan to convince me that he was traveling on my birthday, only to have our friends leap out from behind the furniture and surprise me so much that for a moment I thought we were being robbed. It was the place where we had watched the US election results roll in just a few months earlier, fifteen or twenty of us of various nationalities, from Afghan, Russian, and Yemeni-American to Syrian, Turkish, and Egyptian-British, sprawled across the sofa and floor, gaping at the TV in horror as the map turned red. We cried and primal-screamed together as the sun came up and we realized that the next leader of the United States would not be a woman known for her pantsuits and questionable foreign policy decisions, but a bigot who shouted slurs at Muslims and Mexicans from a bitter mouth shaped like an asshole. I deliriously prepared a pot of coffee that morning, aware that most of the people in my living room were teetering on the precipice of drunk and hungover and still had to go to work in a few hours. I poured a cup for a friend who had stumbled in at seven that morning after a drunken text exchange explaining that he didn't want to be alone when Trump announced his victory. I held out the steaming cup to him and he took a slug of whiskey from the open bottle on the table instead.

Now, the new president was enacting his worst promises, the ones we never thought were possible. A Muslim ban? There were too many Muslim-Americans, too many people with families spread out across the world. It would have such a disastrous effect on our communities. How could the US government measure their Muslimness, much less control it? It didn't seem to matter whether someone prayed five times a day or drank whiskey until five o'clock in the morning. They were on the list, banned, unable to travel simply for being affiliated with a religion that had become synonymous with terrorism in the eyes of the US government.

Salem and I had never seriously discussed moving to the United States, largely because of how difficult it was for Syrians to get a visa even before the ban. Still, I always imagined it as a place that we might end up some-day, a privilege and safety net that I assumed was my right, until it was taken away. Suddenly, with the stroke of a single pen, Trump had banned all citizens from Iran, Yemen, Somalia, Iraq, and Sudan from entering the United States for the next ninety days. Syrians were—of course—banned indefinitely. It felt as if a door that had been ever so slightly ajar had been slammed in our faces, then locked and double-bolted. The green card marriage that we had once joked about was out of the question.

I scrolled through Facebook in horror as I saw the way that it was throwing families around the world into chaos. One Syrian-American translator I knew was desperately trying to get her husband to the United States before it was too late. Airports were scenes of legal limbo as lawyers rushed to Arrivals areas desperately trying to get their clients out of passport purgatory. Hundreds of people had been in the air when the laws changed, trapped by borders that were erected overnight.

Others were waiting for visas at embassies and consulates around the world, counting down the days before they would join loved ones in the United States. One of them was a twenty-eight-year-old Yemeni woman named Amal, who had just traveled three days through war-torn Yemen, and then another three weeks to Istanbul, then Cairo, and finally to Djibouti, where she had her final interview at the US Embassy to move to New York to be with her childhood sweetheart, Mohammed.

"I was so tired after traveling for so long," she told me, her crystal blue eyes becoming wide as she remembers the month-long journey to get from Sana'a to the nearest US Embassy in Djibouti—only to learn that she wouldn't be able to travel after all. "I thought that there had to be some sort of mistake."

Today, Mohammed and Amal Alobahy are happily living in Sheepshead Bay, Brooklyn, with their one-year-old son, Ahmed. I met them for breakfast at their favorite Turkish restaurant, and they look like the perfect little family—Mohammed clearly adores Amal, putting his arm around her as often as he can, and Ahmed is like his Mini-Me, with curly brown hair and hints of the same mischievous smile.

But it took fleeing a war zone and waiting for a year and a half in limbo for them to be able to start a family at all.

"You have to understand, she had to travel through all of the different conflicting factions in Yemen just to get to the airport," Mohammed interjected, reminding me that, at that point at the end of 2016, Yemen had been under siege for more than a year, as the Saudi Arabian–led coalition blocked off the country's airports and ports, effectively confining civilians. "Al-Houthi, al-Qaeda, the Southern al-Hirak—all of them are really dangerous."

Before the war, it would have been easy for Amal to leave Yemen from any of the major cities. But ever since the Saudi-backed coalition air strikes had started, there were no more passenger flights leaving Sana'a. Now, the only way to fly out of the country was through the city of Seiyun, and the only way to reach Seiyun was by bus. "I spent two days in that bus," Amal remembered, a look of disgust on her face. Ordinarily, the road from Sana'a to Seiyun only takes an hour, but now it was choked with checkpoints run by various groups, from the Iran-backed Houthi rebels who controlled Sana'a, to the al-Qaeda militants who were gaining ground in the south. Each time the bus stopped, Amal held her breath, wondering if someone was going to be kidnapped or shot.

"Let me just make it to the airport," she told herself, trying to stop herself from throwing up every time the bus lurched over a pothole or careened through a mountain pass. It would be worth it when the visa was in her passport, and she was on her way to New York City, to finally start her life with Mohammed, whom, even though he was technically her husband, she hadn't seen in almost a year. "I really, really couldn't wait to see him."

Their love story started when they were kids. Mohammed was a short kid with curly black hair and a goofy smile, while Amal was a bit of a tomboy. Every summer, they would see each other when their families would retreat from the city and go back to the village in the mountains where they grew up, and the children would spend the long, carefree summer days chasing each other down the dirt roads.

"We used to play really rough with each other," Mohammed said, laughing as he remembers the way that seven-year-old Amal used to scream like a banshee while running after him, as they tackled and choked one another, with the kind of roughhousing unique to children. "One time, I told her that she couldn't play with me and the other boys," he continued. It got him in trouble—Amal was so angry that she grabbed a stick from the ground and stabbed his hand so hard that crimson blood spurted out of the wound.

"Do something!" he howled, as she stared at him in horror, before running to get her mother. Long after the wound was bandaged, Amal was still obsessing over his finger, taking his hand in hers, caressing the spot where she had drawn blood just a few hours before.

"It really felt like she cared about me," Mohammed said—and I imagined him as a seven-year-old with a toothy grin, unabashedly pining for the girl next door.

Their love might have blossomed from that moment, but in a conservative village like theirs, it is frowned upon for young women to spend time with men who are not their immediate family members, and as Mohammad and Amal grew from children into teenagers, they suddenly didn't know how to act around one another. "Everything got weird," Mohammad said, remembering what it felt like to suddenly be expected to conform to the prescribed rules of being a young man and a young woman in a conservative society, even though the two of them had been inseparable their entire childhoods. It felt like a border of its own: invisible yet damning, the prickly barbed wire of tradition redefining what is and is not acceptable, cutting loved ones off from one another after they had been accustomed to roaming freely together. "We had to suppress those feelings that we had for each other."

A few years later, their separation became even more pronounced. Mohammed's family found out that they won the Diversity Visa lottery— a rare opportunity to immigrate to the United States—and left. Now, the barriers between Mohammed and Amal were suddenly physical: thousands of kilometers of rolling seas and sprawling continents stretched out between them. Mohammed started high school in New York City, as far away in distance and character as possible from the dirt-road villages that barely had electricity where he grew up with Amal.

"We had no way to keep in touch, our communication went totally dark," he continued, his eyes becoming big as he narrates the story—he was so animated when he spoke, their separation still so real to him, that I almost forgot that Amal was right next to him now, softly singing to their one-year-old son, as he played with her cell phone.

But at that time, Mohammed was a teenager in New York City, on his way to becoming a US citizen, while Amal was taking on the responsibilities of a young woman in Yemen. "When you don't see someone for that long, it is almost like they aren't alive anymore," he remembered—still, there was a glimmer of hope every Eid, when his mother would call her mother, using the holiday as an excuse to catch up and gossip. Mohammed didn't know it at the time, but Amal would linger next to the phone, trying to catch snippets of their conversation. "I always wanted to know what was going on with him," she said with a laugh. "I wanted to know if he still remembered me."

Of course, he did. "I knew she was the person that I wanted to be with," he remembered—and maybe it is his retelling of the story, but I am not sure I have ever seen anyone so convinced of something in my life. He was so blindingly certain that in his second year of college, he asked his mother if she would reach out to Amal's family, so that he could formally ask her father for her hand in marriage. It was the only way that it would be possible for them to reconnect.

"Are you sure?" his mother asked him—she enjoyed her friendship with Amal's mother greatly, and dearly missed the days that they were neighbors, but it had been ten years since Mohammed had laid eyes on Amal. A childhood friendship is very different from a marriage—and there was no knowing whether they still would even like each other as people, much less want to spend the rest of their lives with one another. Mohammed couldn't argue with her logic, but he couldn't ignore how persistent his feelings were, either.

"But the first time I asked for her hand in marriage, I was shot down." He laughed, stealing a mischievous glance at Amal as if to remind her of all the hoops that he was willing to jump through to be with her. "It wasn't that her father didn't like me," he quickly added. "He just thought it had been a long time, that we didn't really know each other anymore." Still, he was crushed—and when he opened his computer to aimlessly browse Facebook, he didn't think anything of it when he saw that he had a Facebook friend request from a name that he didn't recognize, with a profile picture that was a single rose.

"I'm a girl from your past," the words popped up on the screen. It couldn't be her, he thought—it was probably just one of his friends messing around with him, trying to play a prank. Still, his heart skipped a beat at even the faintest possibility of reviving the flame, just when he thought it had been extinguished.

"Amal?" he typed, suddenly feeling stupid for holding out hope.

"It's me." Little did he know that when she heard that he had reached out, she asked her aunt for permission to contact him—allowing them to reconnect, with her blessing.

For the next eight hours, Amal and Mohammed didn't stop talking. It was ten years of missed conversations, stories that only the other would understand. As the sun rose in Brooklyn, the sun set in Sana'a, and maybe it was the sleepless night—or maybe it was the sudden twist of fate, the way that, just when he thought their love story might be over before it had begun, she had seized control of the narrative—but Mohammed couldn't wait another second to confess his feelings. "I've always loved you, Amal," he typed into the message box. "I don't want to go another minute without telling you that."

Several continents and an ocean away, Amal smiled, the words she had always known but never heard spoken, written on the screen, indisputable. Suddenly New York didn't feel so far away.

———————

Two years later, Mohammed asked for Amal's hand again. This time, her father had one request. If he was serious, he would come to Yemen to marry her—as soon as possible.

"I hadn't been in Yemen in twelve years," he said, his eyes becoming wide as he remembers preparing to go back to a country that he might no longer recognize. Since he left, the revolutionary fever that captured Egypt and Tunisia in 2011 had spread to Yemen, inspiring young people to take to the streets and demand that Yemeni president Ali Abdullah Saleh step down. Peaceful demonstrations quickly turned violent as snipers opened fire on protestors in Sana'a, turning a protest into a massacre. A year later, the president did step down, but the power vacuum he left behind pushed the country into a war. Now, Sunni extremist groups like al-Qaeda were gaining ground in the south, while the Shia Houthi rebel forces were moving in from the north, turning the already impoverished nation into the location of a proxy war between Saudi Arabia and Iran. "Before the war, I didn't even know what sect I belonged to," Mohammed told me. "All of a sudden, it became if you're Shia, you're with the Houthis in the North; Sunni, you're with al-Qaeda in the South."

Ever since the interim government had asked Saudi Arabia to intervene to help oust the Houthis from Sana'a, Saudi air strikes had become a part of the city soundtrack. Often, they killed civilians instead. Every time Amal heard the low hum of an airplane coming closer, she would drop everything and run to be with her family. "Sometimes we would be chatting online, and suddenly she would just disappear," Mohammed said, remembering what it was like to be safe in Rochester, while the woman he loved was sheltering from an air strike with her family. "If they were going to die, they wanted to die together."

Now, Mohammed was voluntarily flying into a country where air strikes were more common than passenger planes, and living through war was a part of daily life. "What choice did I have?" he laughed, when I ask him whether or not he was nervous to visit a war zone. "It was my last chance to be with her." He booked a flight for New Year's Eve.

"I wanted it to be this new beginning," he said, again laughing at himself. "Of course, the plane was delayed for six hours."

Four days later, he touched down in Sana'a, after a journey that took him from New York to Istanbul to Amman, to a military base in Saudi Arabia, and finally, to Yemen. Immediately he saw the ways the war had disfigured his country. First there was the shattered glass. "None of the windows were intact because of the air strikes," he told me. Helicopters languished on the tarmac, and fighter jets far outnumbered commercial airplanes. One of the passenger planes had been sliced open, the front awkwardly disjointed from the back, singed by an air strike at the exact places where passengers would disembark.

"What the hell have I just done," he thought to himself, looking around at the evidence of total destruction. At first, he had been nervous about being targeted as a US citizen. Now, he was nervous about everything else.

That night, he fell asleep in a hotel room, dreaming that it was his wedding day. "I never remember my dreams, but this one was so vivid," he remembered. His relatives were singing, enthusiastically playing music, as they accompanied him to the wedding hall. Just when he was about to see Amal for the first time in the dream, a peal of celebratory gunfire ripped through the air.

Suddenly, he jolted awake. Outside the window, flames were leaping up the side of a mountain, and the celebratory gunshots that he had imagined were real-life air strikes, bombs dropping from the sky and erupting into giant balls of fire as they hit the ground.

"That was the moment I realized I was in a war zone," he said now, looking at Amal adoringly as she rocked Ahmed on her knee. "I loved this girl enough to travel to a war zone for her."

————

On the day of their formal engagement, Amal had butterflies in her stomach.

"All of my family was at the door, and it was just me and Mohammed in the room," she said, giggling as she remembers the moment that she was finally able to talk to him. It was surreal to see him as a grown man, strong and serious—so different from how she remembered him as a teenager. Still, when his eyes twinkled, she suddenly saw the little boy that she had once chased through the streets, and any barrier that had ever come between them suddenly melted away, leaving just the two of them staring into one another's eyes, wondering what the future would bring.

"I only have one question for you," she said, still trying to process that he really had flown halfway around the world, just to ask her if they could spend the rest of their lives together. "Why me?"

Mohammed smiled, not sure how to tell her that nothing had ever felt more natural than this moment.

"Amal," he said, taking her hands in his for the first time. "It has always been you."

As much as they wanted to celebrate, the wedding had to be small. "Everyone was afraid of large gatherings," Mohammed said, remembering the way that family members warned him that both weddings and funerals were frequent targets for air strikes. There was no live music, no celebratory gunfire. Mohammed's uncle played music from an iPad, as close friends and family cautiously danced.

"We're going to do this the right way in New York," Mohammed whispered to Amal. All he wanted was to take her with him right then and there, to whisk her away from this death trap where he couldn't put his arm around her without being harassed by strangers, to where they could celebrate their wedding without worrying about Houthi gunmen storming the wedding party or Saudi air strikes raining down on their guests. But Mohammed had to go back to New York and apply for a visa for Amal to join him—a process that, even in the best of times, could take up to a year. He hated that she would be waiting in a war zone until then.

When Amal finally landed in Djibouti one year later, she thought it would be just a matter of days before she finally saw Mohammed again. Instead, she learned that she couldn't travel—not because she didn't get the visa, but because she was from Yemen and there was a ban. "I couldn't stop crying," she remembered. "I didn't know what I was going to do."

Mohammed was stunned. "It felt like all of our dreams were shattered," he said, remembering the moment that he learned that Trump's infamous Muslim ban had coincided with the week that they were finally supposed to begin their lives together.

"I'm a US citizen—I didn't think that this was possible."

———

I wish I shared Mohammed's surprise. I always felt like the Muslim ban was the result of hatred that had been simmering beneath the surface in our country for a long time suddenly boiling over. Trump might be the first president who was bold enough to publicly call for a "total and complete shutdown" of Muslims entering the United States, but he was not the first to fantasize about it. For me, it brought me back to the weeks after the September 11 attacks, when it felt as if Muslim, Arab-Americans, and any other even vaguely Middle Eastern–looking person was suddenly seen as a terrorist.

"If you think that the US should invade Iraq, go to the other side of the room," my seventh-grade history teacher instructed our class. Even though I grew up in the Bay Area, it was far enough inland that many of the rainbow flags and FREE TIBET bumper stickers popular in Berkeley and San Francisco became Bush/Cheney yard signs and proudly fluttering American flags by the time you got to my small town.

Some of the parents, like mine, were middle-aged hippies. Others were definitely not.

"If you think that the US should not invade Iraq, stay on this side," she continued. As my classmates pondered their allegiances, I sat squarely on the side of the classroom that was against the war. It would be easy, I reasoned. All I had to do was show them that Iraqis were no different than anyone else.

"There are families just like yours there," I began, pacing as I looked out over the sea of faces on the other side of the room. They couldn't be twelve- and thirteen-year-old war hawks. "It isn't right for the US to drop bombs on their houses—imagine if that was happening to you or me." A few of my classmates shifted uncomfortably in their seats. Still, none of them were moved enough to come to my side of the room. "If we are ever going to have peace, we have to have a war first," said one blond boy, very earnestly. A few of the other students nodded in agreement. Was I missing something? I didn't understand how carpet-bombing an entire country could lead to anything besides more violence. I decided to play the heritage card to make a point.

"Some of my family is from Lebanon, that isn't that far away from Iraq," I said, hopping up on the desk for impact. "Do you really want to kill people that could be my relatives?" It might seem far-fetched to imagine that an air strike bound for Baghdad could end up in Beirut, but something about seeing civilians on television with the same big brown eyes and expressive faces that I recognized from my own family made me feel uneasy. I wondered if my classmates wanted to kill me, as well.

The blond kid shrugged his shoulders. "We have to kill the terrorists," he said. He was about as eloquent as Donald Rumsfeld.

While I was watching the war on terror unfold from the hallways of a suburban middle school, President George W. Bush was drastically overhauling the US immigration system in the name of national security. First, he passed the Patriot Act, which gave the FBI sweeping surveillance powers, which were almost entirely deployed on Muslim communities. Then, he established the Department of Homeland Security—a collection of twenty-two agencies, including ICE—to enforce it.

"Before the September eleven attacks, most Islamophobia was focused abroad," Moustafa Bayoumi, an English professor at Brooklyn College and the author of *How Does It Feel to Be a Problem: Being Young and Arab in America*, told me. "Afterwards, it was refocused into something domestic."

First, there was a registry of emigrants from twenty-four Muslim-majority countries (and North Korea), who were heavily monitored by the FBI and frequently called in for interrogations about their religious and political beliefs. Many were arrested and deported for failure to comply with the draconian registration requirements, which had a ripple effect on their communities.

"A lot of families were split up because the men were the breadwinners and they would get deported," Bayoumi continued. "Their wives and children would stay back, and often struggle really hard because opportunities were still better in the US than they were back home."

Many emigrants from Muslim-majority countries also experienced delays in their naturalization as US citizens because they were subject to extra layers of scrutiny as "potential threats" to national security. Even though Muslim and Arab-Americans were technically protected as US citizens, many of us were subject to new skepticism and humiliation in a way that made it seem as if our citizenship was conditional.

More troubling is that the US has a history of calling the citizenship of different immigrant groups into question, due to national security. "At the time, not a lot of people knew about what happened to us," Chizu Omori, a ninety-one-year-old Japanese-American activist who spent three years living in an internment camp, told me over a bowl of lentil soup at a café near her home in Oakland, California. Coincidentally, the café is Yemeni.

After the Pearl Harbor attacks in 1945, Chizu and her family were among the 120,000 Japanese and Japanese-American families on the West Coast who were evacuated and taken to ten different "relocation centers"—or, as they are better known, internment camps—as a part of Franklin Delano Roosevelt's Executive Order 9066. When Trump announced the Muslim ban, he justified it by comparing himself to FDR, on *Good Morning America,* who, in his eyes, was one of the greatest presidents in US history. But for survivors of the Japanese internment like Chizu, it brought back dark memories.

"The strangest part is that afterwards I just went to high school as if nothing happened," Chizu told me, saying that many families closed that chapter of their lives and never spoke of it again. "They were hell-bent towards assimilation and becoming good Americans so that we wouldn't get picked up again." It reminded me of the Muslim women who quietly took off their headscarves after 9/11 and the Arab and Muslim-American families who raised red, white, and blue flags outside of their homes, as if performing Americanness would keep them safe in a country that could decide they were national security threats at any moment.

As a college student, Chizu quickly got involved with the civil rights movement, but did not connect the dots between the issues that she was marching for and her own experiences until a trip to Seattle many years later, where she met other internment survivors for the first time. She started working with her sister, filmmaker Emiko Omori, on uncovering their own family's story and connecting with other survivors to put together the pieces of the bigger picture, culminating in their film *Rabbit in the Moon,* which examined their own family's story and compared it to that of other survivors. Chizu remembers a research trip to the National Archives in Washington, DC, where she discovered the loyalty questionnaire, a form that was given to everyone in the camps to determine whether their loyalties would lie with Japan or the United States, asking questions about what leisure clubs the respondent participated in and how well they spoke Japanese. The last one asked whether the respondent would declare loyalty to the United States and renounce allegiance to the Emperor of Japan, a question that was inherently problematic as Japanese immigrants were not even eligible for US citizenship at the time, as they were not seen as white. Her family was divided about how to fill it out.

"I didn't feel like I was Japanese," she said, remembering the way it created divisions within her own family. "But my parents didn't think that there was any place for them in this country."

It reminds me of the way that so many Arab and Muslim-Americans felt their loyalty questioned in the wake of 9/11, as if being a certain race or religion automatically meant that they were a threat. Trump's Muslim ban extended to those of us with loved ones in the Middle East, keeping couples like Mohammed and Amal separated for months, living in limbo with no end in sight. Our worst nightmares—of internment camps and loyalty questionnaires—fortunately did not come to pass, but when I asked Chizu about her experience she carries with her to this day, her words sit with me.

"What did I learn?" she asked, rhetorically. "I learned that the US government can do whatever it wants."

———

Stranded in Djibouti, Amal started to wonder if she would ever see Mohammed again.

At first, she reasoned that she would have to be patient for one month, maybe two. It was swelteringly hot, and she felt isolated as almost no one besides the few other Yemenis spoke any English or Arabic. "All I did was eat and sleep, eat and sleep," she remembered. "Every day was exactly the same."

Two months turned into three, and three turned into four, and four months turned into the kind of limbo where one shapeless day bleeds into another, and every day she struggled a little bit more, living in a state of suspended reality. "I was jealous of the women who had babies," she confessed, remembering how she longed to be spending her time caring for a child. Even though she had been married for more than a year, she had only spent two weeks of that time with Mohammed. It felt like their future together would never begin.

After the first few months, Amal's family started pressuring her to come back to Yemen. "Mohammed has brought you nothing but hardship," they would say, trying to convince her that it was not too late to bail. Mohammed was terrified that she would listen to them. He wished that he could have spent more time regaining her father's trust.

"I had to completely push them out of my mind," Amal said, grimacing as she remembers the way every phone call made her feel more and more isolated. Often, she found herself calling Mohammed—sometimes twice, sometimes three times a day, trying to remind herself why she was waiting.

"Just tell me that we are going to see each other again, and I will forget about everything my family is telling me," she told him, feeling as if she were beginning to lose her mind. Without FaceTime, and the constant reassurance of his voice, she didn't know what she would have done.

"Of course we will," he assured her. But really, he didn't know. Mohammed was spending every weekend driving the seven hours between Rochester and New York City, trying to meet with any lawyer or journalist who would listen to the story of two childhood sweethearts who found themselves suddenly separated by the ban. "At first, people were really motivated," he said, remembering the days of people caravanning to the airport, staging sit-ins at airport terminals, enthusiastically chanting "No hate, no fear, Muslims are welcome here."

But after a while, the shock of the Muslim ban faded from the headlines—persisting only for those whose lives had been put on hold. "I was saving up for our wedding," he remembered. "It was supposed to be a huge celebration, but then I had to buy plane tickets, and put down deposits for apartments—and I was just a recent grad, on a starting salary. I had student loans, and car payments, too."

After a while, he moved back in with his family to save money and took on a second job. "I was exhausted all of the time," he remembered—and I wonder how many people were like him, working constantly in order to sustain a life in one country, and support a loved one in another. "I kept thinking that if it weren't for the ban, we could have rented a nice big apartment and gone on a really nice honeymoon," he continued, sharing that they often fantasized about going to Hawaii or Cancún. "We really wanted to do that together."

When I asked him what gave him the strength to keep going, he laughed. "We had already been through so much together," he said, with just a hint of bravado. "We weren't going to let something like the Muslim ban get in the way."

But not everyone shared his conviction. More and more families were starting to pack their bags, weighing the cost of staying in indefinite, expensive limbo against that of going back to a war zone. It was almost impossible for most of the Yemenis to find work away from their own country, and temporary separations from loved ones were starting to feel permanent.

"A lot of people used to call me, and tell me that they were afraid their marriages wouldn't survive the separation," said Curtis Morrison, an immigration lawyer in Los Angeles, who counseled many Yemeni and Iranian families who were affected by the Muslim ban.

"Maybe it was easier for some of the younger people, who were better at using things like WhatsApp and FaceTime, to stay in touch," he mused aloud, and I was struck by the ways that technology transcends borders, allowing people like Mohammed and Amal to be a part of each other's lives—or Wala'a and Ahmed to fall in love—even when physical borders keep them apart. Still, communication over apps like these is not enough to sustain a relationship forever. "I try to give them hope," he continued. "I try to tell them if it is real, they will wait."

One of his clients particularly haunts him. A Yemeni-American like Mohammed, Mahmood Salem had been waiting for several months to bring his wife and their five children to the United States. "I had to tell him that there were no updates, and it was still probably going to be a while," Curtis remembered. But Mahmood was falling deeper and deeper into both debt and depression, worrying that he couldn't keep supporting his family with no end in sight.

A few days later, Curtis learned that Mahmood had shot himself.

Perhaps the most agonizing aspect of this story is that when a spouse becomes a widow or widower, it is easier to facilitate a visa waiver to attend the funeral. Within a few days, Mahmood's wife and five children were on a plane to Louisiana. What would their lives today look like if they had been able to take that plane just a few days earlier, if the money that Mahmood spent on visas and expensive accommodation in Djibouti could have been a down payment on a home that they shared together, as a family?

————

Mohammed had almost given up on ever seeing Amal again when he met Ibrahim Qatabi, a lawyer for the Center for Constitutional Rights, at a Yemeni wedding in Brooklyn. "I knew who he was, so I went up to him and introduced myself. I told him the whole story," he told me. To his surprise, Ibrahim asked him if he would be interested in joining a lawsuit, suing the Trump administration on behalf of families who had been separated by the ban. He immediately agreed to be the lead plaintiff.

One week after the lawsuit was filed—and one and a half years after Amal had landed in Djibouti—she had a visa.

Amal was supposed to call Mohammed during a layover in Doha, but her plane had arrived late, so she ran through the airport to make sure she didn't miss her connection instead. "I couldn't wait," she remembered. "I didn't want to take any chances!"

Mohammad grew nervous when he didn't hear from her, wondering if she had made it onto the airplane. After more than two years apart, he didn't want to get his hopes up that he was going to finally see her later that day. What if she hadn't been allowed to board? Anything could happen to a Yemeni woman traveling in the age of Trump; a visa did not feel like a guarantee that she could travel. But dozens of friends and family members insisted on accompanying him to the airport, eager to see the young couple reunite after so long apart. "I think around fourteen cars came with me that day," he said later, laughing as he remembered the procession of friends and family members who were just as excited to see Amal. "It felt kind of like its own little wedding."

As he drove along the ocean, Mohammed thought back to the thousands of hours that he must have spent on FaceTime with Amal. Most of the time, people have to wait until after they are married to get that close—but somehow, during those long, often painful calls, being there for each other had allowed them to transcend many layers of love. "I didn't know it was possible to love someone that much," he told me. "Our love grew to something beyond what I could have ever imagined."

And Amal? At first, she was nervous—after all, how could she know that they could be husband and wife when they had only spent two weeks together in their adult lives? But when she finally saw him, grinning from ear to ear in the Arrivals area of John F. Kennedy International Airport, somehow both the little boy that she had cared about more than anyone and the man who had proved he would do anything for her, her anxiety melted away. "At that moment, I realized that wherever he was, I would be home."

————

Over the years, dozens of lawyers challenged the Muslim ban, sometimes resulting in happy reunions like Mohammed and Amal's. For every happy reunion, however, there were hundreds of broken hearts: families separated between the United States and the Middle East for even longer than the year and a half that Mohammed and Amal spent away from one another.

One of the first things that Joe Biden did as president was overturn the Muslim ban. Nevertheless, dozens of couples remained separated by the bureaucracy and backlog. Others had long since broken up. Denying people freedom of movement and the right to be with their families for four years has consequences that last beyond an electoral cycle—and even when legislation has been overturned and amended, it is impossible to get back that lost time.

During the ban, some people gave up on the US entirely. I know this because I am one of them. When Trump signed Executive Order 13769, Salem and I were not married, and had no legal right to be together in the United States. Working as a journalist in the Middle East meant that it was not as dire for me to live in my country as it was for many other Americans. Nevertheless, I wished that I could imagine starting a life in—or even visiting—the United States with my boyfriend, rather than feeling like I had to choose between the two of them.

Instead, I had to face reality. If we were going to explore our relationship, it was going to have to be in Erbil.

4 | *A Mouse*

Moving to Erbil felt like a crash course in the messiest aspects of war reporting.

At the beginning of 2017, the Kurdish capital was teeming with journalists covering the war on ISIS—many of whom were old friends of Salem from his time covering the war in Syria. A few years ago, they had all gotten to know each other in Aleppo, where they watched out for one another while they filmed and photographed stories of ordinary people living under Assad's barrel bombs. Many of them had witnessed the beginnings of the group that would go on to become ISIS, and were now gathering in Erbil to document what everyone hoped would be the end of their three-year reign of terror in Northern Iraq.

One of them was Alice Martins, a Brazilian photographer whom Salem had known for years. As soon as Salem got kicked out of Turkey, she prepared a room for us in the house that she shared with a group of journalists, no questions asked. "Salem is like my brother," she said with a laugh when I thanked her profusely. I had long admired Alice from afar—her photographs, of soldiers taking cigarette breaks or children going back to school, had a way of capturing moments that cut through the noise and went straight to the heart of the story. She was also one of a handful of women who routinely covered the most dangerous and difficult-to-access front lines in the Middle East.

I quickly learned that our new roommates were equally impressive. Cengiz Yar was a photographer who would film nail-biting Instagram stories that showed what it was like to run through narrow alleys in Mosul and duck for cover from ISIS snipers in real time. Cathy Otten, a British journalist from Manchester, could carry on full conversations in Kurdish and was chronicling the stories of Yazidi women who had been captured and enslaved by ISIS, which later became the book *With Ash on Their Faces*. Her Iraqi boyfriend, Arshad, dripped with boyish charm and had a magnetic personality that he used to help journalists secure access to Iraq's elite special forces—but really, he was most passionate about creating projects that showed the world that there was another side of Iraq that wasn't perpetual war and fighting. "I'm organizing a drift racing event in Mosul," he told us one day when he stopped by the house. He had a way of speaking so enthusiastically that even his craziest ideas, such as racing souped-up cars on the abandoned streets of a city that had only recently pushed out the world's most notorious terrorist group, seemed possible. "Want to come film it?"

It sounded as reckless as it was intriguing—what if ISIS retaliated or the area was not yet cleared of land mines? Still, it could just as easily be a chance to witness a city rise from the ashes. Not long ago, Beirut was a shell of itself, reeling from the aftermath of a fifteen-year civil war. Berlin had once been strangled by a wall that left people separated from one another for years on end. Cities can crumble in an instant, sometimes remaining forever fractured afterward by people who spend a lifetime seeking revenge. But they can also be built back up again by those who want to pave the way forward into the future. I was curious about which story I would see in Mosul.

"How are you feeling?" Alice asked me the morning we were set to depart. I was anxiously packing and repacking a backpack with bandages, spare underwear, and anything else I thought I might need for my first overnight trip to a questionable war zone.

"Is it wrong that I'm a little bit nervous?" I confessed. As much as I tried to focus on the excitement of being a part of one of Arshad's hare-brained ideas, I couldn't help wondering about the likelihood of ISIS suddenly pushing back, or a rogue suicide bomber detonating himself in the middle of the event. Then I felt guilty when I thought about the number of people who lived under this reality every day. They would probably love to have the option to stay sheltered in a comfortable house in Erbil instead.

"If you are never afraid, you can never be brave," she responded, thoughtfully pouring the last of the coffee into my cup. I had always assumed that some people were born fearless, preprogrammed to run straight into fire without worrying about the consequences. I never considered that bravery could only exist as an antidote to fear.

"Also, you're going to need these," she said, tossing me a package of wet wipes. I hadn't considered that there might not be functioning toilets near the front lines. It brought a whole new meaning to the importance of female friendships.

A few hours later, we piled into Arshad's car and set off down the lonely desert highway toward Mosul. As we drove farther away from Erbil, fear dissipated into intrigue as I started recognizing the names of places that I had heard about from other journalists. Al-Qayyarah was the oil-rich town that ISIS had torched to thwart the Iraqi soldiers' advance, making residents choke on thick black smoke that coated their sheep in layers of soot that made them look as if they had rolled in coal. Al-Bartella—our destination—was a Christian neighborhood on the outskirts of Mosul that had been one of ISIS's first targets—militants stormed the streets in 2014, lighting churches on fire and barging into people's homes, demanding that they either pay a tax to the Islamic State or flee. Anyone who refused was executed in the public square.

Once we arrived, a group of soldiers greeted us, inviting us inside a house whose door had been blown off its hinges, making it look like a rotting carcass. It used to be a family home, two stories with a spacious reception room that used to welcome guests who were not journalists, at a time when Al-Bartella was just an ordinary neighborhood in an ordinary city. Now the walls were scrawled with ISIS graffiti, vestiges of an occupation whose footprint still felt fresh.

I wondered where the family that used to live here was now. Now, the soldiers triumphantly laid out their mattresses underneath walls that had been painted with ISIS slogans, cracking jokes into the night as if they were at a boyish slumber party. "You snore like an elephant!" one of them shouted to another, to peals of laughter. "Don't worry, I won't leave your side," Salem whispered to me as I curled up next to him. We fell asleep to the sounds of laughter and soldiers snoring.

The next morning, we gathered next to the mosque, not sure what to expect from a drifting event in Mosul—even though the area was liberated, Iraqi Special Forces officers had still sealed off the street and were on high alert just in case. One car screeched around the corner, its engine popping like gunfire before speeding off toward West Mosul. A pickup truck followed—with actors dressed as terrorists, meant to symbolize what had happened to the city. Salem jumped into the back of the truck, filming them up close. It wasn't part of the plan. What if soldiers who weren't aware of the event didn't know that they were actors? Suddenly, I heard a popping sound in the distance and hid underneath an awning with another journalist. I thought it might be one of the cars and hoped I didn't look ridiculous ducking for cover. Later, I found out that it was an ISIS drone—which could have been dropping explosives.

"You promised you wouldn't leave my side," I seethed to Salem afterward, shaking with anger. He seemed invigorated by the excitement, unperturbed by the ISIS drone that had just been whizzing over our heads. "I was filming!" he said, riding the high of finally feeling like he was in his element. Practically, I knew that he couldn't both film and stay comfortably attached to my side. Still, I wondered how many explosions

I would have to shelter from on my own, if we were going to build our lives here.

Back in Erbil, the mundane logistics of sudden exile took over our lives. We had to find a place to live—more journalists were coming to Alice's house for the next phase of the operation, and we were starting to feel like we had overstayed our welcome. Still, I was reluctant to move on. As long as we were staying there, we could pretend that we were ordinary journalists, just staying for a few days before going back to our lives in Istanbul. It was our last portal into denial.

"We might need to find someone to forge us a marriage certificate," Salem casually dropped one morning, while we were drinking our coffees in the front yard. Most of the foreign journalists and NGO workers rented big guest houses together, without worrying how it looked that a group of unmarried men and women were living in a conservative country as if they were on an episode of *The Bachelor*. But Salem worried that our particularly odd combination of passports might not afford us the same privileges.

I rolled my eyes at him, suddenly seeing the layers of bribery and corruption needed to survive in contested territory. "I'm not forging any documents," I told him, realizing that if I were to have a marriage certificate, I wanted the commitment of an actual marriage to go with it. Uprooting my life was making me crave stability, and a grand romantic gesture would have made me feel more secure than joyriding around Mosul.

Too many fake documents, and I would have no idea what was real.

A few hours later, we found ourselves in the offices of an apartment complex called Lebanese Village, which looked more like the suburban apartment complex of my nightmares than a bucolic village of the motherland. Still, it had one- and even two-bedroom apartments that we could afford, and promised a housing contract to make it official. I realized that this contract could be important to our future—if we had enough documents to prove that we had continuously lived together, it might help us apply for a spouse visa to immigrate to the United States.

"Where is your marriage certificate?" the manager asked, staring at me over thick glasses. I felt exposed, as if even the formless jeans and long-sleeve shirts I had started wearing so as not to stand out still made him think of me as a Western prostitute. No housing contract without a marriage certificate, no marriage without dozens of housing contracts. It felt like a trap.

"We had to leave Istanbul suddenly and left our marriage certificate in our apartment," Salem responded, the white lie slipping out of his mouth like honey. How easy it was for him to talk his way into and out of situations, while I wondered if we would spend the rest of our lives lying about our relationship.

"Please, it is very important that both of our names are on the document," I added, my American earnestness interrupting their delicate dance. "We need it to apply for visas in the future."

I watched the bespectacled manager turn back to the document and start writing something down. Perhaps our sweet-talking had worked. I imagined the housing contract folding itself into a paper airplane that promised to take us away and give us back our freedom. Our temporary exile was but a minor hiccup. I looked down at the fresh ink, expecting to see our names side by side. Instead, I saw the words: "Salem Rizk and his American wife."

"What does he think I am, a mouse?" I seethed. Our future living anywhere that wasn't a desolate apartment complex perched on the side of a desert highway depended on corroborating our relationship through reams of documents, stamped and notarized to erase any shadow of a doubt over their—and by extension, our—legitimacy. Now there would be a gaping hole in our records, one that Salem could theoretically fill with any fake American wife that he pleased.

"I am just a mouse in the corner. I don't have a name. I don't know how to talk. Why would I? I'm a mouse," I continued, now performing for an audience of empty park benches, perched on an elevated bed of concrete. Each building looked identical to the other; a bulldozer dumped a pile of rubble next to our new building. I did not know how long we would live there, or if we would ever escape what felt like a desert purgatory.

"Okay, little mouse," Salem said, extending his hand toward mine. Sometimes there comes a time when you have to accept your fate. "It's time to go home."

5 | *No Border Can Get in the Way of Your Love*

I always imagined exile as steeped in the romance of days gone by.

It was Leon Trotsky fleeing the USSR only to be murdered with an icepick, Marlene Dietrich sensually holding an elongated cigarette between two fingers, dramatically renouncing her German citizenship to protest the Nazis. It was Mahmoud Darwish fleeing Palestine, writing lyrical poetry to recreate a lost homeland only to realize that perpetual longing was as much a part of him as the land he longed for, adrift with no anchor save for the constant feeling of drifting.

Exile was the dramatic and storied world of poets and political thinkers, intellectuals who challenged oppressive regimes or political prisoners who spent their later years in Parisian cafés, chain-smoking cigarettes, penning op-eds about the true meaning of freedom.

I never thought of exile as the condition of ordinary people who fell in love. Not until I met Ava.

"I have been in exile for almost eight years," she told me over a Facebook voice call from her home in rural Mexico. I first reached out to Ava when I found out that she ran a Facebook group for US citizens whose husbands have been deported from the United States. While there are exiled wives around the world, the vast majority are scattered across Mexico, largely because deportation policies in the United States have historically targeted Mexican citizens. Many have

been living in the United States for decades, falling in love and starting families there—families where some people are US citizens, and
others are not.

"I know at least one woman in every state of Mexico," Ava continued.
Like the women who call her, Ava is also a US citizen, and up until her
husband, José, was deported to Mexico, she had never left the country.
"There are hundreds of others along the border."

The United States census regularly estimates the number of undocumented immigrants living across the country. Agencies such as US
Immigration and Customs Enforcement (ICE) and US Customs and
Border Protection (CBP) regularly gloat over the number of people they
apprehend—and deport—every year. No one has bothered to count the
number of US citizens whose spouses have been deported, who now live
in exile because of their own country's immigration laws.

Ava has the nearest estimates, after eight years of making herself
available to anyone who is considering moving to Mexico after their
partners are deported. Sometimes the women she talks to are still in
shock. Other times, they want logistical advice—how to register their
children as dual citizens, or find a good school once they're on the other
side of the border. "Almost everyone says they're going to come at first,"
she told me, when I asked her how common it is for people to relocate
once their families have been torn apart. "I would say that thirty percent
actually do."

Looking through Ava's photos, it is easy to think that she might have
spent the past years offering guided tours around Mexico rather than
acting as an emergency responder for women whose husbands have just
been deported. She often shares beautiful photos of herself, José, and
their adorable ten-year-old son, Luis, hiking up waterfalls and riding on
horseback through the rolling hills of the Mexican countryside. Many
of them involve some version of José goofing off with Luis, wearing

matching dinosaur costumes or shooting at one another with squirt guns. Ava posts captions joking that she has not one child, but two.

"I love Mexico for letting me have a family again," she continued, the gratitude audible in her gravelly voice. "I just want to show people that there is a life after deportation."

But Ava's journey into exile has not always been as picture-perfect as her photo albums would suggest. It began on a sunny afternoon in 2014, when she was tidying her home and waiting for a phone call from José—whom she had been in love with ever since he first confessed his obsession with *Beverly Hills, 90210* to her while they were on a work site together. "I was his Donna," Ava told me, laughing as she remembered the early days of their courtship. It is easy to imagine when she shares photos from those times—José is young, burly, and broad-shouldered with an obvious sense of humor radiating through his eyes, while Ava is a cute, all-American bottle blonde, smiling as he pushes her around in a shopping cart. "At one point, we worked as a bouncer and a shot girl," she laughed—it was one of many jobs that she and José worked together, giving them ample amounts of time to fall in love with everything about each other. She loved his goofy sense of humor, and the way he could always make her laugh. He loved the way she stuck up for him, and wasn't afraid to get in someone's face. When their first son, Luis, was born, they both melted.

A few months after the baby was born, José drove to the airport to pick up a friend, and had the audacity to drive a few meters in the pickup line without a seatbelt. Suddenly a police siren started going off, and within a few minutes, José was arrested, and being told that he had a deportation order, and would be detained until he was sent back to Mexico and banned from entering the United States for the next ten years.

That night, all Ava wanted to do was eat dinner with José, but an ICE agent insisted on escorting him during her visit. "I told her that I wanted to have dinner with my husband," she remembered. "She told me that she had to have dinner with him—so I told her she would be having dinner with both of us."

As soon as she drove home, she realized that it was just going to be her and Luis from now on. She broke down, sobbing. "I didn't know what I was going to do," she said, remembering the moment that she realized she was on her own, with a newborn baby. "I had to get a job as a nanny, because it was the only way that I could work and bring along Luis."

Back living on the ranch in rural Mexico where he grew up, José desperately missed his family in the United States. Every day Luis grew a little bit older, and José felt like he was missing out on being a father. Still, Ava was barely getting by, as a single parent working two jobs, and it felt like there was no hope for her to reunite with José in the United States, not with a ten-year ban. So, almost two years after he was first arrested for driving without a seatbelt, he set out across the Sonora desert, trekking through the rough, arid terrain, even though he knew it was dangerous to push through the relentless June sun that reaches at least 100 degrees every day. Sometimes, he stepped away from the rest of the group and snapped a picture of the landscape for Ava, knowing that she was counting down the minutes until they would be a family together again.

"Almost home," he wrote, sending along a picture of a mountain rising in the distance. Ava could hardly wait, tidying the house, imagining what she was going to make for dinner. "I was planning a pot roast, since that was always José's favorite," she told me. "We had planned it all so that he would be home just in time for Father's Day," she continued. She couldn't stop fantasizing about the moment that José walked in the door, and Luis saw him for the first time since he was a baby. The minute her phone rang, it sprung into her hand.

But it wasn't José on the other end of the line. "I am with the consulate," a woman's voice told her. "We are calling to inform you that your husband is still alive."

"What do you mean he's alive?" Ava asked, feeling herself become dizzy.

"He was unconscious when Border Patrol found him," the consular officer continued, as if this was the kind of call she made regularly. Ava felt her heart plummet straight to her stomach as the consular officer continued: "He is currently in the hospital and will be released into ICE custody after he recovers." Ava felt her knees buckle underneath her as she fell to the floor.

"No!" she shouted into the speaker, feeling as if she were in a bad dream. "No, no no. We have been waiting for two years for him to come back—his son is waiting for him. He has to come home." The phone clicked with indifference.

Pills. Pills would do the trick—she gulped down a handful, and then regretted the decision the minute that she remembered that Luis was sleeping soundly in the other room. "I called a friend and made myself throw up," she told me, remembering the moment that she almost took her own life. "But at that moment, I realized if both José and I were going to be alive for Luis, it was going to be in Mexico."

A few days later, José called her from Mexico. "I'm so sorry, I'll try again, as soon as I can, baby." Ava wouldn't let him finish. "I won't let you do that," she responded. "We are going to come to you." Overcome with emotion, José couldn't believe he might be able to be with Ava and Luis, again. "You would do that for me?"

First, Ava had to get a passport. "I thought that Mexico was like something out of the movie *Desperado*," she told me, laughing at herself now that she has lived there for almost a decade. Living in the United States, it is easy to absorb the media's representation of Mexico as a giant drug cartel, eager to kidnap cute blonde girls like Ava and hold them for ransom. Most of our media does not offer anything other than images of violence and abject poverty; they forget to acknowledge that ordinary people live there, too.

"Every time I felt myself getting nervous, I just reminded myself that I was doing this so that Luis could have a father," she told me, remembering what it was like to pack up her home—their home—and sell everything until it was stripped bare. *Luis will have a home, not a house,* she told herself—and on a beating hot day in July, she packed up her car and buckled Luis into his car seat, hoping that he would sleep. As she inched out of her neighborhood and turned onto the interstate, she grew nervous. She did not know what to expect. All she knew was that in a few days, the three of them would be a family again.

Once she reached Texas—and saw the saguaro cacti dotting the desert landscape like giant creatures, with their arms outstretched—she started to get excited. Luis ran toward one, yelping in surprise when it pricked his fingers. "I didn't know it could cut him!" she said, remembering getting accustomed to the new landscapes.

But as soon as she saw the intimidating concrete overpasses of the McAllen/Hidalgo International Bridge, the butterflies turned into waves of nausea that made her nearly double over as she inched toward the border. "If I'm meant to be here, they'll let me through," she told herself. After a short inspection, the gate lifted, and she drove across the bridge. José was waiting for her on the other side, as close to the border itself as he could possibly get. "I just melted into him," she remembered. A very hyper Luis ran around in circles.

José looked as if he had just seen him sprout wings. "He can walk now?"

"I hope so," Ava laughed, suddenly feeling light for the first time in two years. "He's two years old!"

It took more than ten hours to reach the two-hundred-year-old cinder block house that was attached to the ranch that José's family had owned for generations. As soon as Ava saw it, her heart sank. Electrical wires hung from the ceiling, and she couldn't stop imagining Luis touching one and suddenly electrocuting himself. "Is there running water?"

she asked, suddenly acutely aware that she was very far from anything familiar.

"We get it from the river," José answered, smiling. He still couldn't believe that she was there. "Don't worry—I'll teach you how." The next day, he showed her how to load the water tank in the back of the truck and drive down to the river—where, for the next two hours, they filled five-gallon water buckets with river water, to dump in the tank. Once the tank was full, they slowly inched the truck back to the house, and then climbed a ladder to hoist it onto the roof. It took between five and six hours. "I never realized how many things I took for granted," Ava told me, remembering those early days, adjusting to things like drawing water from the river for washing and gathering firewood for cooking.

At first, Ava was too scared to leave the house. José helped her as much as he could—buying groceries and translating for her when they went into town—but most of the days he had to work, and left her at home with Luis. "We would go down to the river and skip rocks," she remembered. "We watched a lot of Spanish cartoons."

Even being a housewife was challenging. "Luis was losing weight, and I felt like a terrible mother," she told me, remembering how she even felt overwhelmed by cooking simple meals. She didn't know how to use any of the ingredients that were available, and the altitude difference meant that nothing was coming out right. Trying to surprise José with a batch of snickerdoodle cookies turned into a disaster as she mixed flour, sugar, butter, cinnamon, and eggs together the way that she had thousands of times, only to watch in horror as it liquified into a blob at the bottom of the pan. "All I had to do was add an extra cup of flour, to account for the altitude change," she told me, sharing one of the tips that she frequently shares with other American women who suddenly find themselves trying to recreate their lives. But at the time, it felt as if even the chemistry of cookie dough was plotting against her.

Nevertheless, José was always supportive, even when she presented him with a puddle of sugary mush at the bottom of a pan. "It's even better than regular cookies," he said, smiling. "Let's have them like this from now on."

Meanwhile, Luis was picking up Spanish so quickly that Ava was starting to feel embarrassed. One morning, she opened the cupboard only to find that she was out of eggs and promptly burst into tears. "I decided that was it—I had to start going to the store by myself," she remembered. At first, she cautiously teetered at the threshold of the corner shop, clutching Luis's hand so tightly that her knuckles turned white. "I need seven eggs," she said, shyly. Another customer offered to translate—and it turned out that he was a deportee as well. "You want a medio-kilo," he said, writing it down on a piece of paper. "I pointed to that piece of paper until I got the words right," she told me, and it is easy to imagine her guarding it like a secret code, a key to finally unlock her new life.

A few days later, she ventured to a small clothing shop, where she noticed that two stylish women around her age were working at the cash register. José had pointed them out to her as his distant cousins, and she hoped that they didn't think of her as the American woman who was too afraid to leave the house. "Come sit with us," one of them beamed, introducing herself as Erika. She had shiny black hair that fell over her shoulders in soft waves and a magnificent smile. Meanwhile, Gloria was the daughter of the town doctor and seemed to know everyone. "You need anything? Just ask me," she told Ava, and Ava immediately wondered why she had taken so long to befriend them.

"I started spending every afternoon with them," Ava said, remembering the way that she started picking up bits of Spanish as she learned that shirts cost between viente and cinquente pesos and jeans ran between ciento and dos ciento pesos. After a few weeks of carefully observing Erika and Gloria, Ava tried her hand at the cash register. "I messed up so many times," she said, remembering the way Gloria always swooped in to save her. "But I got to know everyone in the town." Soon, everyone knew them as "las tres muskateras."

"We empowered each other," she continued, remembering the way that they used to take turns watching each other's kids, while the others minded the shop. It was a feeling of community unlike anything Ava had ever experienced in the United States, where the only way to raise Luis as a single parent was to take a job as a nanny and hope that her employer didn't have a problem if she brought him along. Sometimes, after the kids were asleep, a bottle of tequila would make an appearance, and they'd turn up Selena's "Bidi Bidi Bom Bom" until they were dancing on the tables.

"We were just three housewives, but we ran a business together," Ava remembered. "We became sisters."

As Ava told me her story of adjusting to life in exile, I remembered those first few weeks in Erbil, when the shock of being suddenly uprooted from our lives in Istanbul faded into the slow, dull ache of prolonged displacement. I was not isolated on a ranch in rural Mexico, struggling to gather firewood and draw water from a river, but I still felt disoriented, as our romantic walks along the Bosphorus transitioned into walking in circles around the parking lot of our gray apartment complex instead.

"I heard that a TV station needs a correspondent in Mosul," Salem told me, eager to make me see that moving to Erbil might be worthwhile for our work as journalists. "You should do it."

I knew that I needed to start working again to feel like myself, but I was still reeling from the shock of Salem being kicked out of Turkey. "Who do you think I am, Christiane Amanpour?" I joked, not wanting to admit that I was already feeling out of my depth. Everyone around us was constantly going to Mosul, coming back to Erbil at night with stories of nearly being surrounded by ISIS fighters or nearly grazed with a sniper bullet. Meanwhile, in my mind I kept playing and replaying the night that Salem was stopped at the border.

"You'll be so good on camera," Salem pleaded, trying to coax me out of my comfort zone. "Please try. For me?"

A few days later, I made my way to a small house that had been converted to an office, with flak jackets, helmets, and camera equipment strewn across the living room floor, where I met Hussein, an Iraqi journalist who seemed somehow ageless, with wild silver hair that spurted out of his head as if he had been electrocuted and aviator sunglasses that he even wore indoors. Hussein had seen it all—the US invasion and the Gulf wars that came before it—and probably thought that the Mosul operation was child's play.

"Pick one!" he said, wildly gesticulating toward a pile of flak jackets that looked like they were made for men around two times my size. I chose one that said PRESS on one side, and its Arabic equivalent SAHAFA on the other, hoping that it would make people feel comfortable speaking to me in Arabic, and not see me as just another Western journalist, simply there to extract their trauma and get out. "Tomorrow you'll go to Mosul," he said, as if he was telling me about an ordinary morning meeting. "Be here at seven a.m."

At the time, I thought of myself as an expat; I was here because my US passport allowed me to follow Salem to Iraq, and even to easily find a job that would help me be the journalist that I had always dreamed of becoming.

Getting to know Ava years later made me realize that I was also navigating my own unique journey into exile, trying to prove to myself that I was brave enough not only to be a war correspondent, but also to commit to a life where I would not always be able to just go back to the US if things spiraled out of my control. I will always admire the courage of other conflict reporters, but it is easier to be brave when you know that your government will bail you out. Up until now, I had always had these privileges—but suddenly, that protection felt useless, since I could not extend it to Salem. If the war that we were writing about turned into a war that we had to flee, I could always just go "home." But what was home without Salem?

Since then, I have often thought about the idea of romantic exile. It may not be exile in the traditional sense of the word, and yet, *exile* is the only word that correctly places the blame on governments for creating policies that force us to take our lives with our loved ones elsewhere. No one drove Ava and me out of the United States—and yet, at least for me, the moment I fell in love with Salem, the chasm between me and my country began to grow. It was a conscious choice to follow Salem to Iraq—but, often, I find myself wondering: When did free will end and exile begin?

Most blame Trump for trying to ban Muslims and threatening to build a wall, but the United States has a long history of punishing its citizens for falling in love with the wrong kind of foreigner. Even during the time of relatively open borders before the 1924 immigration quotas, American women could be stripped of their US citizenship if they married an immigrant. It left thousands of women stateless, not knowing that they were no longer US citizens until they tried to access social security benefits or travel abroad. Men, on the other hand, could easily naturalize their foreign wives. Suffragettes campaigned to overturn this law, arguing that it robbed women of their autonomy, but even the Cable Act of 1922 that replaced it only allowed women to marry men who were eligible for US citizenship. At the time, this excluded emigrants from East Asia, Africa, and often, the Middle East.

Up until the 1960s, mixed-race relationships—even among US citizens—were still illegal in sixteen states, a hangover from both slavery and the eugenics-informed politics behind the 1924 immigration quotas. Mixed-race couples—typically White Americans and Black Americans, but also Asian Americans and Native Americans—lived knowing that the police could knock down their door at any moment, as they famously did with Mildred and Richard Loving, who were then kicked out of the state of Virginia and banished to live in Washington, DC. Even though they were now living in a more tolerant place, the Lovings still felt as if they had been unjustly ripped apart from their families and community, and famously took their case to the Supreme Court.

Loving v. Virginia became the Supreme Court case that finally abolished anti-miscegenation laws nationwide. Now, these laws seem archaic—but look closer and they are not all that different from the way that ICE can knock down the door of a family home today and decide that a mixed-status couple—like Ava and José—cannot be together. During the 1960s, mixed-race couples were banished to other states— now, mixed-status couples are banished to other countries. Those of us who are forced to follow our loved ones become new versions of ourselves, adapting to our surroundings because we have no other way to be with the people that we love.

————

Three years later, Ava had fallen head over heels with life on the ranch. Every morning, she rose before the sun to wash the clothes by hand in time to let them dry in the morning sunlight, which hit differently than the stronger midday sun. After she walked Luis to school, she would muck the stables and let the dogs run wild, taking in the wide-open spaces that reminded her of the rolling fields she had grown up around, breathing in the fresh mountain air before gathering hay to feed the horses or firewood to cook dinner. She spent afternoons helping Erika and Gloria at the shop, and evenings curled up next to José, finally feeling like herself.

Living at the ranch, Ava realized how much she used to take for granted. "I had to drive an hour and a half just to get tampons," she told me, laughing at the memories. Sometimes she didn't have money for gas—but Gloria taught her how to take a pair of scissors to Luis's diapers and create a maxi pad instead. "We made everything ourselves," she continued, remembering the way that old clothes became dishrags, T-shirts could be dresses, and almost any piece of fabric could become a toy for Luis. "Not a single thing went to waste."

She even started meeting other exiled wives—women just like her who had followed their loved ones to Mexico, hoping to no longer need to live in the shadows.

"I taught them my recipes," she said, and laughed, remembering how good it felt to share everything she had learned. "I wanted them to know they weren't alone."

But nothing lasts forever—not even living a simple life of trying to keep a family together. Even though Ava had grown accustomed to living off the land, she saw how hard José was working to support the three of them and started to understand why so many young people left to try their luck in the United States. "I don't think you truly understand until you are gathering firewood to burn, or drawing water from the well," she said, pointing out that most people who migrate are from rural areas. "People are working so hard, living with so little."

Soon, people she knew started to leave. "First it was the expats," Ava remembered. "All of the exiled wives just went running back to the United States." But Ava didn't want to leave; she had already left everything behind to keep her family together. Going to the United States would mean once again ripping Luis away from his father, and it felt ironic that she was being driven out of her home in Mexico by the same forces that pushed so many to migrate north in the first place.

Nevertheless, she knew that if she could spend a few months in the United States, she could provide a more comfortable life for the three of them. "I didn't want to leave, but I knew I had to," Ava said, remembering making the difficult decision as a family. Ava's mother bought her a bus ticket to the United States—an offer that Ava resisted at first, and then accepted, promising herself she would come back as soon as she had made enough money to support her family for a few months. It felt ironic to take the same trip that José, and so many others, had taken before her.

Instead of paying a coyote to smuggle her across the desert, however, she was able to take a bus to the border, a US passport in her hand, Luis on her lap, heartbroken to be leaving José behind.

"I felt horrible," she remembered. "I felt like I was running away."

————

Once upon a time, where there are now the imposing barbed wire and wrought-iron slats that make up 700 miles of our southern border, there was just a river, and the almost 20,000 Border Patrol agents stationed to intimidate people like José from crossing to the United States did not exist. Most important, Alta California and Santa Fe de Nuevo México— the land that makes up present-day California, Arizona, Nevada, New Mexico, Colorado, and Texas—belonged to Mexico, and the US–Mexico border was not even the Rio Grande, but the edges of the Louisiana Purchase, ending at the peaks of the Rocky Mountains.

But US president James K. Polk had his eye on expanding the United States to the Pacific Coast—and in 1846, he sent troops into disputed territory in Texas, kicking off a brutal territorial war between the United States and Mexico. Two years later, General Winifred Scott's army raised the American flag over Mexico City, and Mexican and American negotiators met in Villa Guadalupe Hidalgo on the outskirts of Mexico City to agree on the terms of a peace treaty. To end the war, Mexico would cede Alta California and Santa Fe de Nuevo México to the United States.

It resulted in chaos. What would happen to the more than 50,000 Mexican citizens, many of whom were indigenous to land that would now belong to the United States? Now, as borders were being redrawn, their lives hung in the balance. Slavery was illegal in Mexico but was common practice in the United States. Mexican negotiators were nervous that their people—who were neither Black nor White—might end up on the wrong side of the color line and be enslaved. As the Treaty of Guadalupe Hidalgo was drafted, they had one request: anyone who stayed on their land would be automatically granted US citizenship, and the privileges that came with it.

"Now, this was full citizenship," Miguel Levario, a Borderlands historian and the author of *Militarizing the Border: When Mexicans Became the Enemy*, told me, over a Zoom call. "It meant they could vote, own property—and that they were legally white."

Unsurprisingly, the Mexicans who decided to stay—the first Mexican-Americans—were rarely treated as white. "While the Texas Rangers were originally tasked with clearing Native Americans out of South and West Texas, they started targeting Mexican landowners, claiming that they were bandits," Dr. Levario continued, pointing out that the original Californio and Tejano communities were directly in the crosshairs of manifest destiny. At this point, the migrants were not Mexicans who stayed on their land, but the Anglo-American settlers who redrew the borders and were now trying to push them off, in order to claim the land as theirs. It is the origin of the popular Mexican-American protest chant: "We didn't cross the border; the border crossed us."

Race also shaped relationships. Wealthier, light-skinned Californianas and Tejanas were encouraged to marry white men to protect their land, and to assimilate into Anglo-American society. Darker, more obviously Indigenous people were frequently assaulted and even lynched. The border might not have yet physically divided people the way that it does today, but it institutionalized the white supremacist culture that continues to influence the way that Mexican and Mexican-American communities are treated in the United States to this day.

Interestingly, Mexican nationals were excluded from the 1924 immigration quotas, but this was largely due to the lobbying efforts of Texas ranchers, who depended on migration for cheap agricultural labor. "It was almost as if the US wanted their bodies, but not them," Dr. Levario said, pointing out that Mexican immigrants have rarely been seen as more than laborers throughout history. "They wanted people to do the work, but not to be a part of communities." It feels like the beginning of a theme that would characterize the relationship between the two countries for years to come: Come, but do not get too comfortable. Give us your best years, but do not start a family. Work until your body falls apart, but take nothing in return.

Up until that point, there were no immigration laws targeting Mexicans. Without immigration laws, there is no illegal immigration. A few symbolic concrete blocks marked the boundary between the two countries, and local sheriffs loosely policed the border, but people continued to cross freely. Border Patrol was just a fleet of seventy-five agents on horseback—but as the 1924 immigration quotas started to push the idea of controlling the kind of people who could immigrate to the United States, they shifted their attention to the southern border, recruiting Texas rangers and Ku Klux Klan members to fill their ranks. Soon, Border Patrol was a police force of white nationalist vigilantes and lynch-mob veterans, experimenting with immigration control tactics of their own. Sometimes, they would douse Mexican nationals in toxic chemicals to "delouse" them before crossing the border. Other times, they branded them like cattle, doing everything in their power to identify them as foreign and make sure that they knew that they did not belong.

Unsurprisingly, many Mexicans who wanted to work in the United States chose to cross the border outside of the official ports of entry. Even though this was technically illegal—and, as of 1924, a deportable offense—it was rarely enforced. People continued to cross as they always had, both "legally" and "illegally," though there were rarely consequences once they were in the United States. Then, in October 1929, the stock market crashed.

"American jobs for real Americans," proclaimed President Herbert Hoover, breathing life into the narrative that Mexicans were "stealing" jobs that could go to unemployed Americans. Department of Labor Secretary William Doak, who oversaw the Immigration and

Naturalization Services (INS), almost immediately addressed Congress, informing them that there were 400,000 people living in the United States without authorization, instructing employers to start laying off Mexican employees. He proposed adding a "Mexican" category to the 1930 US census, for the purpose of rounding up the Mexican and Mexican-American population, using the excuse of getting "real Americans" back to work.

Within weeks, INS officers were storming restaurant kitchens and factories in predominantly Mexican neighborhoods in Los Angeles, demanding to see proof that people had entered the country legally. If people could not produce these documents, they were promptly arrested and frequently thrown onto trains that took them straight to the border. With few immigration laws, there were also few immigration lawyers at the time—meaning that INS officers taking directions from the Department of Labor were able to largely act with impunity.

For me, the most jarring instance of these raids occurred on a sunny afternoon on February 26, 1931, when INS officers stormed La Placita Park in Los Angeles, sealing off every exit, transforming a lively scene of Mexican families enjoying tamales and mariachi music on a Saturday afternoon into every immigrant's worst nightmare. Unlike the factories that were being raided, La Placita Park was not a place of work, but a place of leisure—a respite from racist bosses, and the inevitable discrimination that came with being Mexican in Los Angeles. That afternoon, hundreds of people were held for over an hour and interrogated, causing a scene of utter panic. Seventeen people were apprehended, but the public display of intimidation created a climate of fear that made people pack up and leave—even those who did have papers.

"It all comes back to family separation," Dr. Levario told me, when I ask him why more than fifty percent of the people who were "repatriated" to Mexico were actually Mexican-Americans who could presumably prove their US citizenship. "People were afraid that if immigration enforcement officers came and invaded their homes while someone was at work, the parents might be taken to Mexico while the children stayed in the United States or vice versa," he continued, describing a political environment that feels all too familiar today. Exile, then as now, is the only way to keep a family together.

———————

As soon as Ava had made enough money to support her family for six months, she boarded a bus back to Mexico. Her bags were bulging with clothes and kitchen supplies for everyone that she knew, in hopes that she could bring some of the abundance of the United States to the people that she loved. "I was so excited," she remembered. "I felt like I was finally going home."

Home was no longer a ranch with wide open spaces, but a smaller house in a mid-sized city. Often, tourists came through on their way to visit ancient Mayan temples and Indigenous villages; the presence of the police that are deployed to protect the tourists makes her feel safer than she did on the ranch. Nevertheless, every day she missed the wide open spaces and the community that lived off the land that will always be home.

"I have so much respect for the women who live there, making delicious meals out of almost nothing," she told me, fondly remembering the moment that the elders started calling her pet names, and told her that, as far as they were concerned, she was one of them. "I feel so spoiled when I open a can of beans and pour it into a pot!"

Every year, Ava spends six months in Mexico and six months working in the United States. It is the easiest way to support her family, which, even though they have managed to find a way to be together, is still straddled between the United States and Mexico for half of the year. "One time Luis told me that he wants to go to La Frontera when he grows up," she laughs, mimicking the way that he talks about the border in Spanish, as if it is a far-off land. "I told him, you're a US citizen—you don't need to cross La Frontera. You can just go!"

Still, exile alone is not enough to keep a family together. "I couldn't have done this without José," she continued, gushing as she remembers the way that he showed his love for her those first few months. "A lot of women call me crying, telling me that their husbands are being difficult," she continued, saying that many don't get along with their in-laws, or are frustrated when their husbands are upset that they can't cook traditional meals. Sometimes, she has even had to intervene in situations that became abusive—something that Ava finds is unfortunately common, after someone is deported.

Meanwhile, José has always been excited to bring their cultures together. During her first Thanksgiving in Mexico, José made an excuse that he had to drive six hours for work, only to come back with Kentucky Fried Chicken, just to make her feel at home. One PTA meeting, when Luis's teachers were trying to get the parents to cook lunch for the students, José noticed Ava becoming self-conscious that she couldn't cook the mole that one of the teachers was suggesting. José suggested that they alternate, one week cooking mole, the next shepherd's pie. When one of the women grumbled that she didn't know how to make shepherd's pie, José shot back: "How do you expect Ava to know how to make mole?"

It reminds me of another story that Ava told me, about one of their first dates, when a younger version of Ava with bottle-blond hair sat across from a shy and self-conscious José at a roadside diner: another customer had turned around, snarling at José to learn English. "You should learn Spanish!" Ava shouted back. "There is a community college up the street."

Ava laughed when I reminded her of the story, which must have happened at least ten years ago. "You have to be there for each other," she said, smiling. "It makes everything easier."

———

Exile is not always an option. Sometimes it is too expensive—Ava makes it work by spending six months out of the year working in the United States, ironically separated from her family in order to support them. Other times, it is logistically impossible. I do not know how I would have followed Salem to Iraq if I had had children that I needed to protect or a job that didn't allow me to easily move from place to place. It was not until I started looking for other stories of love and borders that I realized how the ripple effects of a deportation could swell into a riptide, dragging entire families into its depths for years on end.

For every woman like Ava, there are dozens more like Cecilia.

"It has been a long day," Cecilia told me, when I called her after landing in Chicago. Ever since her partner, Hugo, was deported in 2012, Cecilia has worked at least two jobs at a time to support their five children. But that isn't all that she does. Somewhere between these shifts at the local hospital where she works as a medical technician, she volunteers at her church, translating sermons into Spanish and leading "Know Your Rights" trainings for undocumented immigrants. As if this were not enough, she also started a group called Family Reunification Not Deportation, which organizes trips to Washington, DC to lobby politicians on behalf of families who have been separated by US immigration policies. "Activism is my therapy," she laughed, when I asked her how she does everything that she does in a day. "If I don't stay busy, I'll just get depressed."

The day I visited her in Chicago, she had already worked a full shift at the hospital, and then gone to pray over a friend's partner who had recently fallen into a coma—but she still graciously agreed to meet, and suggested a Mexican restaurant downtown. Even though it was our first time meeting in person, I immediately recognized her from her glossy black hair and magnetic smile. She looked particularly beautiful, with perfectly manicured acrylic nails and long, feathery eyelashes. "I'm going to Tijuana soon," she smiled—and for Cecilia, going to Tijuana means getting to see the love of her life.

"Every time I visit him, I just fall in love all over again," she told me as we perused the menu.

Cecilia's trips to Tijuana remind her of everything that she loves about her Mexican heritage, and the values that she grew up with. "I can feel it in my blood when I'm there," she said, smiling as we debated which tacos to order. Taking long walks on the beach with Hugo always reminds her of one of her first visits in 2014, when they spontaneously decided to get married at the border wall—etching "Cecilia & Hugo" into the sand, surrounded by a heart. "It was so beautiful," she told me, remembering the day that they exchanged vows to never let a border come in the way of their love story. "We were surrounded by all these other activists who have been separated by borders. That day, they became our family, too."

But when it is time to fly back to Chicago, the reality hits that he can't come with her. "It is like I'm Cinderella, and my carriage is turning into a pumpkin again," she told me. Even though she is smiling, I can see the sorrow creeping into her eyes.

The story of how Cecilia and Hugo went from being a loving couple, with a big house and a white picket fence in Chicago, who drove their five kids to soccer practice in a Hummer, to being permanently divided by a border is so similar to the beginning of Ava and José's story that it can only be described as systemic. "I don't even remember what I was cooking that night," Cecilia told me, recalling an otherwise ordinary evening in 2012, when she was waiting for Hugo to come home. After a few hours passed with no news from him, she started to worry—but reasoned that maybe he had to work late or had decided to meet up with some of his buddies.

At midnight, her phone lit up with EVERGREEN POLICE DEPARTMENT on the Caller ID. "What happened?" she asked, suddenly wide awake.

"I got pulled over," Hugo said, his voice uncharacteristically anxious.

"That's okay, we can pay whatever fine," Cecilia responded, relieved that he didn't sound drunk. "Just come home."

"No baby," he responded, even more quietly. "They called ICE."

Cecilia didn't sleep that night. As soon as she could the next morning, she went to see an immigration lawyer, who had told her that he would be able to adjust Hugo's status—but it turned out, the process wasn't complete.

"I thought it would be easy since I'm a US citizen," she told me, but she soon realized there was nothing that she could do to keep Hugo from being deported. Still, the lawyer told her that there was a possibility that ICE wouldn't come—and to make sure that Hugo didn't sign anything.

But when she saw Hugo at the precinct a few hours later, it was already too late; he had been pressured to sign a document called a voluntary departure, voluntary only insofar as it stated that the undersigned would *voluntarily* leave the United States and would not be able to enter again for another ten years. His crime? An expired vehicle registration. It didn't matter that she was a US citizen, or that they had five citizen children together. Within ten days, Hugo was processed for deportation. All Cecilia could do was pack him a duffel bag with clothing, toiletries, and no more than three hundred dollars in cash. "I love you," she choked, handing him the duffel bag at five o'clock in the morning, the day before he left. "I love you, too, baby," he said, wishing that he could hold her close. The ICE agent on duty wouldn't allow them to touch.

ICE is the perfect name for it, she thought to herself, as she drove home, tears streaming down her face. It's cold, it's sterile—it's ice.

"Overnight, I had to become a mom and a dad at once," she told me. Before Hugo's arrest, she was thinking about cutting back a few hours at work, and finally pursuing a dream of going to nursing school. Now she was taking on every additional shift that she could, working evenings and weekends so that she could start to make up Hugo's lost wages. At first, it was almost enough. With her mom or her sister looking after the kids while she was at work, she could shuttle between jobs and still make sure that there was food on the table at dinnertime.

A few weeks later, a Department of Children and Family Services worker knocked on the door. "Did you know that your kids haven't been going to school?" the caseworker asked when Cecilia opened the door, breathless, getting ready for another shift. She did not—between working double shifts, Cecilia hadn't noticed that the school had been calling, or that her kids had been deleting the voicemails asking about their absence before she could listen to them.

"Look, their dad got deported and I've been working nonstop," Cecilia said, hoping that the woman would understand that Cecilia was the opposite of negligent, that all she could think about was how she could take care of her children, even if it meant being two people at once.

"What is your plan for if he can't come back?" the caseworker asked, narrowing her eyes. What plan? she thought. There is no blueprint for what to do when the father of your children is arrested and deported overnight, and suddenly a DFS caseworker is at your door, asking if you are fit to take care of your own children.

"I guess I'll move to Mexico," Cecilia answered, reasoning that it would be her last resort to keep her family together, if, even after Hugo's ten-year ban was up, he still couldn't come back.

"After ten years?" the caseworker scoffed. "By then your husband will have another wife and kids."

Moving to Mexico might be the best option, but it wouldn't be easy to uproot her family of five. Four of her kids were already in school, and Mahalea, the youngest, was just about to start kindergarten. There were five mouths to feed, which was hard enough in Chicago, but it would be nearly impossible to earn as much money in Mexico as she did in the United States. Besides, Chicago was home—it was where the rest of her family lived, and where her love story first began, when a twenty-four-year-old Hugo worked up the courage to ask a twenty-one-year-old Cecilia out to spend the afternoon with him on the bank of Lake Michigan, hoping she would say yes.

"He was not the type of person I pictured myself with at all," Cecilia laughed—at the time, she was what she describes as a "metal girl," listening to a lot of Metallica and rock and roll, while Hugo was into hip-hop and rap. For a twenty-one-year-old, this felt like an insurmountable difference. Luckily, the longer she spent with him, the more his presence made her feel so calm that their difference in music taste didn't feel so important—something about being around him just made everything click into place. Within one year, they had their first son. By the time she was twenty-nine, they were a rambunctious and loving family of seven: three girls and two boys.

"We were so good as parents," Cecilia told me, her voice soft as she remembered the way that they seamlessly shared their responsibilities, working together to create a home. "Hugo loved taking the kids to soccer games—I hated it," she laughed. On his days off, he would take everyone fishing at the lake. Even when he was working, Hugo always snuck home to tuck Mahalea—who, according to Cecilia, was always his "little princess"—into bed before finishing his last shift.

Now, Cecilia feels like a single mom, but the most frustrating part is that she is not. "My kids have a dad who would do anything to be with them," she said. "I have nothing against single mothers, but that's not me."

————

Even though the US government partially blamed Mexicans for the 1929 stock market crash and the Great Depression that came afterward, the moment that the US entered World War II and needed workers to replace the soldiers fighting overseas, the US government shamelessly reversed its tone, announcing the Bracero Program to recruit Mexican workers to toil on farms and in factories. Until then, most of the Mexican population was concentrated in the Southwestern United States. But with the new program, more people started coming to cities like Chicago.

"It was really risky to go," Lori Flores, a labor historian and the author of *Grounds For Dreaming: Mexican-Americans, Mexican Immigrants, and the California Farmworker Movement*, told me, explaining that men who wished to migrate to the United States as a part of the Bracero Program had to pay high fees to go to processing centers in Mexico, with no guarantee that they would have a good job with fair wages once they crossed the border. "People needed a way to support themselves and their families," she continued. "So, they accepted the risk, and pursued the ambition of bringing some of that money home."

Only men were allowed to be Braceros, their worth as immigrants contingent on their ability to perform hard labor. Most of the time they were recruited from rural areas of Mexico—and, as University of California—Irvine Chicano-Latino Studies associate professor Ana Elizabeth Rosas points out in her book *Abrazando el Espíritu*, the Bracero program targeted men with families, including a clause in each contract that they would return home. Many wrote love letters to their girlfriends and wives who stayed behind, but these letters often did not reach their recipients. Instead, they were intercepted by US consular officers, who cited "national security reasons" as an excuse to scour the letters for instructions on how to cross the border. "They feared these flourishing romantic relationships might prompt couples to marry and begin families," Dr. Rosas writes, describing the US government's anxieties that the workers they were importing might have the audacity to want to bring the people they loved to join them.

As a result, the US government singlehandedly orchestrated a scenario where women in Mexico assumed that they had been forgotten by their Bracero partners—and when they did not get responses to their letters, their partners undoubtedly assumed the same. Dr. Rosas writes about the way that women often sought support from one another, forming Casas Despiertas, or "Awake Houses," named for the organizers' desire to raise awareness about the emotional toll of the Bracero program on the women who were left behind and to encourage them to be open and honest about their experiences. Learning about these informal groups of women leaning on one another makes me think about Ava and the Facebook and WhatsApp groups of expats and exiles, where members exchange advice on everything from the logistics of deportation to the emotional toll of living with the impact of this cruel policy. Sometimes, the only support that we have comes from those whose stories mirror ours.

Meanwhile, many of the Braceros were falling in love in the United States—and while it was legal to work as a Bracero, it was not legal to stay past the end of a contract or cross the border without the program. "A lack of documentation started catching up with people in the 1950s," Dr. Flores said, pointing out that those who fell in love and started families often ran the risk of violating the narrow parameters of the program. Others wished to work in the United States, without the limiting rules of being a Bracero. To crack down on what he termed an "illegal invasion of wetbacks," head of the Immigration and Naturalization Services (INS) General Joseph Swing unveiled Operation Wetback, which would track down anyone who had entered the country without inspection, with a dramatic showdown of SWAT teams and military-grade helicopters. "People who might have been married or had children or been in the United States for twenty years could suddenly be separated," Dr. Flores continued. Unlike the INS raids during the 1930s, which were concentrated in Los Angeles and along the border, Operation Wetback went after Mexican communities across the United States, in cities like Chicago, proving that immigrants—and the people who loved them—were not safe no matter where they lived.

Sometimes families did not know that their loved ones had been swept up in a raid until weeks later. "They didn't have the kind of quick communication technology that we have today," Dr. Flores continued, reminding me that a world without cell phones is a world where our families can disappear into the night. "People didn't know what happened to their loved ones," she continued. "Even if they did, they might not know where to find them." My heart dropped as I imagined what it would have been like if Salem hadn't been able to call me the night that he was detained, and if Hugo hadn't been able to call Cecilia the night that he was arrested.

A few years later, the Bracero program came to an end. One year later, President Lyndon B. Johnson triumphantly addressed the nation from the base of the Statue of Liberty, announcing the end of the 1924 immigration quotas. "From this day forth, those wishing to immigrate to America shall be admitted on the basis of their skills and their close relationships to those already here," he said, announcing the 1965 Immigration and Nationality Act, also known as the Hart-Celler Act, to great fanfare. "Those who can contribute most to this country—to its growth, to its strength, to its spirit—will be the first that are admitted to this land." Immigration shifted from prioritizing emigrants from Western European nations to creating paths for families to be together, no matter where they were from. For everyone except Mexicans, that is.

During his speech, President Johnson failed to mention that the newly minted legislation would impose quotas on immigration from Mexico for the first time in US history. Mexicans, despite playing an enormous role in keeping the economy alive during World War II and for decades before, were not included in the list of those who could contribute to the country's growth, or its strength. Even though many of those same workers had started families in the United States, their family ties would not be considered as a legal reason for them to stay. Instead, it would make it far more difficult to legally immigrate, causing a spike in illegal—and by extension, punishable—immigration instead. Ironically, the immigration act that opened the United States back up to the world also cemented the southern border as a force for dividing families with loved ones on both sides.

———————

A few days after our first meeting, I joined Cecilia at the Lincoln United Methodist Church, a modest building in Chicago's historically Mexican Pilsen neighborhood. Despite its unassuming façade, the church has a rich history of providing a space for activists, everything from organizing marches for justice for young people of color targeted by the police to campaigning for a path to citizenship for all undocumented immigrants.

"This is where I come on my days off," Cecilia laughed, when she pulled up a few minutes later.

Inside, the church feels more like a summer camp than a place of worship, with high school–age kids painting the walls and showing off giant squash they harvested from a community garden as part of an initiative to bring healthy food to low-income communities. Cecilia kicked off her shoes and got to work—sharing information about an upcoming delegation to Washington, DC, where she was hoping to get a few other people to lobby politicians to overturn the 1996 legislation that led to the ten-year bans that have kept families like hers separated for so long.

"Can you join me in Washington, DC, in September?" she asked one of the students who had expressed interest in the trip. Everyone crowded around her, and you could see why she can rally huge numbers of people, as she shared parts of her story and invited them to connect on social media. A few days before, she had even made her first TikTok video.

"My kids make fun of me," she laughed, as she shows me the video of herself, playfully swaying to the music, while sharing information about the upcoming trip to Washington. "But maybe if we can be influencers, we can influence politics," she pointed out. "Maybe that way we can get our law."

After most of the high schoolers had left, Cecilia and I sat together on a small bench outside of the main hall. "Borders divide what God brought together," she told me as we looked up at an engraving of Jesus on the cross. "I used to think that God was punishing me," she continued. "Now I know that He was testing me."

Even though it feels as if Cecilia's faith in God has always been unwavering, she didn't always feel comfortable coming to church. At first, she thought that God was punishing her for having children before she was married—but when even marrying Hugo didn't do anything to help reunite him with his family, and lawyers told her that her case was too complicated, she turned to Facebook, where she found a video of an auburn-haired woman named Elvira Arellano talking about how she was living in a church to resist being taken away from her US citizen son.

"She lived in a church for a year to keep her family together," Cecilia told me, her eyes becoming wide in reverence. Churches, along with schools, hospitals, and other places of worship, are one of a handful of places in the United States where ICE is not authorized to conduct raids. For this reason, Elvira was able to stay in the church. The first time that Cecilia reached out to her, Elvira invited her to a service. At first, Cecilia was nervous about attending a Methodist church service as a Catholic, but as soon as she walked in, she saw a room where everyone looked like her.

"It saved me," she said, smiling as she remembers meeting dozens of other immigrant families who knew exactly what she was going through. Soon, Cecilia was hosting "Know Your Rights" trainings for the congregants, organizing protests and demonstrations for those who were interested in lobbying politicians, and even training as a pastor so that she could pray for families split apart by deportation. Often, her kids join her at rallies—and the first time that Mahalea spoke, and told the crowd her story and finished by saying "We didn't cross the border, the border crossed us," Cecilia was overwhelmed with pride.

"She's feisty!" she laughed. "I'm passing it on to the next generation."

Even though Cecilia has found her calling fighting for other separated families, she wishes that she didn't have to keep telling her story over and over again. "I never thought he would be gone this long," she told me. "Mahalea was only four and a half years old when he was deported, and now she has just had her quinceañera. For us, that means she is a young woman, but all of this time she has been without her dad." Now that her older children are becoming adults—moving out of the house, and even starting relationships of their own, Cecilia wonders how Hugo's prolonged absence will affect them, too. "My oldest daughter just moved in with her boyfriend and my son has a girlfriend," she told me, as her younger son, Enrique, comes over to us, planting a giant kiss on her cheek then scampering away. "I know they don't want families yet, and that is fine—but I know that our experience is part of why they're hesitating," she continued. "We were this loving family and the system just completely ripped us apart."

More than 22 million people across the United States live in a mixed-status household, meaning that at least one member of the family does not have papers. While US citizens like Cecilia and her children cannot themselves be deported, there is nothing stopping their spouses and parents from being taken away—not to mention grandparents, aunts, uncles, siblings, cousins, and anyone else who doesn't necessarily fall into the narrow definition of a nuclear family. No one knows the number of people whose families have been torn apart by the system, the tally of broken hearts.

"I am grateful that I was born here, and can travel back and forth," Cecilia continued, insisting on counting her blessings. Many undocumented couples and families are faced with an impossible choice if one of them is deported: Follow your partner and give up everything you have put into building a home in the United States, or stay and accept that you might be separated from the person you love for the rest of your life.

Without a US passport or green card, it doesn't matter that Mexico is just across the border; it may as well be on another planet.

Even with the privileges of being a US citizen, Cecilia bears the dubious honor of being one of the only people that she knows whose marriage has lasted this far into a ten-year ban. "You have to let go of all of your insecurities," she laughed, when I asked her for her secret. At first, she used to worry that Hugo might reconnect with an old girlfriend or move on. Too many missed phone calls or holidays spent apart could easily cause two people to drift apart until they become strangers—often, it does.

But it has not been the case for Hugo and Cecilia. "We just know each other so well," she mused out loud, telling me that every time she is even a little bit sad, Hugo can hear it in her voice, and talks to her until she feels better. They support one another in every way that they can, even when they cannot physically be together. Hugo FaceTimes her whenever her car breaks down, walking her through exactly how to fix it. Just the other night, he called just to hear her voice before he fell asleep. "I had a dream about you the other night. You looked so beautiful," he said, dreamily looking into the camera. "Are you saying I'm not pretty?" she responded, flipping her long, luxuriously dark cascading waves as if to prove that she is anything but stunning.

"No! You're always beautiful," he said, quickly backpedaling. She loved how flustered he got when she teased him, flirtatious banter bringing them back to exactly why they fell in love in the first place. "But you looked so young!"

"So, you don't think I look young anymore?" she shot back, and as Hugo put up his hands in mock exasperation, it suddenly felt to her as if there were no border between them, hardly different than it was twenty years ago, when it was just the two of them on the bank of Lake Michigan, wondering how she, a girl who liked rock and roll, ended up on a date with a boy who liked hip-hop. "I always say no border can get in the way of your love," she told me, smiling as she remembered the phone call from just a few nights ago. "You fight for who you love," she continued. "I love my husband, and I love my family, and I will always fight for them."

Spending time with Cecilia brings into focus the way that borders have been shaping the lives of couples and families for decades. Even though Trump became notorious for separating families at the US–Mexico border in 2018, many presidents before him have cruelly ripped people apart from the people that they love, as evidenced through both Ava and Cecilia's stories. Bill Clinton created the Illegal Immigration Reform and Immigration Responsibility Act in 1996—the legislation that implemented three- and ten-year bans for people who were arrested and deported, even for crimes as innocuous as driving without a seat-belt or with an expired registration. George W. Bush's Department of Homeland Security "secured the border" by birthing agencies such as ICE and CBP to push the idea that all foreigners were threats who should be kicked out of the country. More people were deported during Obama's administration than under any other president, and more than the total of all other presidential administrations of the twentieth century combined. José and Hugo were both deported during his time in office.

And Trump? Trump normalized it, building an entire presidential campaign around building a wall that dozens of people before him had already built, constantly reminding undocumented families that their days together were numbered. He even gutted the political asylum system that had been built to welcome the world's "poor, huddled masses," and tried to "deter" people from coming to the United States, most famously through separating mothers from their children at the border, as "punishment" for seeking refuge.

For people fleeing gang violence, economic collapse, and the growing impact of climate change in countries like Honduras, Guatemala, and El Salvador, this was hardly enough to dissuade them from coming. Over the past few years, their countries had become so dangerous that the United States, even with Trump in power, was their last hope for freedom and safety. While the number of people migrating from Mexico to the United States has decreased in recent years, the number of people coming from Central America has increased, particularly as political instability and gang violence have spiraled out of control there, leaving people with few other options.

Historically, most of the people crossing the southern border have been people like Hugo and José, those hoping to make a better living than they could in Mexico, and staying—or trying to stay—once they start families. People also come from Honduras, Guatemala, El Salvador, and many other countries, often fleeing failed states and organized crime that have claimed the lives of so many like them.

And some are fleeing for love—at the end of 2018, Oscar and Darwin, a young queer couple from Honduras, were two of them.

"I was afraid of the journey," Oscar Juárez Hernandez, who was only nineteen years old at the time, told me, when I asked him what it was like to make the decision to come to the United States as a couple. "It was technically my idea," Darwin Garcia Portillo interjected—he is a little bit older, and Oscar clearly looks up to him. "Unfortunately, in our country, you can be killed for being gay," he continued. "It is very sad."

Homosexuality is technically legal in Honduras, but homophobia and discrimination are everywhere, and it is not easy to live together as an openly gay couple, especially in a city like San Pedro Sula. Oscar tried to apply for jobs, only to have potential employers look down on him, asking him why he shaved his eyebrows and wore such tight-fitting clothes. He had tried to come out to his mother when he first met Darwin, but she couldn't wrap her head around the fact that he was falling in love with a man, so he moved out. Once they were living together, they tried to include their families in their relationship—but were frequently met with snide remarks and cold shoulders. "Often, they told us our relationship was a sin," Darwin remembered.

And then, there were the gang members who started harassing them, every time they left the house. "Maricón," they shouted after them, even during the day when they were just going to the grocery store. "Fucking faggots." Gangs like the Mara Salvatrucha, commonly known as MS-13, and their rivals, Calle 18, are notorious in Honduras, particularly in areas where the government is weak, slipping into power vacuums to recruit new members and intimidate anyone who is not with them. As a queer couple, Oscar and Darwin were easy targets.

"We can't keep living in this country," Darwin groaned to Oscar one night, when it felt as if the harassment might never end. Ever since more people started joining the caravans going to the United States in 2018, he had been pushing for the two of them to leave. As the oldest son in a family without a father, Darwin felt enormous pressure to provide for his younger brother. After his mother passed away when he was young, he no longer felt like it made sense to do it from Honduras. Besides, he wanted to live somewhere where he could be himself for a change.

But Oscar had heard stories of people dying after tumbling from trains, falling victim to corrupt police officers who shook them down for bribes. Stories of exploited and extorted migrants hung vividly in his imagination. Besides, he didn't want to leave his mother and sister behind. But staying in San Pedro Sula was becoming a little bit more dangerous every day. Oscar was just growing accustomed to the way that armed men shouted at them from a distance when they started sending him threatening messages on Facebook, making him feel like he was being personally targeted. One night, he was leaving a party with Darwin when they turned the corner to see a group of men waiting for them outside, guns cocked in the air. "RUN," Darwin shouted. Oscar took off in one direction, Darwin in the other, his feet pounding the ground so quickly that he hardly noticed his heart racing inside of his chest. He peeled around one corner, and then the next, trying to lose the gang members and failing every time. Gunshots crackled behind him, as a bullet whizzed past his ear. Somehow, around the next corner, he found Darwin, who was clutching his arm as blood poured on the street.

"We have to leave," Darwin said, tightening his grip on the blood-soaked T-shirt wrapped around his arm. "As soon as we possibly can."

So, their journey began—first, across the border to Guatemala, and then through Mexico, where they would make their way to Tijuana and wait to turn themselves in at the US border. "So many people showed us kindness," Oscar told me as he recalled the journey, which was peppered with as many people offering them a free meal or lodging as it was with intimidating police officers and nights spent sleeping in the street. But that kindness stopped the moment they crossed the border into California and were escorted by a Customs and Border Protection (CBP) officer to a detention center that felt like a prison. "It was a cell just for LGBT people," Oscar said, remembering the first few hours when they were detained with another couple, who were equally confused about what was going on. A few hours later, another CBP officer came and took one of the men away, leaving his partner alone, hysterically sobbing. "I could feel his pain," Oscar said, remembering the moment that he realized that they were separating people from their partners. "I just knew at that moment that they were going to take Darwin away, and that was going to be me, too."

A few hours later, his worst nightmare came to life: a CBP officer came and took Darwin away, leaving Oscar completely alone.

"I just watched them taking him away," he told me. "They didn't even let us hug goodbye."

———

For two months, Oscar didn't hear any news from Darwin.

"I didn't think I had enough money to make a call," Oscar remembered. Even if he did, the only way to contact anyone was through the detention center's pay phones, which charged extortionate fees to even make local phone calls. Personal cell phones were prohibited, as was access to the internet. It was easy to feel as if he had disappeared.

After keeping him one week in Arizona, ICE had transferred Oscar to a different detention center, in Colorado. One of the men that he was detained with in Arizona had given him five dollars, but he didn't think it was enough. Nevertheless, he decided to try, and dialed Darwin's aunt, whose number he had memorized in case of an emergency. To his surprise, she picked up. "If Darwin calls you, please give him my address," he said, spitting out the words quickly, fearing that the call could drop at any minute.

Darwin had been taken to a detention facility in Mississippi, where he was trying to reach his family, but he didn't have any money either. "I befriended a guy who was from Peru," he remembered. "As a gift, he offered to pay for a phone call." Darwin immediately called the same aunt—and when he found out that not only had she heard from Oscar, but that she had also gotten an address, it felt like the clouds were parting and he could see a ray of light.

"Please let me call my boyfriend in Colorado," he begged one of the guards. But it is against ICE's rules for a detainee to call someone in another detention center. The only thing that he could do was write him a letter.

"Dear Oscar," he began. While he and Oscar had texted and talked extensively while they were living apart from each other in Honduras, he realized at this moment that this was his very first love letter.

I hope you are keeping your spirits up and are in good health. I am at a detention center in Mississippi and I miss you every day. Do you know anything about your case? Please write to me and let me know.

Love, Darwin

_____

"Oscar Juárez Hernandez?"

Oscar wasn't expecting to hear his name called. Sometimes the guards called him in for a medical check, but he wasn't expecting a letter. As soon as he heard the name of the sender, he jumped out of bed for the first time in weeks, not quite able to believe that he wasn't dreaming until he was pressing the envelope to his chest. "My hands couldn't stop shaking," he told me. "I wanted to open it, but I was crying too much." Finally, he managed to open the envelope, not quite able to believe that the words in front of him were written by Darwin. After two months of not knowing where Darwin was, if he had been sent back to Honduras or even if he was alive, he finally had a way of being in touch with the person that he loved so much.

That night, Oscar wrote him three pages, front and back.

_____

Oscar's story of writing Darwin love letters from inside of a detention center sits at the far end of a timeline that started with the raids along the US–Mexico border in the 1930s, followed by the US government's interception of love letters between the Braceros and their girlfriends and wives, before Operation Wetback normalized INS immigration raids across the country. Next, President Nixon declared a "war on drugs" in 1969, which, in an act of pure political theater, allowed warrantless searches of every car driving across the border, while increasing minimum sentences for marijuana possession. This made it easier to deport immigrants for minor drug crimes, and it especially targeted both Black and Latinx immigrant communities.

Soon, Nixon turned his attention toward people who were attempting to cross the border via other routes—specifically those who were coming to the United States by boat from Haiti, fleeing political repression under François Duvalier's dictatorship. Many had survived torture as political prisoners and had no other choice but to leave Haiti on makeshift boats courageously pushed into the Caribbean Sea. No one with any other safer option would undertake that journey, but Nixon refused to accept them as refugees—doing so would sour US relations with Duvalier, who was their ally in the global fight against communism.

Instead, he authorized the INS to build the first immigration detention centers, which would imprison Haitians—sometimes for years at a time—until they could prove that they were worthy of asylum in the United States. Cubans, most of whom were fleeing Fidel Castro's Communist government, were granted asylum much more easily, even given stipends to start a new life in the United States. People's real lives were caught in these political crosshairs.

Even though the Refugee Act of 1980 was drafted to right these political wrongs—stating that anyone, regardless of where they were from, had the right to ask for asylum in the United States—Ronald Reagan later used this to crack down on people who were fleeing Honduras, Guatemala, and El Salvador, claiming that many were actually "economic migrants" and should not qualify for protection. Never mind that many were fleeing poverty that had caused them to be in danger, and violence that had then created poverty. Instead, they were indefinitely detained, testing the policy of incarcerating people until their hearings, all the while making flimsy, arbitrary distinctions between economic migrants and refugees that could affect the rest of their lives.

Since then, immigration detention has not only expanded but has become a three-billion-dollar industry that fuses for-profit prisons with immigration policies built around "securing" the border. Now there are more than two hundred immigration detention centers across the United States, detaining a total of more than 500,000 people. Trump became notorious for separating children from their mothers in 2018 as a part of his "zero-tolerance policy," but even before—and after—Trump, the system separated and continues to separate couples and families by default. A straight couple is automatically separated from each other by gender—and while children are typically detained with their mothers, they are still ripped apart from their father. If a queer couple is detained together, it is purely dumb luck. For most, like Oscar and Darwin, CBP will interview and process them as two individuals, even if told that they are a couple.

Even the term "detention centers" is misleading. As immigration "violations" are a civil—not a criminal—offense, these facilities are not technically prisons, and immigrant detainees are not technically "prisoners." However, they are prisons by another name: immigrant detainees are held together in cells, with limited access to the outside world. Unlike prisoners with criminal convictions, immigrant detainees do not have a fixed sentence, and do not know how long they will be in jail. They do not have a right to a public defender, or a fair trial. Instead, those who are seeking asylum are often expected to plead their case without representation, in a language that they do not speak and a system that they do not understand.

Nevertheless, Darwin continued to embrace pen and paper and, with it, hope. "Have faith, mi amor," he would write, thinking of Oscar opening his letter. "Soon, all of our nightmares will be over, and we will be together again."

————

Three months after Oscar first arrived in the United States, it was time for his asylum hearing. He wrote everything that had happened to him down in a notebook, and then gave it to a lawyer, who gave it to a judge. But the judge barely glanced at it.

"I believe you," she said, as Oscar tried to follow along the lagging Spanish translation, perplexed at how it could possibly be this easy.

"I have no objections to your asylum request," the prosecutor confirmed. "Welcome to the United States!"

Oscar had spent the past three months dreaming of this moment. Now, all he had to do was collect his belongings, and he would be free to leave. He even had a sponsor—a retired teacher named Margaret Bobb, who had started visiting him after they became pen pals. She had agreed to let him stay with her and her husband until Darwin was free.

Meanwhile, Darwin was still behind bars.

———

Every day, Darwin found it a little bit more difficult to keep his spirits up.

"I was so scared," he told me, when I asked him for his side of the story. "I tried to stay positive, but every day that was harder and harder," he continued, remembering the endless days spent in his cell, when he started to feel as if he might lose his mind. "Maricón," one of the detainees hissed at him while he was walking to the restroom, sending shivers down his spine, "I hope your faggot ass gets deported back to Honduras." It felt like he had never left San Pedro Sula.

"I stopped eating," he told me, remembering the way the homophobic slurs made his stomach turn, bringing back memories of the gangs that wanted to kill him. "I grew so weak that I barely recognized myself." Even though Oscar and Darwin had nearly identical asylum cases, the fact that Oscar had won his asylum in Colorado meant almost nothing for Darwin. At this point, Darwin had been transferred to a detention center in Louisiana, a state that was notorious for having some of the most conservative judges in the country. Every day, they ordered people to be deported to countries like Honduras, no matter how compelling their claim. Darwin was terrified that he would be one of them.

A married couple—even a same-sex couple—can sponsor one another, but an unmarried couple cannot. As most queer couples who travel through Honduras, Guatemala, and Mexico to reach the United States have never been in a country where they could legally marry, most are processed separately, with no guarantee that they will be able to reunite. If one person wins asylum, while the other does not, their separation could become permanent.

"How we define family is at the heart of this," said Yael Schacher, a practicing lawyer, immigration historian, and deputy director for the

Americas and Europe at Refugees International, when I asked her how these policies affect couples and families seeking asylum. "We have a very narrow definition of family as a nuclear family," she continued, explaining that many other cultures, particularly indigenous cultures from Central America, define family and the caretaking roles that they represent much more broadly. "We do not define fiancés as family. We do not define people who are partners, but not married, as families." But these are the people who are being torn apart by the immigration system, and by laws that make it nearly impossible for them even to visit each other.

At least, now that Oscar was out, Darwin could talk to him on the phone. "It was the only thing that kept me sane," he said, remembering his long conversations with Oscar, where he would tell him about the people that he was meeting, and what they were going through. Many did not have access to lawyers, or have anyone to help them gather the documents that they needed for their asylum hearings. Some hadn't been able to contact their families at all.

"What if I was able to help from the outside," Oscar asked him. He couldn't give anyone legal advice, but he could give them the phone number of the pro bono legal clinic that had helped him prepare his case. Most of all, he knew he could help people connect with their families—and wanted to bring them the same feeling that he had had when he finally received that first letter from Darwin, after so many months apart.

"When I was in prison, I wanted to see a picture of my family so badly," he told me, remembering the three months that he spent, essentially behind bars, in a detention center, i.e., prison. "Outside of prison, it is so easy to download a picture of someone's family from Facebook, print it out and send it over to them. Receiving something like this is so meaningful—and for us, it was easy." Even though most detainees have access to libraries, they cannot use the internet—thus, logging onto social media to keep up with loved ones is impossible. Again, it's a prison by another name.

A Cuban man that had befriended Darwin asked Oscar if there was any way to find his wife on Facebook—he had a phone number that he was trying to reach her with, but no one picked up. Oscar typed her name into Facebook—*Maria Luisa Valdez*—and wrote to each person who came up in the search results until someone replied. "Please let him know my new number," his wife wrote back. "I haven't heard anything from him in five months."

Whenever Oscar received a letter or message from someone on the inside for their loved ones, he would type each word into Facebook Messenger, reminding himself of the two months during which he had heard no news from Darwin, and the moment he received his first letter in the post. "It made me realize just how many people are separated by borders," he told me. "Just these small pieces of land, separating so many stories—mothers, fathers, brothers, sisters, partners. It was so emotional."

Ten months after Oscar and Darwin were first separated from one another in January of 2019, Darwin finally had his first asylum hearing.

Oscar's hearing had taken ten minutes. Meanwhile, Darwin's lasted almost ten hours. "I was just sitting there wearing that ugly prison uniform," he remembered. "I hated that uniform." Oscar's judge immediately believed his story, and barely had any questions. Darwin's judge was skeptical, and had many questions.

"Why can't you live in one of the safer parts of Honduras, such as the Islas de la Bahía," he asked, referring to a group of remote islands off the Caribbean coast. Darwin was confused—if gang members could threaten him in San Pedro Sula, there was nothing that would stop them from finding him in the Islas de la Bahía. Still, this is a common tactic of asylum officers around the world: try as hard as possible to argue that a country is safe, even when it is known for having an ongoing war or the highest murder rate per capita in the world.

"I used to work as a salesman," he responded, measuring his words. "I know that I can experience homophobia anywhere in my country, and that my partner and I would not be safe."

Darwin did not receive a decision that day. Instead, he went back to his cell, where his cellmates continued to taunt him. "I guess the faggot is finally getting deported," they jeered. He grew so despondent that, for several days, he didn't check to see if there was any news about his case— but when he finally called, a few days later, he had an appointment for the final hearing.

"I didn't tell anyone where I was going," he remembered. If anyone asked, he planned to tell them that he was going to a doctor's appointment, but as he prepared his documents, he secretly prayed that it would be the last time he saw any of them ever again.

"We cannot grant you asylum based on the grounds of religious or political persecution," said the judge, as Darwin struggled to follow the Spanish translation. Was it not enough that he had fled gang violence in San Pedro Sula, that someone had broken a glass bottle over his arm simply for his having the audacity to live openly with the person that he loved? Darwin started to worry, wondering what would happen if they decided that he didn't deserve protection at all. Just before they switched off the screen, the judge turned to him.

"Congratulations," he said. "You won your asylum. Welcome to the USA."

"I was screaming out loud with happiness," Darwin tells me, remembering going back to his cell to gather his belongings. Even though he had been fretting about all the reasons his asylum could be rejected, ultimately he won, on the basis of being persecuted for his sexual orientation. Finally, he could be with the person he loved.

"Most of my cellmates were still laughing at me—but when the guard came and congratulated me, they all clapped." Suddenly, Darwin didn't care about them anymore. He was going straight to Denver to reunite with Oscar.

———

"I had to buy balloons! I had to buy flowers!" Oscar said, remembering the way he rushed to the supermarket, picking up every cheesy Valentine's Day balloon that he could find, feeling as if nothing was enough to celebrate.

But when Darwin landed at the Denver International Airport, he could not see Oscar anywhere. Instead he saw a mass of heart-shaped balloons running toward him. "I will never forget that moment in my entire life," Darwin says, laughing as he remembers the moment that he saw Oscar—who is no more than five two—emerge from a bouquet of red tinsel, just as overwhelmed with love as he was.

"If you truly love someone, you will not give up on someone just because you cannot see them for a long time," Oscar told me. It is a few years after their tearful reunion, and Oscar and Darwin are living happily in Denver, now reunited with Darwin's little brother and Oscar's little sister, as well. Every once in a while, I check in on them—and every time, they seem a little bit more like an old married couple. Nothing makes me happier.

"Truly, love can cure many things," he continued, squeezing Darwin's hand as he nuzzles into him, their love oozing through the video screen of our Zoom call. "If love makes you this happy, you are going to be there in good times and bad times, and the worst times as well."

6 | *Finding Light in the Darkness*

One thing no one ever tells you about being a war correspondent is how much time you'll spend waiting.

I did most of my waiting at Hamam al-Alil, a military base just south of West Mosul where soldiers often sprawled out on paper-thin mattresses, taking a well-deserved rest while huddled around a single cheap floor fan that they treated as an oasis, even when it seemed to circulate only hot air. Meanwhile, journalists sat around anxiously biting their nails, waiting to hear whether they would be given permission to pass the checkpoints and travel to the front lines, salivating at the prospect of witnessing the fighting that soldiers were trying so desperately to escape.

Salem often made fun of the journalists who were just visiting—particularly the overly macho ones. If a new journalist came to town, he would lean back, size them up, and ask them with a perfectly straight face: "Did you take selfie in your flak jacket for Tinder yet?"

Most of my days were spent smoking cigarettes and drinking tea with Mohammed, a cameraman from Baghdad who worked for so many different news agencies that everyone treated him as if he were the mayor of the military base. Mohammed had watched much of Iraq's recent history unfold through the lens of his camcorder and was accustomed to life in a conflict zone. He could weave in and out of firefights so smoothly that I blindly trusted him. I ran if and when he told me to, making sure to wrap up my broadcasts before the sniper fire started again.

But most of the time, we waited.

"Let's go see the cars," he said one particularly blistering afternoon. We had nearly given up on hearing any news and were starting to look on the bright side of not having to spend the rest of the afternoon sweating through Kevlar. My bladder was bursting with sweet tea and I had smoked all the cheap cigarettes that my lungs could handle.

By "cars," Mohammed was referring to a nearby parking lot of partially exploded car bombs. It looked like a Picasso painting come to life, ordinary Toyotas and Nissans rigged into death machines by ISIS fighters who drove them straight into buildings to explode into smoke and flames. One of the Iraqi army's duties was identifying cars that were rigged with explosives and defusing them before they became weapons of war. Sometimes it was too late, and the burnt carcasses of family sedans ended up in the Hamam al-Alil parking lot, melted plastic consoles and burnt seat cushions spilling out of them like entrails.

Mohammed positioned himself next to a particularly disfigured Toyota. "My lady," he said, in halting English that I didn't even know he spoke. "Can I get you a car?" I laughed so hard that I nearly forgot that we were standing around a bunch of would-be car bombs.

Ever since my first stand-up in a flak jacket, my bosses had been begging me to keep embedding with the soldiers, obsessing over the theatrics of the front line. While I knew these stories were important, I couldn't help feeling like I was getting in the way of the actual war, dodging bullets for a news package destined to become background noise in a dentist office in Hong Kong.

I preferred to spend time with ordinary people doing ordinary things, which were suddenly extraordinary to them as they emerged from three years of living under the Islamic State. It felt magical to witness people rediscover the simple pleasures of welcoming customers into a shop or smoking shisha on the riverbank. Mohammed and I even went to Mosul's first bar reopening. At first, it didn't look like much—a nondescript building in a Christian neighborhood, with barely any signs, to protect it from possible suicide bombers. But inside, a man was belting out "My Heart Will Go On" next to a jukebox at 2 p.m., next to a few picnic tables and a counter with a selection of cheap beers.

"I haven't been able to see my friends like this in two years," the Celine Dion impersonator told me, slapping the table with drunken enthusiasm. A few hours ago, he had driven three hours from Ramadi to meet a friend from Mosul and a friend from Baghdad—three cities that had been either choked by checkpoints or occupied by ISIS over the past three years, making a visit like this impossible. Now, they all sat around the same table together, grinning inebriated grins, not quite able to believe that they were together again. I couldn't believe that I got to share the moment with them—or the fact that, at one point, he offered to sing me a song, dedicated to my channel. Mohammed filmed the whole thing.

Driving back to Erbil always felt like a comedown. Mosul was alive with the buzz of friends reuniting over once-forbidden beers; Erbil felt like its inverse, its soul sucked dry by overpaid security consultants and NGO workers making a killing off the war economy.

Most nights, I would have preferred to stay home, but I was in love with an extrovert, who refused to accept that our social life was inevitably doomed just because we were stuck in Erbil. Sometimes, our friends from Istanbul flew in for assignments, and it almost felt like old times. Salem rarely admitted it, but I could tell that he felt nostalgic every time someone went back to Istanbul, or talked about our favorite places. One night, he sighed, "I wish I could go party in Istanbul." It was as close to despondent as he would ever get.

Meanwhile, I could go to Istanbul—or anywhere else—whenever I liked, but the thought of jetting off to Istanbul while Salem was stuck in Erbil made me feel as if I were no better than the NGO workers who threw all-night parties and posted pictures on their Instagram accounts of luxurious vacations while the people that they were employed to help were starving. Most of my resentment was jealousy. I wanted to travel the world as a couple, as others did, without being limited to the handful of countries that would accept a Syrian passport without a visa. I wanted to pick a country, any country, without worrying about whether or not they would accept my boyfriend the way that they accepted me. I wanted Salem to experience that freedom the way that I did, and see the world as boundless.

I started to wonder again if marriage was an option. Salem had made it abundantly clear that he would not marry me for a passport, but I didn't see how we were going to escape Erbil otherwise. While the US Embassy was in Baghdad, Erbil had a consulate—a barbed-wire-en-crusted building, filled with diplomats who were not allowed to leave for "security reasons," who hosted cringe-worthy Bingo nights. The few times I visited them, the diplomats reminded me of prisoners of war, held against their will.

"Do you perform marriages?" I asked when I called the consulate. I winced at the thought of exchanging vows in front of an officiant who was still hungover from Bingo night margaritas, but reasoned that it was a small price to pay for freedom.

"You have to go to the Embassy in Baghdad," she responded—and while this was simply a statement of fact, it plunged me back into an existential crisis. Salem couldn't go to Baghdad, and even I would need a visa to get married there. I started to obsess over places we could go. I was a journalist. More important, I was a geography wizard. At the age of seven I had memorized the entire globe and became a local celeb-rity when I showed off my knowledge at a map store. The owner was astonished that I could find Bosnia and Herzegovina in a fraction of a second. Little did he know that I could also find Lesotho. But my knowl-edge of obscure countries did not lead me and Salem to a romantic sanc-tuary. Most European countries require a visa, and the United States was unreliable as long as both the Muslim ban and "extreme vetting" were a cornerstone of immigration policy. Lebanon—along with Jordan, Turkey, and even Northern Iraq—had closed their borders to Syrians three years ago. Most Asian countries required a visa for Syrians, with the exception of Malaysia, but even Malaysia wouldn't let anyone stay beyond three months. A handful of other countries—Maldives, Ecuador, Dominica—allowed visa-free tourism, but all of these felt unrealistic as a permanent home.

It was starting to feel like we were running out of countries.

"Put on nice clothes," Salem told me one day when I got home from work. "We are going to the Rotana Hotel." I was more accustomed to wearing the same two shirts to work, and trusting that they would be covered by a flak jacket, than of paying attention to fashion. I racked my brain—and my closet—to find something nice enough to wear to an upscale hotel.

I didn't bat an eyelash when someone pulled Salem aside, after the hotel metal detector went off. Living in a city that is acutely aware that it is living in the shadow of ISIS makes these kinds of moments routine.

"I want to talk to you about something," Salem told me, once he had been sufficiently patted down and we were sitting down at the hotel restaurant.

I assumed it was about work. "Sure," I responded. "What's up?"

"The past two years have been the best years of my life," he began. I looked at him quizzically, wondering if he was having a stroke. "I hope I can spend the rest of my life with you—if you will accept." He pushed a small red box across the table to me. I opened it and inside was the most beautiful little ring—and while I had always imagined a romantic proposal where I said something along the lines of "Yes, yes, one thousand times yes," instead I said, "Baby, this is way too expensive!" and started giggling at the thought that someone had mistaken the ring for a bomb just a few minutes ago.

It was too big for my ring finger, but fit snuggly around my middle finger. "Now I can be glamorous when I flip people off," I laughed, as I playfully flipped him off. Nevertheless, I felt nervous. The weight of the little band of stones felt heavy and unfamiliar, and I couldn't help wondering how we were going to get married, when we were still stuck in Erbil, and hadn't even met each other's families. We had been getting ready to visit his parents in Southern Turkey when he was suddenly deported, and my family was in California, thousands of miles away. I had always pictured all of us coming together for this moment, but it felt like we were navigating this milestone alone.

Nevertheless, when I admired the way the ring caught the light, I saw the most beautiful expression of commitment, a refusal to give up in the face of a system that was trying to keep us apart.

"Do you see the Abu Jalal supermarket?" Samih asked me, when I called him from a noisy intersection in Beirut, Lebanon.

It was an uncharacteristically rainy afternoon when I made my way to Shatila—a Palestinian refugee camp in Beirut's southern suburbs—to meet Samih Mazien Mahmoud and Rayan Sokkar, a young Palestinian couple who became internet-famous when their engagement photos, taken along the narrow alleyways and iconic Palestinian artwork in the camp, went viral. Most young couples in the Middle East stage their engagement photos in ornate living rooms or hotel lobbies, but Rayan and Samih insisted on paying a tribute to the refugee camp where they fell in love.

"Walk down the alleyway next to it, and then round the corner," he continued, making me a little bit nostalgic for Beirut-style directions. Here, most people do not rely on addresses or street names, instead directing people with landmarks, a hangover from the fifteen-year civil war that destroyed the city. Sometimes, the landmarks meant to give directions only exist in people's memories and have long been replaced by something else. It is as romantic as it is dysfunctional, not unlike the city itself.

Once I turned the corner into the camp, I felt as if I had been transported into the memory of Palestine. The noisy intersection of Beirut faded away and was replaced by the sound of bakers luring in customers with freshly baked kaak, conversing in noticeably Palestinian-accented Arabic, stronger and more textured than the feminine lilt of Lebanese. Even though almost everyone in the camp was born in Lebanon, almost no one has Lebanese citizenship—a simple fact that means that Palestinians in Lebanon have been marginalized for generations. Now, Shatila is a refugee camp that has existed for so long, it is basically a neighborhood. At the end of the street, I saw Samih, his boyish face and impish smile peeking out from a bright pink windbreaker. Rayan was right next to him, wearing a polar fleece zip-up jacket with her hair pulled back in a stylish, turban-style hijab, little hoop earrings peeking out from underneath.

"Is it your first time in Shatila?" Rayan asked, as we walked through the narrow alleyways between cinder block buildings built so high they were starting to lean toward one another. I told her that I used to come here all the time when I lived in Beirut, in awe of elders who still remember the day they left Palestine. Meanwhile, subsequent generations lived through the Lebanese civil war, when the Maronite Christian forces massacred Palestinian and Lebanese Shiite Muslims in the camp, which is no more than one square kilometer in size.

"Everyone here is a survivor," she said. Also a journalist, Rayan shares my fascination with living history. At twenty-five years old, she was too young to have lived through the civil war herself, but remembered when Israeli jets bombed the nearby Dahiyeh neighborhood in 2006, and the fear that rippled through the camp that another violent civil war was about to erupt. Even though she has lived her whole life in Beirut, she was born a refugee—and knows all too well how Palestinians in the camp, even if they were born in Lebanon, are not afforded the same rights as Lebanese citizens.

Meanwhile, Samih was born a Palestinian refugee in Syria, which also doesn't have birthright citizenship, making him stateless. He became a refugee once again when he fled Syria. "I grew up in Yarmouk," he told me, referring to the Palestinian refugee camp in Damascus, which was often thought of as the capital of the Palestinian diaspora before it was bombed and besieged by Bashar al-Assad during the second year of the now-ten-year-long Syrian civil war.

"I am sure you know how terrible the war in Syria is," Samih continued as we made our way through the intricate maze of the camp, which has also become home to thousands of Palestinians from Syria in recent years. "Everyone always talks about Beirut as this amazing place," he said, remembering how, as a seventeen-year-old leaving Syria for the first time, he imagined Beirut as a city of thumping discos and all-night parties. His heart sank when he saw houses that looked on the verge of collapse and electrical wires that crisscrossed the alleyways and sparked in the rain instead.

"I thought, that's it." He laughed, remembering his first impressions of the notorious refugee camp. "Let's turn around and go back to Syria!"

Still, fleeing the war—and even finding refuge in Shatila—is what put his love story in motion. "If it weren't for the war, I would have never come here." He smiled as he looked toward Rayan, who had stopped to chat with one of the elders.

"I might have never opened my mind to falling in love with someone like Rayan."

Samih first laid eyes on Rayan at a journalism workshop, put on by the Lebanese NGO Basmeh & Zeitooneh. "At first, I hated the idea of journalism," he remembered. "I thought all journalists were liars, because that is all I saw on TV in Syria." But, unsure of what he was going to do after his education was cut short by the war, Samih figured he would give the workshop a chance.

Rayan had already been studying journalism at the Arab University of Beirut, and was eager to gain more experience and get to know some of the new people in the camp. "Maybe at first we were stereotyping each other a little bit," Rayan said, remembering how most of the people that she grew up around had never met a Palestinian person from anywhere besides Lebanon, and thought that they might somehow be different. "But then, all of these walls fell down, and it was like we had always known each other."

At first, Samih thought Rayan had a big ego. "You have to understand, back in Syria, I always thought that if a girl raised her voice, it was a problem," he said, remembering his first impressions of Rayan, interpreting her confidence as bossiness. "But as I got to know Rayan better, I started to see that she was this strong woman who made everyone listen to her, and it completely changed my mind," he continued. "I started standing up to my father, because I did not agree with the way he was treating my sisters."

But Samih didn't admit to himself that his admiration for Rayan was starting to become romantic until he saw her walking through the camp with someone else. "I started acting like such garbage," he remembered, shaking his head at how he fulfilled every jealous stereotype. "I would either be constantly trying to get her attention or ignoring her completely."

Rayan had a feeling that Samih wanted to be more than friends. All the signs were there, particularly his intolerable behavior. "Why are you acting so strange with me?" she asked him one afternoon, hoping that they could open an honest conversation together. His heart skipped a beat, wondering if this was finally his chance, all the while worrying that she might reject him. "You are my idol," he fumbled, instead. "I wish I had a big sister like you."

"I knew that he was lying to me, and I found it very immature," she remembered. Besides, she wondered what people would think if she were with someone like Samih. At twenty-one Rayan was decidedly a young woman, but at eighteen, Samih still looked like a little boy. "He didn't have any hair on his face at all," she said, laughing as Samih comically stroked the stubble that had grown in its place since then.

"I know how hard it is in the camp," she explained, suddenly becoming serious. "I thought it would be better to be with someone who was also educated, who also had a good job, to know that we wouldn't have to struggle as much." She had a love interest at the time—the same guy that Samih had so expertly clocked—but when she noticed how moody he was, and how he dragged her into his depressive episodes, she started questioning whether he was the right person for her. Eventually, she called it off.

Even though Samih was aware of Rayan's many admirers, he never stopped pining for her. One day, he was having a coffee with her, just as friends, when her sister called—her mother had just given birth to a baby boy. "Why don't you come with me?" she said, anxious to get back to the camp and meet her new brother. But Samih saw it as his chance to talk to her father about the possibility of exploring a relationship with Rayan.

When she found out about the conversation, Rayan flew into a fit of rage. "We have been friends for two years," she shouted at him. "Why do you keep doing this and making everything complicated?" Still, Rayan didn't want to fracture their group of mutual friends—in a place as tight-knit, sometimes claustrophobic, as Shatila, it doesn't serve anyone to burn bridges.

But not loving Rayan felt even more complicated than loving her. During the first days of Ramadan, Samih tried to find solace in the way that the city transformed around the holiday, neighborhoods decorated with little copper moons that twinkled as soon as darkness fell, the streets coming to life with people breaking their fast. Instead, he only thought about her more—so much so that, during Laylat al-Qadr, he prayed for one last chance.

"Please God, let it work between me and Rayan," he thought, imagining the power of prayer carrying his desires into the universe, setting them in motion. Laylat al-Qadr is the night that the Quran was first revealed to the Prophet Mohammed, and it is said that the power of prayer is so palpable that you can feel it in the air.

Meanwhile, in the women's section of the mosque, Rayan was realizing that she needed to set him free. "We need to talk," she texted him, proposing that they meet for a coffee. As she waited for his response, she thought about what she needed to tell him. *Samih, I love you, as my friend, but I want you to be happy*, she rehearsed, trying not to think about how he would respond.

But she also wanted to protect him. It was already so difficult to find work in Lebanon, particularly when Palestinians were already systematically kept out of many professions and made to get work permits from the Lebanese Minister of the Interior as if they were foreigners. Rayan had gotten around this by working as a freelance journalist and translator, hustling to snag as many jobs as she could, but most people didn't have these opportunities and could only work menial jobs around the camp. Samih had a few journalism gigs as well, but they didn't pay him enough to sustain a future and start a family.

Besides, his family was so different from hers. While Rayan had grown up always knowing that she wanted to study and have a career, Samih grew up with a mother who was only sixteen years older than him, in a family where women were expected to be mothers and wives. Rayan valued her independence and expressing her opinions—and while Samih might accept her for the woman that she was, she did not know if his family ever would. It was better to set him free, and hope that they would still be friends.

But the moment she saw him, everything changed.

"I had never seen a man look so gentle," she remembered. "It felt as if the look in his eyes went straight to my heart." At that moment, she folded her hands and looked deep into his eyes.

"I have made a decision," she said, not quite able to believe the leap of faith that she was about to take. "Samih, I want to be with you." Samih could barely contain his excitement—after more than two years of pining after her, Rayan was telling him that he was the one for her. It felt like he needed to pinch himself.

Still, Rayan was already concerned about the practicalities of being together. "I don't want my father to think that you can't provide for me," she continued, as if she could already hear her father's reaction to the news. "If we are going to be together, we are going to be equals." Samih was already taking notes, willing to show her father that he was the right person for her.

"I'll do anything, Rayan," he said, already imagining the rest of their lives together. "Anything so that I can spend the rest of my life with you."

––––––––

A few months later, Rayan and Samih decided to officially announce their engagement. Rayan had one condition.

"I want to take our engagement pictures in Shatila," she told Samih. He was taken aback. After working this hard for her family's approval, the last thing he wanted to do was take their engagement pictures underneath the electrical wires that sparked in the rain, posing on staircases that felt as if they might crumble at any minute. "Rayan, I do not think it is a good idea," he said. "People will just laugh at us."

"I want this, Samih," she responded. "I want to take our pictures in the place where we fell in love, so that we will always remember that love can blossom, even in Shatila." He couldn't say no to that.

On the day of the photo shoot, Rayan dressed in a long, light gray dress with delicate beadwork on the bodice and a silky navy blue hijab thrown over her hair. Omar, one of their friends from the workshop, agreed to take the photographs, borrowing a camera from the NGO for the occasion.

"I was nervous," Rayan said, remembering the moment that she started second-guessing herself. "I thought that Samih might be right and that everyone would make fun of us." But the minute they started recreating some of their favorite memories from their time together, her anxieties faded away. First, they started in the square—the place where they had eaten lunch together every day during the workshop, not knowing that they were falling in love as they became inseparable. Next, she hopped into a three-wheeled tuk-tuk, parked in one of the alleyways. "What do you think?" she asked, relishing the feeling of posing behind the steering wheel in a flowing evening gown. Samih jumped behind her, and Omar snapped his shutter, capturing Samih's coattails flying in the wind.

Meanwhile, Samih felt as if he were seeing the camp with new eyes. "Look at this poem," he said, pointing out a line from Mahmoud Darwish that someone had painted onto the wall of one of their houses.

> And we have our small dreams
> Like we wake up cured of disappointment
> We do not dream of insurmountable things
> We are alive, we survive and we dream on.

For the final shot, they posed on the rooftop at sunset, gazing into each other's eyes as the sun set over Beirut, a magical glow spreading across the sepia-toned buildings.

"It is my favorite spot in the camp," Rayan told me, as we both look out the window—by now, the rain has cleared, and Beirut is again bathed in a golden glow, which sometimes is so beautiful it makes you forget the way that the streets stink when the trash piles up, and that it's impossible to get anything done when the power spontaneously goes out. "I wanted to share it with him."

After the photo shoot, Rayan uploaded the pictures to her Facebook page just in time for the power to cut. "Just another night in Shatila." She laughed as she remembered going through the motions of lighting candles, waiting in the darkness for the lights to come back on. "And then . . ." Samih said, smiling his impish smile.

"The power came back on, and I turned on my phone," Rayan continued, picking up his cue, as if it were a performance. "I didn't believe my eyes." Their photos had gone viral—first, friends sharing the pictures, then friends of friends, and then their friends, and soon people she didn't even know were sharing the album and she was fielding requests from media who wanted to profile the young Palestinian couple who showed the world that love could blossom even in a refugee camp. As a journalist, Rayan was thrilled. But it was the comments from her own friends and family that filled her eyes with tears. "Congratulations" popped up dozens of messages. "Our two love birds in Shatila," said another. "We love you so much."

As long as she was as happy as she was right now, nothing else mattered.

"Look at our two celebrities of Shatila!" cooed one of the elders the next morning, leaning out her window, as Rayan and Samih walked side by side through the camp—this time wearing their sweatshirts. Others cheered them on, as if they were on their way to their wedding that day. "We were the heroes of the camp," Rayan said, smiling as she remembered recognizing the pride in people's faces that she didn't know she craved. "But it wasn't because we were actual celebrities or something like that," she laughed. "It was because we looked like them."

It is difficult to imagine Beirut without Shatila—or Lebanon without Palestinian refugees. For as long as I can remember, Shatila has been Beirut's most poorly kept secret. Even though it is not listed on any maps, it is hiding in plain sight, just behind Abu Jalal's supermarket. Palestine has also been erased from most maps—but in Shatila, it is alive, through people telling their children Palestinian folk stories and embroidering Palestinian designs onto their clothing, teaching the new generation that Palestine still exists—even if, for them, it is only a patchwork of memories. What *is* important is that these memories are alive.

Once upon a time, the site of the imposing concrete barrier along Lebanon's southern border was simply an olive orchard, with nothing but rolling hills of ancient trees that have nourished the Mediterranean basin for centuries. No one cared about the point where Lebanon ended and Palestine began, because people traveled between the two countries every day, on trains connecting Beirut and Jerusalem, Jerusalem and Damascus, in a way that only exists in people's imaginations today. Palestine was once an ordinary country, where Palestinians were ordinary citizens with ordinary love stories.

"My parents' love story wouldn't be possible today," Suhair, a seventy-five-year-old Palestinian activist who has spent most of her life advocating for Palestinian refugees' rights in Lebanon, told me when I visit her office in the Corniche el Mazraa neighborhood of Beirut. Because of the worsening political situation in Lebanon, Suhair is a pseudonym.

Born to a Lebanese mother and a Palestinian father, Suhair grew up in Beirut at a time when the Nakba was still fresh, when Palestinian refugees did not know if they would be staying in Lebanon or going back to Palestine.

"My father was very rich, and his family had a lot of land in Palestine," she explained, as I helped her prepare a pot of tea and arrange cookies on a plate. "My mother was supposed to live there—but when the Nakba began, they fled to Lebanon." The Nakba. The Arabic word for "catastrophe," which is also known as Israeli Independence Day, showing that one country's celebration can just as easily be another's tragedy. For Palestinians, it caused extraordinary displacement, driving them to seek refuge in Lebanon, Syria, and Jordan, in hopes that they could go home after the violence subsided.

"Of course, there was discrimination in the beginning, but that is ordinary when there is sudden competition for jobs, and competition for housing," Suhair told me, when I asked her what it was like to be Palestinian in Lebanon, in the immediate aftermath of the Nakba.

Economic anxiety can so easily manifest as xenophobia, as seen in the United States when Mexicans were scapegoated for the Great Depression. Later, Syrian refugees that came to Lebanon were blamed for stealing jobs, too, even when they were systematically kept out of the workforce, like the Palestinian refugees who came before them.

But I am not an economist as much as I am a romance anthropologist, and when I asked Suhair if this kind of racism got in the way of any love stories, she laughed at me. "It didn't stop anyone from having relationships," she said, regaining her composure. "What was a problem was the nationality." Jus soli—more commonly known as birthright citizenship—is standard throughout the Americas but far rarer in other parts of the world that primarily follow jus sanguis, or citizenship by blood. Citizenship must be inherited, instead. And in the Middle East, several countries, including Lebanon, only allow men to pass down their nationality, meaning that a Lebanese woman who marries someone that is not Lebanese cannot pass citizenship on to her children. If the father has a strong passport, often it's not a problem— but if he is stateless, it is.

Palestinians have also been systemically kept from Lebanese citizenship out of a fear that if they were granted citizenship, they would never go home. But without a country to go home to, Palestinians without another citizenship are born as refugees without rights. Statelessness becomes a generational curse.

Despite this injustice, Suhair does not blame Lebanon. "If we were in Palestine, we would have our land," she told me. "Most of us would be able to live from our land and wouldn't have to work." I have often shuddered at the images of Israeli bulldozers uprooting ancient olive trees, but I never realized how much this kind of violence was blatantly pillaging Palestinians of not only their livelihood and homes, but generational wealth. Photographers capture romantic images of Palestinian farmers clinging to their trees, but there is nothing romantic about being robbed. A Palestinian family with land can easily make a living through orchards and crops that have been cultivated for generations; Israeli bulldozers can destroy it in seconds. Meanwhile, Palestinians who hurl rocks at Israeli soldiers and settlers are framed as terrorists and jailed as criminals, simply for protecting what is their own.

"Now, in Lebanon, Palestinians have to work constantly. We live in camps, stacked one on top of the other," Suhair continued. "I don't blame Lebanon for this. I blame Israel. I blame the occupation."

Fewer and fewer people remember a time when Palestine was a country and Palestinians were citizens with rights instead of stateless refugees. "Most of the ones who are still living are so old that they have Alzheimer's disease and are starting to lose their memories," Rayan told me a few days after we first met as she prepared to go visit one of the elders in a neighboring camp. Coincidentally, she was also gathering the stories of people who fled the Nakba as children, hoping to document their lives before that living memory is lost. For her, it is personal. "I want to record their stories, because we are the result of them."

Standing in the shadow of this history, I wonder if she finds it meaningful that she and Samih are both Palestinian. "I feel like if we started a family, we would be this little committee of Palestinians ready to fight for our cause," she said, smiling—and for a minute, I imagine their living room filled with little kids speaking Arabic in Palestinian accents, creating art and music together just like their parents. "But we do not want to have children, just for them to live this life."

Samih shook his head, as if to echo her words. "No kids," he said, smiling but serious.

"We can't travel and Samih doesn't even have an identification card," she continued. Rayan and Samih's grandparents also fled the Nakba, and yet, the young couple is still feeling the impact of that flight, seventy-five years later. Still, Samih chooses to be optimistic. "We don't have any feeling of security or freedom here," he told me. "But one of the things that keeps us going is love; not just romantic love, but the love that we have for our friends and our families."

But for Rayan, love is inextricably connected with statelessness. "Love should be easy," she said, earnestly. "But as Palestinians, our nationality constricts us. As refugees, the laws are difficult, life is becoming more difficult, our circumstances are becoming more difficult," she continued. Even though she and Samih had a beautiful religious wedding, they still haven't been able to register their marriage with the state. "His papers say that he is still single," she said, laughing as he shrugged his shoulders.

Lately, Rayan has started looking into visas to try to go to Canada or Germany. Even if she is able to move to another country with Samih, she feels heartbroken at the prospect of leaving her family and community behind. "We should be able to plan our lives without worrying about trying to go abroad," she said. "I should not have to fight this hard," she continued, reflecting on the choice between either stability without community or community without stability. "We dream to have freedom, but why is it a dream when it should be my right?"

Every day, this idea of freedom becomes a little bit more elusive. The ongoing repercussions of Lebanon's 2019 economic collapse means that even Lebanese citizens are feeling the impact of a corrupt government on their livelihoods, with a passport that gives them limited options to flee. For Rayan and Samih, it has made it that much more difficult to plan their future, when the currency is becoming more and more worthless every day and everything is increasingly unstable around them.

"If we were free, we would be able to travel wherever we want, live wherever we want, and study whatever we like," Rayan finished. "We would be able to love whomever we choose."

———

Listening to the stories of how the Nakba has trickled down through generations in Shatila, it can feel like statelessness is a uniquely Palestinian experience. But statelessness wraps itself around people's lives every time that borders are drawn and redrawn. Countries that people once called home suddenly disappear, only to be replaced with new ones where those who once inhabited the land no longer have rights. It happened with Israel and Palestine, but it also happened when Hitler stripped Jews of their citizenship through the Nuremberg Laws in 1935, leaving them with no option but to flee or risk being deported to concentration camps. Jewish writer Hannah Arendt famously criticized the notion that human rights should be contingent on citizenship. "The right to have rights, or the right of every individual to belong to humanity, should be guaranteed by humanity itself," she wrote, upon learning that she had the right to a US passport after being stateless for eighteen years. Reading her words, I can't help thinking about Rayan fighting for her freedom, and the way that papers dictate so many people's lives today.

Ironically, the Zionist movement manipulated the Jewish sense of statelessness after World War II to bolster emigration to Palestine, and created the state of Israel, the Jewish state, to end all statelessness. It had international support, particularly from Great Britain, which had supported the idea of a Zionist state as a homeland for the Jewish people since World War I, when the Mandate of Palestine was still under British colonial rule. While their vision was of a Jewish homeland that would not interfere with the civil or religious rights of indigenous Palestinians, in practice, the formation of the state of Israel violently pushed Palestinians off their land, expelling them from the newly drawn borders of Israel. Soon, a Palestinian passport became useless as either a document to signify citizenship or travel freely, and freedom of movement and other rights were based on Israeli citizenship, and were drastically reduced for Palestinians with residence in what is now known as the West Bank and Gaza. Meanwhile those who left were not able to come back at all. Exile, as Mahmoud Darwish famously philosophized in many of his poems, was the only place a Palestinian could feel at home.

Rather than become a thing of the past, Darwish's idea of exile as an identity has since expanded to include people who fled the Balkan wars that fractured the former Yugoslavia and the former Soviet Union,

Rohingya refugees expelled by Myanmar, and thousands of people impacted by sexist citizenship laws in the Middle East. Historically, others have been stateless, too—including the Bolsheviks fleeing the Russian revolution and Armenians who survived the Ottoman genocide—but this was at a time before borders were controlled and passports were needed to cross them. Statelessness, according to Mira L. Siegelberg's *Statelessness: A Modern History*, once carried the cachet of being a citizen of the world, blending in with the ease of a chameleon, able to make a home anywhere.

A few days after walking around Shatila with Samih and Rayan, I reached out to Joey Poladoghly, a researcher in Beirut who is also stateless, hoping that they could shed light on how these laws affect people outside of the camps, as well.

"The question of nationality always comes back to state formation, and what a state is," Joey explained, over a glass of pink lemonade in the Geitaoui neighborhood of Beirut—the power was out, so the espresso machine wasn't working at the coffee shop. Unlike Shatila, Geitaoui is one of the more upscale neighborhoods in Beirut, populated by trendy cafés where Lebanese hipsters work from laptops between power outages. Still, living here doesn't make Joey any less stateless—being born to a Lebanese mother and an Armenian father meant that they weren't able to inherit Lebanese nationality. Growing up outside of Armenia meant that Joey couldn't get an Armenian passport unless they served in the army for two years—something that felt unsafe to them as a queer person, and unnecessary for someone that had lived in another country for their entire life.

"Often when people talk about statelessness, they speak about states and citizenship—these bone-dry academic words," Joey continued. "But statelessness is a lived reality—often, people just want to work. They want to have the freedom to take opportunities and see the world, but borders become prisons." Lebanon is a particularly small prison—surrounded by Israel, an enemy state in the eyes of the Lebanese government, to the south, and war-torn Syria to the east, there is no room to breathe, much less escape. Emigrating to Europe is the only way that Rayan can imagine starting a family, but getting a visa to travel is so difficult that Palestinians—and increasingly, Lebanese people—are following in the footsteps of people like Wala'a: paying to be smuggled across the sea.

"The problem with Lebanon and Palestine is a very typical problem, because here is a state that existed, and now it has been wiped off the map, and replaced with another state," Joey continued. "There was a state of Palestine, but now it is redefined as Israel with new borders, and a new identity—but the old identity is up in the air." It is not unique to Palestine—Crimea, as Joey pointed out, has been historically contested territory between Russia and Ukraine. Ever since Russia annexed Crimea in 2014, Russia granted Russian citizenship to anyone born in Crimea, or holding a Crimean residency permit. At least 3,500 Ukrainian citizens refused Russian citizenship and kept their passports—but, particularly with Russia's invasion of Ukraine in 2022, it became all too clear how quickly these borders could shift again, leaving people in the lurch.

"As long as there are new states being formed, people are always going to fall through the cracks," Joey continued, drawing on the example of the former Soviet Union, which dissolved in 1991 and became fifteen new countries, including Ukraine, Kazakhstan, and Estonia. Many of these new countries did not extend citizenship rights to the millions of people who fled the Soviet Union before its fall, often escaping violence at the hands of the KGB, which was notorious for torturing people in gulags or expelling them to Siberia. "Where do you belong when the only country that you belong to no longer exists?"

———

On the opposite side of the world, Karina Ambartsoumian-Clough has pondered the same question for most of her life. "I always thought I was undocumented," she said the first time I met her at the Open Borders Conference in New York City in 2019, sponsored by the Free Migration Project. "It turns out, I'm also stateless."

People at immigration conferences often assume that Karina is a public defender, not an immigrant herself, something that seems to amuse her as much as it frustrates her. She is tall and fair-skinned, with rosy cheeks and bright blue eyes that twinkle when she laughs. When she opens her mouth, she does not speak English—she speaks *Valley girl* English. "I'm always the whitest person in the room," she joked. At the same time, she wishes that more people understood that there is no "look" of an immigrant, no one place of origin or kind of experience.

Karina was born in Odessa, then part of the Soviet Union, and fled with her family when she was three years old. During the time that I was interviewing her for this book, Russian president Vladimir Putin had just launched a full-scale assault on Ukraine, and many members of her extended family were fleeing air strikes.

"Sometimes I wonder if I was always meant to be displaced," she mused, reflecting on how much the pictures of children fleeing Putin's bombs remind her of her family being smuggled out of the USSR thirty years ago. "I have a lot of memories from then," she told me, during one of our several Zoom calls. "I remember my grandmother, hunched over in the kitchen, making kholodets," she continued, describing it as a savory gelatinous dish with chicken, served with horseradish and mustard sauce. "I wanted to just stick my hand in it." She also remembered the feeling of being unsafe—her mother is Ukrainian, while her father is Armenian, but born in Tblisi, Georgia. As ethnic minorities in the USSR, they both experienced violence and discrimination. "My mom was beat up when they tried to live in Tblisi, but then, my dad was also targeted for his ethnicity and couldn't establish himself in Odessa. It was dangerous for all of us."

To escape the USSR, her family paid smugglers to reach Germany, where they purchased tickets to Cuba with a layover in Newfoundland, and then were able to leave the plane during the layover and apply for asylum in Canada. "I just remember being so tired when I woke up in Canada," she said. Unlike many of the Ukrainian refugees who are leaving today, Karina's family's asylum application was rejected—even though her parents had been repeatedly beaten up and subjected to ethnic persecution. Out of fear of being sent back into danger, they decided to try their luck in the United States. "I could feel in my bones that it wasn't safe," Karina said, remembering driving to the border in the dead of night and walking across. "I think my parents were scared, too." Shortly after they crossed, they were stopped by US border patrol agents, and they asked for asylum. "I know they were scared of being returned, or deported."

Once they were in the United States, Karina and her mother, father, and younger sister made their way to Philadelphia, where they knew that there was a Russian-speaking community that could support them while their asylum application was considered. Five years later, their request was denied for a third time, and they were ordered to leave the country, but when they went to the Ukrainian embassy to get passports, they were told that they didn't qualify for Ukrainian citizenship. Even though they were trying to leave, they had nowhere to go—and the country that was listed on their documents, the USSR, no longer existed. Now, their only choice was to stay in the United States, which was not kind to undocumented immigrants. "Sometimes I wonder what would have happened if we had stayed in Canada, and tried again," Karina mused, noting that there is a stronger social safety net and more care for asylum-seekers and refugees there than in the United States. Instead, they stayed in Philadelphia, her mother cleaning and her father painting rich people's homes to support the family, and Karina taking whatever waitressing job she could, to help out. She felt hopeful when one of her mother's clients generously offered to pay for Karina's first year of college studying prelaw at Villanova University, with the understanding that after that first year, Karina would "figure it out."

"Of course, I did not know this then, but there were no ways to figure it out," she said—undocumented immigrants are not able to apply for Federal Student Aid, and without scholarships, it is almost always impossible for them to afford college, essentially trapping them in service industry jobs that pay under the table. Once her college admissions office found out about her status, they started charging her international tuition and let her go from her job on campus. She dropped out and got a job at Starbucks. "I thought, there has to be more to life," she said—on top of everything else, she had recently been diagnosed with type 1 diabetes, and even though she had access to health insurance at her current job, she didn't know how she was going to get treatment in the long run. "I wanted to be an ordinary nineteen-year-old," she remembered. "I wanted to find love."

Karina had never thought much about dating, beyond a fantasy. Growing up in a conservative Armenian family meant that boys were strictly off-limits. "My dad barely gave me permission to attend my prom," she told me, remembering how much she wanted to be an ordinary American teenager. Instead, her family assumed that they would find her a husband within the Armenian community, as was traditional. The idea made Karina so uncomfortable that she decided to take matters into her own hands.

"I went on OkCupid!" she laughed, remembering filling out the questionnaire of more than 100 different questions, wondering if she would find someone that she liked. At first, no one wanted to meet up—but then she got a message from a guy named Kevin.

"I like the colour of your eyes," it read. "I spell colour with a 'u' because I'm British."

Karina was immediately smitten. "One of my favorite movies is the 1995 PBS Masterpiece *Pride and Prejudice*, so I immediately thought of Colin Firth," she explained, flushed and excited just remembering their conversation—which ended in Kevin asking Karina out to a tapas restaurant in Philadelphia's Northern Liberties. "I thought, you're doing this, Karina. You're going on a date."

As soon as Karina was sitting across the table from Kevin, she learned that he was only British in the American-of-British-descent kind of way, but he was so sweet and kind, and curious about Karina—it seemed like he wanted to know everything about her. But when the conversation turned to where she was from, she shifted uncomfortably in her seat.

"I was born in Odessa," she started, not sure how much of her story she was ready to tell. It was such a loaded question, "Where are you from?" Innocuous when the answer is straightforward, a minefield when it is not.

"I'm Armenian and Ukrainian," she added quickly, hoping that her ethnicity might redirect the conversation. "My family had a lot of problems in the USSR, so we left and asked for asylum," she continued, trying not to look Kevin in the eye, even though it felt like he wouldn't stop staring at her. "Our case got rejected, so now I'm undocumented," she continued, suddenly deciding to lay all her cards on the table. "I just dropped out of school because they found out I wasn't born here and couldn't pay the international fees," she continued, the words now tumbling out of her mouth. "Also, I just found out that I have type one diabetes." There it was, all her baggage, laid out on the table right next to the tapas. She imagined that Kevin would excuse himself, and she would never see him again. It didn't matter if he did, she told herself. There were other guys on OkCupid.

Instead, Kevin smiled shyly. "Maybe we should get married?"

For their next date, Kevin invited her over to his apartment. "He clearly had his shit together," Karina said, remembering the beautiful, spacious loft in the Old City with high ceilings and big bay windows. It was pouring rain outside that day, one of those East Coast summer storms when the clouds break and the rain pours down, rendering all umbrellas useless.

"I don't really like umbrellas," he said, suddenly seeming irresistibly suave. "I guess they always break, don't they?" she replied, trying to maintain her cool. It was the type of bizarre conversation that always preludes a first kiss. For the rest of the afternoon, that was all they did.

"We started spending every weekend together," Karina said, recalling how happy she was to spend time with him, trying new restaurants and exploring the city. He showed her films, like *Pulp Fiction*, and she introduced him to Indian food and world music. "I was so excited," she said, remembering the way that falling in love showed her there really was more to the world. "I felt like I was finally living the life that I wanted."

A few months later, Kevin asked her to move in. "We like living together," Kevin offered, hoping that he wasn't coming on too strong. "Do you want to move in with me?" At first, Karina worried about their power dynamic. "I was always insecure that I wasn't bringing enough in," she said, remembering how self-conscious she was that she would never make as much as he did, as long as she was waiting tables. But Kevin didn't mind, and while anyone else he had ever dated had gotten under his skin, he realized that spending time with Karina was different.

Karina couldn't open a bank account or buy a cell phone plan without a photo ID, so Kevin added her to his, hoping that it would make her life easier. "He really took on this burden and shared it with me," she told me, as Kevin nodded on the screen. "She had to trust me so much more than if we had had an ordinary relationship," he added, remembering being acutely aware of how these kinds of power imbalances could become abusive. "At the time, most of the people I knew who were living together without being married had some kind of arrangement where they would share expenses," he continued. "I had a lot of anxiety that we weren't really saving or able to plan like some of the couples around us." Nevertheless, he was adamant that whatever money he made was theirs—and that they would decide what to do with it, together. "That was huge for me," Karina remembered. "Huge."

————

Karina always wanted to get married. "It had nothing to do with my immigration status," she said, laughing. "I was twenty-four years old and I wanted that life, I wanted to be a married woman."

Meanwhile, Kevin was more skeptical. He always thought that marriage caused more problems than it was worth, and thought that two people who were legally bound together would inevitably outgrow one another. Watching Karina be carted off in an NYPD paddy wagon after the two of them had been caught smoking weed on the sidewalk during a weekend trip to New York City made him see it differently. Luckily she was released, but it could have turned out far worse. What if being legally bound to someone could protect them from harm? Suddenly it felt less like being bound together and more like liberation.

"I wanted to see an immigration lawyer before we did anything," he said, forever the practical, methodical one of the two of them. Karina only knew one immigration lawyer—the Armenian-American lawyer that her parents had found when they first came to Philadelphia, who promised to help her family win their asylum case, and then was forced to tell them to leave the country once it was rejected.

"I remember you when you were only this tall!" he beamed as soon as she walked into his office. Karina couldn't help noticing how much chummier he was acting now that she was seemingly attached to a white man, as if she was suddenly more worth his time. "So, you found yourself a US citizen?" he said, leaning back in his chair. "I just did one of these last week for a girl from Armenia," he continued. "Easy! So when are you going to get down on one knee," he said, turning to Kevin, as if this was some kind of joke.

"I'm ready to at any minute," Kevin said, trying to deflect the sleaziness that seemed to radiate through his office. "Great!" the lawyer responded. "Drive down to Maryland and pick up a marriage license over the weekend, and I'll see you in my office on Monday morning."

It wasn't quite the romantic wedding Karina had envisioned. "I had always wanted to get married at Philadelphia City Hall," she gushed to me, when I asked what she had imagined instead. But anyone who wants to get married in the state of Pennsylvania needs an identification document, and Karina's USSR birth certificate was not enough. Elkton, Maryland, was a far cry from the ornate architecture of Philadelphia's City Hall, but that state allowed them to get a marriage certificate without an ID for her. She still felt a rush of excitement when she squeezed Kevin's hand and signed the papers.

"It was the first time I saw my name on a legal document," she remembered. "It really felt like I would finally be recognized."

First thing Monday morning, Karina and Kevin went back to the lawyer. "You entered without inspection?" he asked her, raising an eyebrow as he sifted through her file. Karina nodded, suddenly concerned—although she thought that he already knew her family's convoluted struggle with the immigration system. "This is going to be a lot more complicated," he frowned. "You would have to leave the country and enter with a new visa."

But without a passport—without any country that would give her one—this was impossible. Even if she were to leave, the final removal order on her record would mean that she was automatically barring herself from coming back for at least ten years. Almost fifteen years after she first crossed the border, it felt like that moment was still dictating her fate. It wasn't enough that she couldn't have a normal childhood, or attend college and pursue the law degree that she had always wanted. Now she couldn't even get married—even though she had been advised for all her life that this was her only way out. She looked at

Kevin, and he looked at her, with the unspoken agreement that they should leave.

"Don't forget to tell your parents that they still owe me twenty thousand dollars!" the lawyer shouted after her as she walked out, reminding her of all the times that he had given them false hope. That night, Karina stared at the ceiling, wondering if she would always be a citizen of nowhere.

———

As soon as Karina realized that she was not only undocumented but stateless, she realized that she had to investigate her case by herself. "No one knew what I was," she remembered. She couldn't find any similar or relevant experiences online at first—but then she saw a video of a petite, middle-aged woman with cropped brown hair who was explaining that she had fled the former USSR only to have her asylum rejected, spending three months in immigration detention when the authorities couldn't figure out where to deport her.

"That is me," Karina thought, stunned as she recognized herself for the first time. Even though she frequently went to immigration rallies, most of the people she met were from Latin American or Asian countries and could get green cards if they married a US citizen. It always made her feel like an outsider, as if a story like hers couldn't exist.

"That is exactly me."

Armed with new information, Karina started approaching immigration lawyers, determined to finally solve her case. Instead, she was met with skepticism. "Are you sure you are stateless?" one asked her, as if she would make this up.

Eventually, she connected with a lawyer who suggested that she apply for DACA, then a new initiative from President Barack Obama that had gone into effect in 2014 and granted two-year work permits and protection from deportation to immigrants who came to the United States as children. Karina was nervous that a marijuana arrest from when she first started dating Kevin would come back to haunt her, but the lawyer encouraged her to fill out the paperwork anyway. Eight months later, a tiny envelope arrived in the mail. "I couldn't believe my eyes," she said, remembering the moment that she saw her name, printed underneath her picture on a little piece of plastic for the first time. "I was like—*holy shit*," she remembered. "I have an ID. I'm twenty-four years old and I have an ID for the first time."

She went out and bought a bottle of wine to commemorate the occasion.

"It just felt like everything was going to be okay because I had an ID," she said, remembering celebrating with Kevin. "It felt like freedom like I had never had before," she continued, sharing that they booked a belated honeymoon to Puerto Rico, and she finally had the chance to travel—at least, domestically—on a plane. Most important, she finally was able get paid for her work at the community space where she was already volunteering.

Gradually, Karina started opening up to others about her experience. "I realized a lot of people didn't know about DACA, or thought that they had never met an undocumented immigrant," she said, recalling conversations with coworkers, where they told her that they thought all immigrants were Mexican or they didn't realize that an undocumented person could be white. She finally felt safe enough to tell them that they were wrong.

Once a year, members of the coworking space where she worked would host an event called Ignite Philly, which Karina described as "TED talks, but less of a cult of personality." Watching the events made Karina realize that she could share her story and engage the community around her. So, she drafted a slide presentation, trying her hardest to condense everything—from her family's persecution in the USSR, to their journey to the United States, and then their battles with the immigration system—into five minutes.

"I was born in the USSR in a country that is now Ukraine," she began, addressing the crowd during a night that would set the tone for the rest of her life. "Unfortunately, this talk is too short to go into detail about the persecution that my parents and grandparents faced under the communist regime, suffice it to say that they bribed their way out of the Soviet Union when I was just three years old so that we could enjoy a life of freedom."

From there, she told the story—the failed asylum claims, living without papers, marrying a US citizen only to find out that she was stateless and his citizenship wouldn't change anything. "I never chose to come to this country," she continued, knowing that she was coming to the end of her five minutes. "But while I am in this country, I am paying taxes. I am a contributing member of society. But I feel like a political prisoner—the knee-jerk reaction to 9/11 around the world has put me in a position that I may never have a path to citizenship, ever." She had chosen her words carefully after years of not knowing where to begin. "My biggest fear is to be deported—away from the country that I call home, and away from my family," she finished, to soaring applause.

"I just felt this weight lift from me," she said, remembering the feeling of releasing her story for the first time. "Kevin was waiting for me in the green room, and I just collapsed into his arms."

As soon as the video was online, she posted it to Twitter, with the hashtag "#stateless." A few hours later, she received a direct message, from someone who said he was also born in the former USSR, before coming to the United States on a student visa—and when his visa expired, the USSR no longer existed. "I suddenly realized that there must be so many of us." Karina shared that, a few years ago, she had reached out to a representative at UNHCR, the United Nations refugee aid organization. Now that she had evidence that she was not the only one, she felt like she had to do something.

A few months later, she was in the UNHCR offices in Washington, DC, meeting six other stateless people—it was the first time she had ever met anyone like her who wasn't in her family. "At first, we just shared our stories and cried together," she told me, remembering what it was like to recognize one another in each other's experiences. "Then we realized we needed to do something, we needed to organize."

———————

Four years later, in December 2021, Karina was frantically running around a conference room in Washington, DC, preparing to welcome fifty people from across the country for the largest-yet United Stateless convening—the product of the circle of seven people who first cried in recognition of one another's stories three years ago. "I can't believe you made it," she said, hugging me before running off to greet the other guests. "Get yourself some coffee and find a seat."

Some of the people who gathered that day were also born in the former USSR, but others represented stateless populations from across the world. There were people from across the Middle East who were unable to inherit a nationality from their mother, and people from contested territories such as the Western Sahara region in Morocco and the Tigray region of Ethiopia. One was a twenty-year-old college student who was born in a refugee camp after the Balkan wars. Another was an eighty-two-year-old Holocaust survivor.

"I really think that this year is our year," Karina, who is now the executive director of United Stateless, began once everyone was seated. She is a natural public speaker; anyone who sees her with a microphone in hand would find it difficult to imagine her as a nervous twenty-year-old telling her OkCupid date that she was undocumented. "We are the leaders because we are the experts on our own stories," she continued. "So, it is up to us to inform the policies that could shape our futures."

Listening to Karina, I thought of the tens of thousands of stateless people around the world who would feel empowered by her words. Many people mistakenly believe that they are suffering alone. Unable to travel abroad, too many are separated from their families for years at a time, leaving them isolated from the people who make them feel whole. Today was like a reunion of chosen family—the pressure release provided by the sense of community was palpable. One of the themes that consistently came up over the course of the three days that we all spent together is that if one person in a family is stateless, the entire family is effectively stateless, even if some members have passports. I wondered how Karina and Kevin have experienced this in their own relationship.

"It affects you and it affects your marriage, absolutely," she told me later, when I asked her about it. "For a long time, I was depressed, and I brought that into our home. I was so ashamed about my status, and I let it control me," she continued. "But now I just don't care anymore. I care about Kevin and our marriage, and I care about the United Stateless family and want the best for them." For Karina, the community she has built through United Stateless feels like a love story of its own.

"I don't want to be the one who is always talking about money, but there were times when I thought that our only way out of this was for me to make enough money to buy off a politician and get them to pass some kind of private bill," Kevin shared. He apologized every time he brought up money, but I was glad he did. Finances are one of the biggest points of tension in any long-term couple. A partnership where one or both people is systematically kept out of the workforce is bound to feel the ripple effects of this in their relationship, the same way that Rayan and Samih's relationship is affected by their efforts to build a life in a country that has systematically denied Palestinians the right to work.

"Also, I don't think that I want to have children," Karina added, once again echoing Rayan. "I know what it is like to have parents who are undocumented, and I see my sister struggling to raise her kids in these circumstances," she continued—even though she is protected by DACA, it can be rescinded at any time, as it was briefly during the Trump administration. The political winds could change again, and in fact, in July 2022, DACA was once again being challenged in court and continues to be on thin ice, politically speaking. A child born in the United States is automatically a US citizen, but, as seen with Hugo and Cecilia's family, this does little to protect parents from being deported.

There are other concerns, too. "I feel like planning for retirement is already difficult for our generation," Kevin said, again bringing up the kind of logistics that many couples consider when planning a life together. "But we have to find three or four contingency plans, because what if she can't collect the social security that she is paying into? What if she can't collect life insurance benefits or equity from any of the various companies that I have worked with?" Undocumented immigrants across the United States pay an estimated $13 billion in federal income taxes every year, but are unable to collect social security benefits once they reach retirement age. Even countries with much larger social safety nets, such as Sweden and Germany, do not extend these benefits to foreigners without papers.

"It feels like laws are always changing or policies are going into effect that block us from things that we have paid into or that I've already earned," he continued, describing a feeling that many have undoubtedly felt when they realize the system is not built for them or the people that they love. But most of the time he tries to help her look on the bright side. "We can't go to France together, but we can go to Puerto Rico," he offered. "It's a weird balance—we are living a nice life, but it is still a human rights violation."

After fourteen years of being together, I wonder if Karina and Kevin have any advice for others to help them navigate the uncharted territory of being stateless in the United States. "Don't isolate yourself," Karina told me, without hesitation. "It is easy to become withdrawn because experiencing statelessness or any kind of forced displacement affects you and your marriage absolutely. But it doesn't define you. We are so much more than that."

8 | *The Gift of Wings*

My mom found out that I was engaged through Facebook.

It was not ideal. I always imagined getting engaged would be a public celebration, like Samih and Rayan's, sharing beautiful photos of us falling in love, celebrating both of our families coming together as one. Instead, Salem had updated his Facebook status—and first my cousin found out, who told my other cousin, who told my dad, who told my mom: the perfect recipe to truly piss my mother off.

"Are you really engaged?" she texted me, while I was caking TV makeup onto my face at five o'clock in the morning, in preparation to film in Mosul. This was not how I pictured telling her. Salem and I had celebrated with a few of our friends shortly after he proposed, and his family had graciously welcomed me as one of their own through a deluge of excited WhatsApp messages and Facebook phone calls, but I wanted to tell my mom in person. She still hadn't met Salem, and I knew that she would prefer to get to know him a little bit more before he became her son-in-law.

"Yes," I wrote back, hoping she would forgive me. "Damn it, Salem," I thought to myself, as I furiously rubbed blush into my cheekbones. I was so tired of layering on the foundation, my pores closing a little bit more with each dusting of cheap powder, and grime from spending days in the field. I was even more tired of having everyone I loved strewn across borders, unable to know and love one another the way that I knew and loved them.

"I guess he didn't do the part where he asks your father for permission," she responded—even though it was a text message, I could hear the words exactly as she would say them: acerbic and snarky, already making a judgment that might take years to reverse. My mom had envisioned me bringing someone home for the holidays, her gradually getting to know first him, then his family—and while she was accustomed to the way that I traveled and spent long periods away from home, she never imagined that I would meet someone who couldn't travel at all, keeping me away from home for good. Why would she?

I wanted her to meet him so much, but I also wasn't going to fly her to Iraq while there was a war going on, and he couldn't visit her in California. I was starting to think that elaborate family celebrations were just another privilege that I had mistakenly always assumed was a right.

I didn't know how to tell her that I was afraid there might come a day when my patience would run out. Even though Salem and I had fallen in love over our desire to experience the world, we now lived in a city where his wings were clipped and where I had clipped mine in solidarity. I wanted to tell her that I wondered how long I could do this before I resented him, he resented me, and we inevitably drifted apart. Of course I was excited to slip a ring on my finger, but I was also afraid that love was not enough to keep us together. I was also afraid of being heartbroken for the rest of my life.

Instead, I responded like a teenager. "I do not belong to either of them!" I wrote, taking my frustration out on the keypad. It was incredibly mature.

My anxieties multiplied a few weeks later. Before we got engaged, Salem applied for visas to Portugal and the United Kingdom, hoping that we might be able to at least go on a trip together. We filled out countless forms and gathered everything from bank statements to letters from commissioning editors to prove that Salem would not commit the cardinal sin of flying to Portugal or the United Kingdom and staying there, as if being Syrian was somehow the equivalent of being a leper.

The Portuguese embassy returned his passport with a rejection letter. "We think that the applicant is a threat to national security or public health," it read. I anticipated that they might have thought he wouldn't come back to Iraq as promised—but that checkbox was blank. Somehow, he had proven that he had enough reasons to return to Iraq. The Portuguese just didn't want him in their country, and so decided that he was either a terrorist or a virus, though they didn't have the common courtesy to tell us which one.

"I have a disease!" Salem laughed, while my eyes filled with tears, imagining the rest of our lives trapped in an endless night out at the Classy Hotel, eternally tortured by the sound of journalists stroking their own egos while drinking away their PTSD at one of the only watering holes in town. Salem would never meet my family, and I would never meet his—we would be forever trapped in a desert purgatory.

"I'm a Syrian," he continued, insisting on making it into a joke. "It is very contagious."

I coped the way that I always coped, throwing myself into work, filing two, sometimes three news packages every day, making stories out of anything that I could find. Many of them were utter garbage, but my news channel was so enamored with my willingness to work around the clock that they sent me on an assignment to Baghdad, which I found incredibly exciting. Unlike Erbil, which feels like the worst of American suburban strip malls, Baghdad is a magnificent, sprawling city filled with fascinating history and interesting people, each with a unique story of living through wars, and of even creating beauty while doing so. I was on my way to interview a ballet instructor who trained dancers to defy ISIS's rules against artistic expression when Salem messaged me.

"I got the UK visa," he wrote, along with a picture—shiny and new, in his passport. I was stunned—I always assumed that if you were considered a national security or public health threat in one country, that would logically mean you had the same unfortunate status in another, but apparently one country's terrorist is another's tourist.

Salem had traveled to the United Kingdom before. Around the time that we met, he had been invited to an awards ceremony honoring one of his films. "The ceremony is in London," he told me, as we lazily lay in bed together in Istanbul, oblivious to the fact that our days in the city were numbered. "Do you want to come with me?"

At first, I was annoyed that he seemed to think that I had nothing better to do than to be his arm candy at an award ceremony. Later, I realized that he was trying to pretend that it would be just as easy for him to take his new girlfriend to an event in London as it would for any of his other foreign correspondent friends—which, of course it was not. He had to go through a long and painful visa process, answering questions like "Have you ever participated in a terrorist activity?" I still wonder what kind of self-respecting terrorist would say yes.

Once he was in London, without me, he quickly became confused. After growing up in Iraq, where, largely due to its colonial history, Great Britain was seen as the pinnacle of civilization, Salem was having trouble understanding what made this place better than anywhere else.

"I have a question," he said, calling me a few days into his trip. Coincidentally, I was in Paris, covering the ISIS attack on the Bataclan. "Where do they keep the shatafa?" I nearly fell over myself laughing—he was looking for a hose that attaches to the toilet, popular in the Middle East for hygiene purposes.

"We don't really have those in the West," I told him, revealing our most embarrassing secret. He was in shock, as if I had just told him that we occasionally practiced cannibalism.

"Does everyone in the UK live their lives with a dirty ass?"

"I'm afraid so." I laughed, intrigued by how disenchanted he was with a country that most of the Middle East worshipped with the throbbing pulse of a postcolonial hangover. Even though countries like Egypt and Iraq had gained independence from British colonial rule more than half a century before, many of the conversations I had while traveling around the Middle East were laced with some kind of implicit belief that the West was somehow better, cleaner, and more civilized than the Middle East.

Salem was one of the only people who didn't buy the hype. During that first visit to London, he decided that the West was boring and had no idea what he would do with his life there if there wasn't a war to cover. While he had once considered joining the tens of thousands of others who were taking boats to Greece—the way that Wala'a did—and applying for asylum in a country like Germany or Sweden, he was now glad that he had not. "Why would I sit on my ass in Germany when I can work on stories here?" he told me during one of the early days in Istanbul, when we were canoodling like teenagers on a staircase overlooking the Bosphorus. I happily nestled into the crook of his arm, suddenly at ease with the promise of a life that would be anything but traditional.

But as soon as Salem was kicked out of Turkey, I realized that we couldn't live in a country that could decide someone was disposable overnight. My first thought was his UK visa, which I naively thought would grant these kinds of protections. I knew exactly where it was, carefully tucked into a plastic sheath, locked in a drawer as if it were some kind of family heirloom we kept hidden to barter for gold in case of emergency. As soon as it was in my hand, my heart sank. It had expired just a few days before. It was no more valuable than any other scrap of paper.

Now the visa was renewed, sitting in his passport as if nothing had ever happened. Six months, multiple entry. Oddly, neither of us thought of it as an escape plan, and it remained in his passport for several months, unused. London felt inaccessible—while I could always pick up stories around the Middle East, I didn't know how I could find a job in London, and as a US citizen, it wasn't like I had the right to work there either. "I don't want to have to worry about your visa and my visa," I told him, the one time we discussed it. "Besides, what would I write about in the UK—Brexit?"

Meanwhile, Salem would have to apply for asylum, a process that could take years. Still, the ability to travel to London opened doors for Salem that would have been closed otherwise. "I can sell the smuggler story," he said excitedly. We had recently met a man who told us that he was working with a network of smugglers to help Yazidi women escape from ISIS-controlled areas, and Salem had pitched the story to a number of channels, hoping to make their story into a documentary. One editor had offered him one thousand dollars to work with a British journalist on the story as a fixer, providing all his contacts but with no guarantee of any credit. If Salem could meet the editor in London, he could show him that he was capable of being the director, not a fixer doing the grunt work while a British correspondent got to be the star.

I could already tell that the visa made him feel less like a refugee and more like an award-winning journalist.

On the day that Salem flew to London, I flew to San Francisco, eager to see my mom, and make sure that she wasn't too angry at me for getting engaged without her or my father's permission. I was flying over the Pacific Ocean when Salem was pulled aside at Heathrow Airport. "What kind of passport is this?" the border guard asked him, as if he was confused that a Syrian had somehow made it to the passport control line and wasn't drowning somewhere in the Mediterranean.

"It is an original," Salem replied, bracing himself, remarkably cavalier about the lawless space between arrival gates and passport control. "What are they going to do, torture me?" he responded, when I had asked if he was nervous to fly for the first time in almost a year.

"We think it is fake," the guard responded, thumbing through the pages with real stamps—some of them even evidence of travel back and forth from the United Kingdom. Salem had never had a problem coming to the UK before; the first time the passport control officer stamped his passport without any questions, and the second time someone tried to recruit him to the British intelligence service. "If you know anyone that the British intelligence services should know about, please write down their name," the officer had said, pushing a piece of paper toward Salem as if he were in a spy movie from the 1970s—we all had a good laugh about it later.

Something about this interrogation felt different, as if an hourglass had been flipped upside down, and time was running out. For the next four hours, Salem waited as the border guard disappeared behind closed doors and reappeared again, his passport in hand, looking more perplexed with every trip. Normally calm and collected under pressure, Salem started to become agitated and nervous. He would have given his left testicle for a cigarette.

"Listen, I know you have a little jail somewhere here," he said as soon as the guard returned. He was so exhausted that he didn't even notice the guard looking at him as if he had just whipped off his pants.

"Can I just spend the night there, have a cigarette, and we pick this back up in the morning?"

Perplexed, the border guard handed him his passport without comment. He would not be escorted into the maze of interrogation rooms carefully tucked out of sight of most of Heathrow's travelers. Not this time. He could make his way toward the taxis and undergrounds that would take him into the city. He was free to leave.

It felt like a narrow escape. What if the border guard had not been so flabbergasted that he forgot how to do his job, and instead of stamping his passport had put him on the next plane back to Erbil? Over the previous few months, Kurdish politicians in Erbil had started rallying for an independent Kurdish state—a change that could destabilize the delicate balance that kept Erbil shielded from the suicide attacks and rogue militias that were starting to seize control of other parts of the country.

Our sliver of contested territory that had given us refuge for the past nine months could disappear overnight, leaving us at the mercy of new borders and unknown rules.

"I have to tell you something, and you aren't going to like it," he told me over the phone a few days later.

"I think I have to apply for asylum."

I was so relieved that I burst into tears. I always respected the way that he stubbornly refused to be seen as a refugee, but his denial was starting to feel more like a burden than liberation. Political asylum would put him on a path to UK citizenship—and most important, to a passport that would let us live wherever we wanted.

"I think that's a great idea," I said, between sobs, as my mother looked at me, as surprised as I was by my uncontrollable outpouring of emotion. "I am so proud of you."

9 | *Migrant or Refugee?*

A few weeks later, I found myself slumped in a chair at the Doha International Airport in Qatar, waiting to board a flight to London.

"Do you think Uber will be working when we get there?" a girl with a British accent and long blonde hair that tumbled down her back asked her boyfriend. I blinked my eyes. Uber. I couldn't imagine living in a city where I could hail a taxi through a smartphone. What would it be like to ride in a taxi without a meandering conversation in broken Arabic where the driver interrogated me about whether or not I was married, and graciously offered his opinions on my personal life as we drove through the city? I couldn't tell if I was excited for what was ahead of me, or already nostalgic for the world that I was leaving behind.

At that time, black-cab companies in London were trying to push Uber out of the city, blaming the start-up for driving down prices. It was a quietly gurgling cold war between the largely British-born cab drivers who had been a part of the city since time immemorial and the mostly immigrant Uber gig workers, a metaphor for shifting demographics, though I didn't realize it at the time. Instead, I sat there, dumbfounded and exhausted, wondering what it would be like to live in a city where the top news story was about a rideshare app, both nervous and excited to see who Salem and I might become once we were finally standing still.

"You're finally in London!" my friend Sarah Giaziri squealed, squeezing me the moment she saw me. I first met Sarah several years before at a journalism conference in Beirut, where I had stared at her googly-eyed as she spoke about safety trainings for local journalists and translators, silently willing her to be my friend. Now, she was inviting us to stay in her house while Salem waited for asylum to be granted—and it reminded me of our old apartment in Istanbul, dinner seemingly always on the stove, journalists passed out on the sofa, sometimes for weeks at a time. Only this time, we were the couch sleepers—and we weren't on our way to an assignment, but a new adventure entirely: political asylum. I had recently found out that in addition to being every freelance journalist's personal hero, Sarah used to be an immigration lawyer, and she had already been helping Salem prepare his asylum case while I was packing up our old apartment. At first, I had thought she was the coolest person I had ever met. Now I thought she might actually be an angel.

"Almost everyone from Syria gets asylum here, no problem," she assured us, pointing out that Salem could easily prove that he had been personally targeted by the Syrian regime and that he worked as a journalist, both of which made for a solid case. Still, we would need to gather as many documents as possible to show that he had a *reasonable fear of persecution*, or in other words, prove that he could not, under any circumstances, return to Syria.

Political asylum as a concept goes back to ancient Greece, when political exiles, debtors, and people escaping slavery sought refuge in ancient temples and statues, thought to be imbued with divine protection from the Gods. Churches became the next logical sanctuaries, protecting fugitives from arrest and execution, but leaving the sanctuary space often meant that fugitives had to go straight into political exile in another country, or risk death. After World War II, when an estimated 60 million people were displaced across Europe, the 1951 Refugee Convention officially defined *refugee* as someone in need of protection from political persecution, and solidified the right to seek asylum. Now, Salem was following in the footsteps of a long line of persecuted peoples: Jewish refugees fleeing the Nazis, Ugandan Asians expelled from their country during the 1970s, and Bosnians who fled the genocide during the 1990s. All sought protection in the United Kingdom, making it one of the most diverse countries in the world. Even though Great Britain took more asylum-seekers than any other country during the early 2000s, asylum-seekers had recently started getting a bad rap, smeared in the widely-read British tabloids for everything from driving down wages to barbecuing the Queen's swans. Salem had to make sure that his case was ironclad: dates had to line up and documents had to support his story; any slight inconsistency or omission could result in a refusal. My stomach turned when I thought about what could happen if this didn't work.

"I just can't believe you guys came here right before Brexit," Sarah laughed, saving me from spiraling into imagining a scenario where Salem got sent back to Syria, and never got to barbecue a swan.

Brexit. I tried to wrap my head around it. Around the time that Salem and I were moving into our first apartment together in Istanbul, in April of 2016, the European Union had struck a deal with Turkey to crack down on the smuggling route across the Mediterranean, leaving thousands of people stranded in refugee camps and temporary accommodation across Europe. That June, Britain had voted to leave the European Union. It was a political campaign that was inextricably tied to immigration anxieties—UK Independence Party leader Nigel Farage used images of refugees crossing into Hungary to push the idea that Britain's membership in the European Union made it vulnerable to a "demographic threat," that immigrants would simultaneously steal "British" jobs while sucking the welfare state dry, all the while converting the entire country to Islam. Naturally, those were Salem's exact intentions.

For those who cherished the multicultural fabric of the country, it was a disaster. Others—particularly those who have long been against Britain being a part of Europe, a movement that delayed construction on the Channel Tunnel that now connects London and Paris for years—saw it as a victory. But most of the people we met behaved as if they had lost a lost loved one. "We are going to lose all of the beautiful women," mourned a British journalist named James whom we quickly befriended. His anxieties about Brexit were mirrored in a popular meme, showing a mouthwatering spread of French cheeses and Spanish cured meats, replaced with a single slice of white toast, slathered in baked beans next to a jar of Marmite.

Still, while Great Britain might have been losing some of its greatness, at least for those who had enjoyed freedom of movement in any of the twenty-seven member states of the European Union for the last forty-five years, for us it was the only place in the world that had opened its doors—Brexit, or no Brexit.

"I grew up in Iraq, and it turned to shit. Next I went back to Syria, and it became shit," Salem joked whenever someone brought up their Brexit anxieties. "I went to Turkey—well, it was shit. I met an American, and what happens? Trump. Shit."

"Now I am here, and what happens?" he would continue, pausing for dramatic effect. "Brexit."

A segment of the British electorate seemed as if it might be having buyer's remorse. Many of those who had originally championed Brexit were starting to realize there were economic consequences to closing borders—economic consequences that could affect them. Who would have a right to the fish that swum freely across the English Channel? What would British farmers do without European subsidies?

More important, no one knew what would happen to the approximately three million EU citizens who were already living in the United Kingdom. Irish citizens were particularly nervous; an open border between Northern Ireland, which is a part of the United Kingdom, and the Republic of Ireland, which is a part of the European Union, was a key part of the Good Friday Agreement that put an end to the Troubles, a conflict that defined Ireland in the 1970s and beyond, with terrorist attacks similar to what Salem and I were used to hearing about in the Middle East. Now, many Irish and Northern Irish feared that the possibility of a hard border between the two territories could open old wounds and lead to more violence.

I personally thought Brexit was a terrible idea, but still struggled to sympathize with the way the new friends we were making were mourning their breakup with the European Union as if it were the most grievous political crisis in the world. Having lived in the Middle East long enough to witness the ways that most passports felt more like handcuffs than a laissez-passer, I struggled to comprehend how a continent of open borders could even exist. What would it look like if there was such freedom throughout the world? Before the Nakba, it was possible to travel by train from Damascus to Beirut, and Beirut to Haifa, but now, a Lebanese MEA flight will not even fly over Israel—and Palestinians living under Israeli occupation are almost never able to visit countries like Lebanon and Syria, where many of their families live, as a result. Meanwhile, Palestinians who grew up as refugees, like Samih and Rayan, might never have a chance to lay eyes on their homeland. Even within one country, there are checkpoints controlling who is allowed to move and who is not. Borders have become so widely accepted that they even restrict our imaginations—we don't consider what it would be like to share our cultures without people getting arrested at a checkpoint or turned away at a border they cannot cross.

I understood why people spoke so passionately about Brexit, but often those same people acted as if refugees drowning in the Mediterranean was a far-away problem, not a tragedy that was inextricably connected to the European Union's open borders.

As the European Union started to implement the Schengen Agreement during the 1990s, which began the long-anticipated process of abolishing internal borders between member states, it also began to fortify its external borders. To allow citizens of the European Union to move freely, it had to make it that much more difficult for anyone else to enter, pushing a visa requirement for countries wishing to join the EU and cracking down on the unregulated immigration that inevitably pops up instead. Nowhere is that more apparent than in Italy, where, ever since more people started crossing the Mediterranean to ask for asylum in 2015, the Italian government started shutting down rescues at sea and making it more difficult to apply for asylum, leaving thousands of young people—most of them young men from West Africa—living in a state of indefinite limbo.

"You have to understand, in Africa, we don't see Italy—we see Europe!" Mona, a soft-spoken twenty-nine-year-old, told me when I met him in a park in Frosinone, a small Italian town just an hour outside of Rome. Every weekend, Mona comes here with his friends—a group of guys he affectionately calls "the family," most of them also from West Africa, hailing from Nigeria, Gambia, Senegal, and Burkina Faso, among others. Nearby, a few of them were passing around a soccer ball; others were preparing a joint. Since it was the Holy Month of Ramadan, one of the Gambian guys brought a speaker and was playing Quranic verses on loop. Others were drinking beer.

"When we see Europe, we don't necessarily even see Europe—we see white people!" he said, as we made ourselves comfortable. I smiled at the way he says "white people," his eyes getting wide as if they are a kind of mythical beast. "I have always loved white people," he continued. "But when I got here, I realized that white people don't love me."

At first, I was hoping to come to Italy to find a story about romantic love and the rise of right wing populism that was driving so much of the hostility toward migrants and refugees—but since most of the people who take the harrowing journey across the Sahara Desert and then the Mediterranean Sea are young men, and not necessarily young lovers, this is a story about friendship. It is a story about the families that we leave behind, and the families that we create around us—but it is also a story about Europe's colonial legacies, and the unequal world that they left in their wake.

"Back in Nigeria, we had a farm," Mona began, with the air of a natural storyteller. "We were able to live off of our lands—we had crops, exactly like they do here, and didn't have to work." When his father's brother grew jealous of his family living off what he saw as his rightful inheritance, he sent a group of henchmen armed with machetes to intimidate Mona's father into giving up the land. "He went after his own brother," Mona continued, shaking his head. One of the armed men attacked his father, and he collapsed to the floor. Mona watched him bleed out.

"I ran to get my mother, but it was too late," he remembered. While the men didn't attack his mother, he distinctly remembers them telling her that she had to give up the land, or else.

Now, Mona was the head of the family—suddenly responsible for providing for his mother and four younger siblings, at only twenty years old. First, he moved to Lagos, Nigeria's largest city, where he drove his uncle's car as a taxi, trying to make enough money to help his mother make ends meet. But when a strange car started following him around the city one day, he got scared and started to worry that what happened to his father might happen to him. He tested them by driving down a small alleyway, and then again down an even smaller one. When they followed, he knew he was no longer safe in Nigeria.

"I need to go somewhere that I can make money," he told a friend one night. Mona had Libya in mind—plenty of Nigerians went there to work and earned more money than they did at home. His friend had another idea.

"Let's go to Europe," his friend responded. "We can make so much more money there." Mona didn't like the idea of being so far away from his mother, but he liked the idea of being able to make a living. According to his friend, they would ride in a truck to Libya, then from Libya cross the sea to Italy. "He made it sound so easy," Mona remembered. First, they had to get to Niger—and in Niger, they would meet a smuggler who could take them across the desert to Libya. "We were all crammed together in the back of a truck," Mona said, recalling the twenty-eight-hour journey from Lagos to Agadez.

As soon as Mona saw a group of other Black people, he relaxed. "I knew we were all going the same way, that we would be safer together," he remembered. But as soon as they reached Libya, his friend sold him out to a Libyan trafficker, who took him to a detention center. "It was my first time in a prison," he said, remembering the way that his stomach dropped when he realized that his friend had betrayed him.

"There were thousands of Black people there—thousands," he continued. "Every day, they beat us, asking for more money." Some of the prisoners who couldn't pay started working for the guards, shifting from oppressed to oppressor in the blink of an eye, beating people for not being able to pay new ransoms in addition to those that they had been extorted for just a few days before.

Hearing these stories, it is easy to think that the fault is with the smugglers and traffickers who inevitably profit off ordinary people's desperation. While they are undoubtedly evil, their jobs would not exist without the restrictive border policies that fuel their demand, leaving people like Mona with no other options.

By now, Mona's friend who had sold him out had crossed to Europe, leaving Mona broke, calling his mother, asking her to wire him money. "I felt so betrayed," he told me. He hated himself every time he called his mother—she was already struggling to take care of herself, and now had to borrow money from her neighbors to pay off the ransom. "I was supposed to be taking care of her," he continued. But if he didn't pay, the guards would write his name on a piece of paper along with the other prisoners who had run out of money. Then, they would call them outside and shoot them, one by one.

"First they would shoot them in the head and then in the heart," he said, remembering the harrowing scenes from inside of the detention center. "They would say your family doesn't need you—they don't even want to send you money." It felt as if they didn't deserve to live.

"I wish someone had told me that this journey was life and death," he said, looking off into the distance. "If I knew that, I wouldn't have come." The idea of Europe as a beautiful place without poverty or corruption is mesmerizing to so many struggling families in countries like Nigeria, Gambia, and Burkina Faso, or Eritrea, Somalia, and Sudan, but when 180,000 tried to make the crossing in 2016 alone, many found themselves locked up in a Libyan prison instead—a practice that continues to this day. Around the world, hundreds of thousands of people migrate for better work opportunities. But often, I find myself wondering why a European or US citizen who moves to Abu Dhabi or Dubai is often called an expat, typically earning an inflated salary, while a Nigerian or Gambian trying to leave their country to make more money is a "migrant." Both people are trying to make a better life for themselves. One is risking human trafficking and being sold in slave markets. The other doesn't have to pay taxes.

"I think about my mother and I don't want her to worry," Mona continued. "I want her to have everything so that she can live a long life." He knew that he had run out of options to support her in Nigeria—and if he went back at this point, he wouldn't be able to make enough money to pay off his debts. "Once you start the journey, you can't go back," he said, remembering the feeling of trying to hold on to his faith. "I had hope because I knew that I might survive."

Mona spent one year and eight months in that detention center.

On the day that he was released, he was too shocked to be afraid of the sea. There were rules for boarding the boat, a rubber pontoon that was built for around fifty people but would be carrying over double that. Don't wear any jewelry—it could puncture the boat. "We were basically naked," he laughed, remembering being shirtless with around 120 other people, many of whom had also survived being in the detention center. "We had to stand straight inside of the boat—like soldiers!" But as they drifted at sea, more and more of the people onboard grew hopeless, the vast sea stretching out around them like an endless abyss. "Some of the people died on the ship, right there in front of my eyes," Mona remembered. "I saw hell and I saw death," he continued. "But I also saw life. I knew that I could survive."

After two days at sea, a rescue ship appeared on the horizon. While the sea route between Turkey and Greece only takes forty-five minutes when the water is smooth, the route across the Central Mediterranean is longer, more treacherous, and results in even more shipwrecks. Almost none of the inflatable pontoons and ramshackle fishing boats that smugglers use are equipped to reach Italy—the nearest European country—by themselves. Instead, they drift at sea for days at a time, hoping to encounter a rescue ship. If they are unlucky, they are caught by the Libyan coast guard and sent back the way that they came.

Others are not rescued at all. During 2015, the year that Mona finally crossed, 2,000 migrants drowned in the Mediterranean. Between 2015 and 2022, the International Organization of Migration's Missing Migrants project counted almost 25,000 deaths at sea. When in 2016 the EU-Turkey deal started cracking down on the "safer" route between Turkey and Greece, more and more people turned to the dangerous three-day journey that Mona took, instead.

"Don't move," shouted the rescue workers. "We are here to help."

As soon as Mona recognized the English words, he smiled for the first time in two years. "Life is going to be easy," he thought to himself. "Apparently they speak English in Europe!"

———

As Mona talked, I couldn't help thinking about how this was just the beginning of the long and difficult road that lay before him. In the spring of 2018, just three years after Mona arrived in Italy, Matteo Salvini—a far-right fringe political personality who had built a following by hosting rallies where he hurled insults at immigrants (sound familiar?)—was appointed as Italy's Minister of Interior Affairs, allowing him to enact his wildest and most xenophobic fantasies.

"Italy must stop being the refugee camp of Europe," he announced to a crowd of supporters of the far-right Northern League party in Italy, shortly after he took office. Like Trump, Salvini was known for practicing a politics of buffoonery—often posting selfies or engaging in stunts such as posing for a magazine shirtless, wearing only a green tie.

But when it came to cracking down on migrants, he was incredibly serious. First, he waged war on rescue missions, announcing a fifty-thousand-euro fine for any migrant rescue ship that docked in an Italian port without permission. Next, he turned to the migrants themselves, stripping away all humanitarian protection visas, meaning that, unless someone won their asylum case and could prove that they were a refugee in need of protection, they would not have the right to live and work in Italy.

It furthered the narrative that refugees are worthy of protection, while "economic migrants"—like Mona—are not. It is a popular binary—a refugee is fleeing a war, while a migrant masquerades as a refugee to take advantage of the system. But what would you do if you came from a country where the average monthly salary is forty-three dollars and a healthy adult's life expectancy is fifty-four years? As Mona pointed out to me, Nigeria is the richest country in Africa—and yet, it is impossible to make money there unless your family is already rich. Upward mobility is an impossible dream.

"If you aren't rich and you don't have a farm, the only way to get by is to steal or come to Europe," he told me, when our conversation turned to corruption and the way that it fuels poverty. Mona came to Europe because he wanted to be able to support his family—but he was also fleeing criminals who were threatening him, and a cycle of violence that poverty creates.

"Of course, I would prefer to live in Africa," he continued, looking wistfully in the distance. I could tell he missed his mother and his younger siblings—he wouldn't be working so hard here if he didn't. "We have everything in Africa," he continued. "We have oil, good climate— the kind of soil that can grow any crop. But we will never forget that Europeans came and stole it from us," he pointed out, once again taking on the air of a philosopher. "So, we have no choice but to come here."

Around a century and a half ago, King Leopold of Belgium tore through the jungles of the Congo, inspiring Europe's most powerful leaders to do the same, dividing up Africa for their own benefit. Mona makes it clear how much the "Scramble for Africa"—and the seventy years of colonial domination that ensued—shaped the relationship between the European Union and the African continent today, where EU governments support "freedom of movement" among member states only if it is contingent on the union's external borders shutting out "economic migrants." Meanwhile the very reason that people are forced to migrate from Africa is the colonial exploitation that pillaged their economies for decades, robbing them of a future in their own countries.

"Europe's wealth was not built in Europe," Gurminder Bhambra, a professor of Postcolonial and Decolonial Studies at the University of Sussex, told me one morning when I called her on Zoom, after staying up most of the night before watching YouTube footage of her arguing that global inequality must be understood in the context of colonialism. I was eager to ask her about whether she thinks that these histories—and the widespread refusal to acknowledge them—contribute to the way that young men like Mona are treated, once they reach Europe's shores.

"We understand these histories as national histories, but they should be seen as imperial histories," she said, pointing out that all six of the founding members of the European Union—known at first as the

European Economic Community, or EEC, when it was founded in 1957—were not individual nations, but colonial powers profiting from vast empires spread out across Africa, Southeast Asia, and the West Indies. It drives a wrench into the popular narrative that the European Union started solely as a trailblazing peace project that would heal the wounds of the Great Wars by creating economic collaboration between nations, making future wars impossible. Thorbjørn Jagland, then chairman of the Norwegian Nobel Committee, said while presenting the 2012 Nobel Peace Prize to the European Union: "We can see that the political framework in which the Union is rooted is more important now than ever. We must stand together. We have collective responsibility. Without this European cooperation, the result might easily have been new protectionism, new nationalism, with the risk that the ground gained would be lost.

"We know from the inter-war years that this is what can happen when ordinary people pay the bills for a financial crisis triggered by others," he continued. "But the solution now as then is not for the countries to act on their own at the expense of others." He fails to address entire continents profiting at the expense of others in the speech.

"Insisting on a national history erases everything that happens outside of those borders, even though it is drawing on the resources, labor, and taxes of its territories," Dr. Bhambra continued, adding that many of the founding members of the EEC were just as invested in benefiting from one another's colonial spoils as they were in maintaining European peace.

Technically, the colonies of the member states—which covered large swaths of Africa and Southeast Asia, ruled by Belgium, France, Italy, Luxembourg, the Netherlands, and West Germany—were considered part of the EEC, but they did not enjoy full access to the privileges of membership. "Even though the EEC was established on the basis of equality of wages, social insurance, and free movement, this was explicitly refused to populations within its borders," Dr. Bhambra continued, drawing upon the example of Algeria, which, as a French colony up until it won independence in 1962, was just as much a part of the EEC as West Germany or Luxembourg—yet Algerians were not allowed freedom of movement across the six member states or equal wages as French citizens.

As soon as Algeria declared its independence in 1962, following a bloody war with France—which, as Dr. Bhambra pointed out, is not acknowledged in the "sixty years of peace" narrative of the European Union—France responded by implementing a visa requirement for Algerian citizens, which many saw as a "punishment" for independence.

Over time, this pattern was replicated across Africa—and, for that matter, the Middle East and Southeast Asia. As more and more countries fought for their independence, the former colonizers responded by sealing their borders to their former subjects, requiring visas for them to work, immigrate, and in some cases even visit. During Nigeria's days as a British protectorate, a Nigerian could freely travel to work or study in the United Kingdom, without needing a visa. Today, these kinds of opportunities are reserved for a small segment of the elite, those who are rich enough to be approved for visas.

"More than ninety percent of people who come to Europe are coming from countries that Europe colonized," Dr. Bhambra continued—and yet, citizens of every African nation, with the strange exception of Mauritius and the Seychelles, need a visa to travel to the European Union today. When Britain—or perhaps, more accurately, the British Empire—was trying to join the EEC in 1969, several member states were concerned that anyone from its colonies would then be able to move freely throughout the empire, leading to migration from the Caribbean and Southeast Asia. Rather than honor the people who had come to Britain and helped rebuild after the war, Britain chose to ally itself with the EEC, drafting legislation that began to systematically shut people out, even while they were still under British rule.

Now, the European Union is trying to protect its wealth built off the backs of its former colonies by fortifying its borders. Colonialism is largely over, but its legacy is not—and while European citizens in countries like Germany and the Netherlands continue to enjoy a social welfare state that contributes to the well-being of its citizens, even the richest African countries—like Nigeria—cannot afford to give its citizens even the most basic social security. Politicians like Matteo Salvini and Nigel Farage—and more recently, Sweden Democrats leader Jimmie Åkesson and Austria's Herbert Kickl—weaponize the fragile welfare state as the very reason why borders should be closed to migrants, but ignore the fact that many of those who are migrating for economic reasons are coming from countries whose resources they pillaged.

"There is a relationship between the two places," Dr. Bhambra went on. "How does that relationship change the way that we—as Europeans—should consider what we owe others?"

I wonder what the world would look like if Europe had never colonized Africa. What would cities like Paris or Lisbon look like, had their unique architecture not been financed by a combination of the transatlantic slave trade and the exploitation of raw materials and labor from the African continent? Would Belgium have perfected its devastatingly rich chocolates without Congo's cacao plantations? Maybe the two countries could have set up a mutually beneficial trade agreement that would have allowed both economies to thrive, and made it less of a necessity for young people in the Democratic Republic of the Congo to seek opportunities elsewhere. What would Africa look like if it had always had sovereignty over its own raw materials, and its history of being bound, shackled, and beholden to Europe and the United States was erased? As with the United States, Europe would be significantly poorer, without the raw materials and manual—more often than not, enslaved—labor that built its lauded capitals. As Dr. Bhambra put it, "Europe would be a lot less wealthy—and the world would be a lot more equal."

Mostly, I find myself thinking about what would happen to people like Mona if the balance of power had not been skewed from the start. Would his family be able to stay together in the face of hardship? If there were good jobs in Africa, there would be no need to migrate to Europe—and perhaps Europe itself, its streets no longer paved with purloined gold, wouldn't be that attractive after all.

"It is interesting because it is not as if other places have not been involved in trade or exchange or moving and settling in places," Dr. Bhambra told me, pointing out that there is a difference between traveling and being influenced by other cultures, and conquering them. "But this is different," she continued. "This is the systematic appropriation of resources from one place that are only used to better another place."

Open borders could be a form of reparations, a gesture to acknowledge a historical injustice and repair the power imbalance between the colonizer and the colonized. But when I asked Dr. Bhambra if she thought this might be the answer, she shook her head.

"When the world had open borders, Europeans had free reign of the world," she pointed out. "That is how European colonizers appropriated land and resources in Africa and the Americas in the first place."

Up until this conversation with Dr. Bhambra, I had always fantasized about a world with no borders, where loved ones wouldn't have to be separated and anyone could live as they pleased, but as she pointed out, open borders could once again facilitate the exploits of the most powerful at the expense of those who have already been disenfranchised. Instead, she suggested a more methodical form of reparative justice. "We would need to think about reparations and the redistribution of resources, particularly given that so much migration is prompted by global inequality," she told me, explaining that migration should be addressed at its source. "One thing would be to make places livable so that people didn't feel like they had to move to live fulfilling lives."

It is difficult to imagine a world where resources are redistributed in a way that would allow Mona to live a fulfilling life in Nigeria, but being able to travel and make a living in Europe, and still visit his family in Nigeria—without worrying about living without papers in Italy, or making the dangerous journey to get there—would be a start. Open borders, as Dr. Bhambra suggested, might prime the world for exploitation, but others—such as E. Tendayi Achiume, the UN Special Rapporteur on contemporary forms of racism, racial discrimination, xenophobia, and related intolerance—point out that it is the only meaningful way to address the global wealth disparity that drives migration today. Some economists, such as Milton Friedman, have argued that open borders cannot work in the modern age, given the proliferation of the welfare state, and political anxieties over who benefits from it. Others, such as Michael Clemens, argue that immigrants have the potential to create the very wealth that supports the welfare state, and that borders trap their talent in countries where it will not be appreciated.

Even without open borders, free—or freer—migration would still democratize movement in a way that would make greedy smugglers and dangerous journeys a thing of the past. Spain provides an interesting model by facilitating migration from most of its former colonies in Latin America, allowing visa-free travel for most citizens of Latin American countries, and a path to citizenship after only two years of living and working in the country. Many Venezuelans have used this loophole to flee the country's economic crisis brought on by Nicolás Maduro's dictatorship and US sanctions, showing that displacement does not have to be as painful and destabilizing as it is for so many others. Still, even in this example, immigrants with money benefit the most; those who migrate and cannot find work risk losing their status, leaving them vulnerable to exploitation as soon as they can no longer pay into the welfare state. While visa-free travel is an important first step to curtail dangerous journeys in rafts and across deserts, policies that ensure the right to live and work without restrictions are needed to redistribute this wealth in a way that actually grants freedom and prosperity to all.

———

Mona quickly realized that life in Italy was not going to be as easy as he thought it was going to be. First, people didn't speak English. "I would try to speak English to people, and they would say, 'Vafanculo—parle Italiano!'" he told me, remembering the way that he was frequently greeted with "Fuck you! Speak Italian!"

"Back in my country, many people do not have documents," Mona explained, saying that even birth certificates are rare in some communities in Nigeria. "But in Italy, you need documents for everything." At first, the idea was strange for him—why should a document make the difference between whether or not you can work? But soon, he started to notice the way that police around Frosinone stopped other Africans, always asking them for their documents. "One time, I saw a Black man who was sick—he wanted someone to call an ambulance," he remembered. "Instead, the police showed up and sent him back to Africa. Just because he didn't have documents!" Stories like this are sickening reminders of Salvini's promise to "sweep the streets clean" of African migrants, a kind of rhetoric that has become fashionable across Europe ever since 2015, and has only intensified since then. Since I visited Mona in April 2022, Italy has elected Giorgia Meloni as its prime minister, who suggests a "naval blockade" in Africa to stop migration and has openly referred to immigration as "ethnic substitution." She is frequently referred to as Italy's first fascist leader since Benito Mussolini, suggesting that migrants in Italy could face even harsher conditions in the years to come.

At first, Mona was cautious about leaving the migrant shelter where he was staying—he saw the way that Black men were stopped by the police, and it seemed easier to keep his head down and stay out of trouble. The few times that he tried to meet friends in a nearby park, he felt self-conscious at the way that the locals were looking at them, and quickly changed his mind and left. "We noticed they were angry when they saw us," he remembered, the sting of casual racism still fresh. "But then we found this park," he smiled. "At first it was just for children, but day by day, we started meeting here, and it became our spot."

Now, it feels like a family gathering—someone always coming or going, knowing that whatever time of day they stop by, there will be someone there, ready to pass around a soccer ball and let off some steam, or help them if they're in a bind. "It is boring to just stay in your house," said Mudalamin, a Gambian friend of Mona's with bright eyes and a wide smile. "Italians like to meet in a bar or café, but it doesn't work for us," he continued. "I much prefer to come here." At first, I assumed he meant that most of them couldn't afford to meet for a coffee or a beer. Later, I learned it is because of racism—almost all the guys have a story of being kicked out of somewhere, accused of "smelling bad" or making the other customers uncomfortable.

"We have become like a family because we don't have anyone else here," Mona said, smiling as he looks out over the group of guys. "This guy is my brother—that guy is my brother, because we watch each other's backs." But even in the park, the family is frequently harassed. Sometimes, police vans line up along the perimeter, which is no more than one city block. "When you see them, you think there is a really serious criminal here," Mona said, explaining that they are often looking for anyone who is smoking weed, or doesn't have documents. "If they weren't registered in Frosinone, they would ban them from coming back." Borders and papers are already keeping them from visiting their home countries and families. Now, they can't even see their friends.

What about their love lives? "Here, in Europe, I notice relationships don't last very long," Mona said philosophically. "My Italian colleagues are always talking about fighting with their wives, or getting divorced," he continued. "They don't know that not everything comes easily—they just want their lives to be perfect all of the time."

Mona dreams of finding the right person—and exploring what it means to fall in love, and start a future, fully aware of all the ups and downs that it might entail. "I think a relationship should be like school," he mused. "You should always be learning new things about her, and she should always be learning new things about you. I want to know what makes her happy and what makes her angry—and I want her to know the same things about me." Most of all, he wants to be a father. "I want to give my mother a girl, because we are all boys," he smiled. "I know that if she has a girl she will be so happy." But he doesn't see it happening any time soon.

"Everything would be easier if Italians liked Black people," he said. "If you see a white woman dating a Black man, she isn't Italian." While he knows of a few mixed relationships in Rome—which is bigger, and more cosmopolitan—he knows of far more instances of Italian families who stopped a relationship in its tracks the moment that they found out their daughter was dating someone who was Black. One of Mona's friends has a court date approaching, for saying "Ciao, Bella" to a girl outside the train station. "I kept telling him not to say anything," Mona remembered, shaking his head. But his friend insisted that he had seen dozens of Italian guys doing the same, that that was the way they courted women here and showed a girl that they liked her. The girl called the police.

But Mona doesn't tell his mother any of this when she calls him. "When are you going to let me talk to your girlfriend?" she asks him. "When are you going to make me a grandbaby?"

Mona misses her a little bit more every time.

"Any day now, Mama," he says. "Any day."

10 | *"The American Refugee"*

Four months after Salem first asked the passport control officer at Heathrow Airport to put him in jail "just overnight," he was granted political asylum in the United Kingdom.

"You have been granted five years leave to remain," read the letter. For the first time since Salem was kicked out of Turkey, I felt the pressure release. We threw a party in Sarah's kitchen to celebrate. "I would like to sing a song," Salem told a room full of both old and new friends, gathered for the occasion. "I'm not a Syrian," he began, to the tune of Britney Spears's classic anthem, "I'm Not A Girl, Not Yet A Woman."

"But not yet a British!" he continued. "I neeeeeed time. To not have anyyyyyy problems for fiiiiiive years. Until, I am . . . a British." That is the thing about Salem—he knows a lot about jihadis, but he also loves Britney Spears.

"No fist fights for five years!" Sarah laughed, sitting cross-legged on her kitchen counter, enjoying the performance. Even four drinks in, she gave sound advice. "Once you have a British passport, you can do whatever you want."

Having a British residency permit—the equivalent of a US green card or, as we more commonly call it, "papers"—meant that Salem was back on the grid. He could do the things that most people take for granted, like apply for a job or rent an apartment. Now, I was the one who didn't have the right documents—and while I could visit the United Kingdom for up to six months, I couldn't do things like rent an apartment or open a bank account, which was reserved for UK citizens and residents. Most important, I could not legally work—and London was more expensive than any place we had ever lived. I tried to get away with freelancing, taking assignments abroad and coming back to spend a few weeks in London. It did not take long before UK immigration caught on to the fact that I wasn't a tourist and started threatening to deport me.

"It is clear that you're living here," a passport control officer said, as if this was a crime. According to immigration authorities, it is—and that, alone, is enough to deport someone. "You have six more months—if you don't get a visa, you won't be able to get back in."

I reasoned that there were dozens of newspapers and media outlets based in London. I covered the war on ISIS, I thought to myself. Surely someone will want to hire me and want to sponsor my visa. I had the haughty confidence of an expat journalist. I could charm anyone into giving me a job.

As it turned out, no one gave a shit.

"Do you have the right to work?" an editor that agreed to meet for a coffee asked me. As a freelancer, I was used to asking editors for meetings when I was in New York, but something about doing the same in London made me feel out of place.

"I would need you to sponsor my visa, but I know that I can write anything," I responded, wanting to add, I am a conflict reporter who speaks three languages! I am tough enough to report from active front lines, wily enough to convince soldiers to let me cross checkpoints when they are not letting anyone else through. Please just let me be in the same country as my fiancé.

Instead, he cut the meeting short. "I can't hire you if you can't work here," he said. "But let me know if you go back to the Middle East and want to freelance." It was humbling, and I hated it. It was also just a tiny taste of what so many immigrants experience: working to earn advanced degrees and with prestigious accomplishments in their home countries only to move and be judged for a lack of papers or the lingering presence of an accent.

Meanwhile, Salem was falling in love with London, and the more I felt like the city was rejecting me, the more I found it annoying. "London is actually a very beautiful city," he would randomly announce, even if he had just watched a pigeon defecate on a park bench. I wondered what had happened to the wise-cracking cynic who was appalled that everyone in London ran around with a dirty ass.

Looking back, I realize I was burnt out. Burnt out from constantly adapting—first to Iraq, and now to London, burnt out from trying to make the best out of what was happening to us, without letting myself process how suddenly Salem was deported and our lives changed. Instead, I had dived straight into covering the war on ISIS and, somewhere along the way, convinced myself that it would be easier to go through the motions as a robot, making decisions for love, yet turning off my feelings about everything else.

Now I was trying to adapt all over again—only this time, I had convinced myself that it would be easy. It would be quiet and calm—there would be no soldiers harassing me for selfies at checkpoints, no taxi drivers inquiring about my marital status. Maybe I had also drunk the post-colonial Kool-Aid and believed that London was somehow better than the Middle East, overflowing with opportunities—ignoring how the majority of the British public had literally voted to make sure that foreigners couldn't take advantage of them. Somehow, Salem had carved himself a place in Brexit Britain, but I didn't know if there was a place for me in it. I had exhausted the privileges of being an expat with a US passport, and now was subject to immigration rules, just like everyone else.

"What if I get kicked out of the UK," I asked him during one of our walks. I tried to keep my anxieties to myself, but I felt myself begin to open up after he got his papers. Now that his situation was not as dire,

I could take my own feelings into consideration again after months of bottling them up.

"That isn't going to happen," he responded, shaking his head. I didn't know if he believed this or was just trying to make me feel better. Either way, his confidence always made me suspend my disbelief, and see possibilities that I didn't see before.

If I couldn't get a work visa, I had two options: I could go back to school, or we could get married. Hilariously, the power dynamic had now flipped. As soon as I presented this option to Salem, he doubled over laughing.

"Don't worry, my American refugee," he said, enjoying it all a little bit too much. "I will marry you and protect you from Trump."

As long as Trump was in office in the United States—and the Muslim ban was still in effect—it might be the only option that we had left that would let us live together in the same country. I visited Ana Gonzales, an immigration solicitor in North London, prepared to be laughed out of her office.

"It is certainly unusual—but it is not illegal," she said, as I held my breath. If Salem could sponsor me, we would no longer have to worry every time I went through passport control. I could apply for a job and be considered, along with the other candidates. Maybe—just maybe—we could start living an ordinary life together.

"I have been working as a solicitor for a long time," she said, breaking out into a smile. "But I have never seen a US citizen marrying a refugee for papers."

Even though it is legal, it isn't as easy as going to a courthouse. If Salem was going to sponsor me, he needed to make at least £18,600 in the next year, a policy known as the "minimum income requirement," to prove that I would not be a "burden to the state." It was a relic of Prime Minister Theresa May's "hostile environment" immigration policies, designed to make life so difficult for undocumented immigrants that they give up and go home.

It was intimidating, but it was not impossible—though I wondered how Salem was going to make £18,600 as a recently arrived immigrant, when even people who were born here were struggling. I decided to enroll in an MA in Investigative Journalism, which I hoped would expose me to the world of journalism outside of war zones, with the added benefit of giving me a student visa for one year. I wanted to use my time in the course to investigate the government's hostile environment policy, which seemed to impact not only immigrants, but also UK citizens, as if it had been expertly designed to punish people for falling in love with someone from another country.

As it turned out, the minimum income requirement was just the tip of the iceberg.

11 | *A Hostile Environment*

"You say you met your boyfriend online?"

Marissa Marius did not expect the UK passport control officer to start asking her about her relationship, not when she had visited London so many times that it felt like home. After flying more than eleven hours from Port of Spain, Trinidad, to London Gatwick Airport, all she wanted to do was reunite with her sisters and cousins at Wagamama.

"You don't understand, my mouth was *watering*," she told me, as she recounted the story to me, a musical Caribbean lilt to her voice on the other end of the WhatsApp call. I couldn't help laughing—Wagamama is such a specifically British craving, an unspectacular chain restaurant where office workers go to scarf down stir-fry on their lunch breaks. But for Marissa, it is the site of warm memories of gossiping all afternoon over soupy ramen and spicy curries with friends and family on Kensington High Street.

"I really wanted to surprise them that day," she told me. "I felt like I was missing all of these family occasions, living so far away."

Even though she grew up in Trinidad, she had always felt connected to London—she had often visited her grandmother there, as well as her sisters, who were born there. As a teenager, she had spent five years living there, enrolling at Hammersmith College to study business and complete her GCSEs, hoping it might allow her to stay around the people who felt like home. Paying international tuition was expensive, so she made the difficult decision to go back to Trinidad, but always wondered if she had the right to UK citizenship, particularly given that her parents had lived there at a time when they were considered subjects of the British Empire—and even had British passports.

Nevertheless, when she went to a lawyer in 2017 and asked him about her parents' status, he said that they were not British. "It was very confusing," she remembered—but a few months later, when she started talking to her boyfriend, Tony, on a dating website, it felt like a sign to try one more time.

"We were so excited to finally meet each other," she told me, remembering the way he used to send her flowers and little gifts, just to let her know that he was thinking about her. "He just knew exactly how to make me feel special, like his princess or his queen." So she decided to try to visit again, packing her bags with whatever documents that she could find, hoping that she could prove that she had the right to stay.

Now, the passport control officer was making her nervous. "What is this," she asked, coming across university records and a UK driver's license, which Marissa had perfectly organized in a file folder, showing the five years of her life that she spent living in London. "I used to live here," she explained. "My father used to live here, too," she continued, as she watched the officer uncover his documents. "I am looking into whether or not he has a right to British citizenship."

As soon as Marissa mentioned her father, she was escorted to another room. Another officer came and took her picture. "It was like I was a criminal, and they were taking my mugshot," she told me, remembering what it was like to be shuffled from interrogation room to interrogation room. "I've never had any kind of interaction with the police before. I was absolutely terrified."

Between interrogations, she had to wait in another room—where she immediately noticed that everyone else was Black. "There was a girl there, she couldn't have been more than fifteen years old," she remembered. "I thought of myself because I used to come visit my grannie when I was that age—and here was this child, detained alongside people who could be criminals."

Over the next few hours, the Border Control agents continued to question her, first about her relationship with Tony and then, more seriously, about her family. "For me, it felt like racism," she told me, remembering how humiliated she felt when they called Tony and questioned him about their relationship. "It felt like they were punishing me for being in love with someone who is white and for researching my family's status."

A few hours later, the head of Border Patrol at Gatwick Airport came and threw her folder at her; the documents were crumpled and folded, carelessly handled. "Whatever you are trying to research, you have no right to be in the UK," he said, before escorting her to another room, where she spent the night. The next morning, she was put on the first plane back to Trinidad.

"Whenever I told them that my parents had citizenship, they told me that I was lying!" she told me, remembering how they almost convinced her that she really was a liar and a criminal. "They just said, 'You're lying, you're lying, you're lying!'"

It only made her more curious about what had really happened with her father. She never had much of a relationship with him when she was younger, but she knew that he used to live in London before a mysterious interaction with the British High Commission while he was visiting Trinidad during the 1980s, after which he hadn't been able to go back to the United Kingdom, even though he had a British passport.

"My biggest mistake I ever made was thinking that I was home," Richard Black told me over a crackly phone connection. I spoke to him from my apartment in North London, which felt ironic given that Richard would have loved to be there with me, but instead was in Trinidad, where he has lived for more than forty years. "Can you imagine?" he asked me, animatedly. "I was dumped in a country that wasn't even my own!"

Richard was born in St. Lucia, a small island in the Caribbean archi-pelago, at a time when most of those islands were still British colonies. At six years old, Richard and his mother boarded a steamship to Great Britain, joining many others from across the West Indies to travel to the "Mother Country," then known as the center of the British Empire, where there were work opportunities for anyone who was willing to leave the warm sea and tropical breeze of the Caribbean behind for a much drearier island, in hopes of filling some of the many positions that were desperately needed to help rebuild the country after World War II.

"We didn't lead an easy life," Richard told me, remembering a time when racism was commonplace, and his mother struggled to make ends meet for the two of them. "My mother worked as a waitress, and I remem-ber we used to eat the scraps that she brought home from her waitressing jobs." Nevertheless, London, and specifically Notting Hill, the bourgeon-ing capital of Black London, became home, where other people from across the Caribbean came together to create their own kind of British identity. "It was good times," he laughed—and suddenly it seemed like he was no longer a gaunt, almost seventy-year-old man who has spent the majority of his life in a strange state of bureaucratic exile, but energetic and youthful, picturing what it was like to fall in love.

One particularly epic night out in 1974, when Richard was twenty-one, a Trinidadian woman caught his eye. "I liked her," he told me, recalling an evening that involved copious amounts of rum at a house party. "We enjoyed sharing bits of our culture together," he continued. "I would tell her something about St. Lucia, she would tell me a little something about Trinidad. We clicked."

Within a year, they were married—and soon had two daughters. But when they decided to take a family trip together to Trinidad to visit Richard's in-laws, he had no way of knowing that he wouldn't be com-ing back. "I realized I had to renew my passport," he told me, recalling an errand that was no more complicated than going to the British High

Commission, the equivalent of a passport office. However, similar to the way the passport control officers at London Gatwick Airport told his daughter Marissa thirty-five years later that she had no right to be in the United Kingdom, the clerk behind the desk told him that she could not renew his British passport, because he was not a British citizen. "Get a St. Lucian passport, or a Trinidadian passport," she advised—but Richard was in shock. "I always thought I was British," he said, remembering the moment he realized he wouldn't be able to go home. "I went to primary school there, I got married and had two children. I always thought that was the end of it."

But that is the thing about borders—they can change at a moment's notice, without even notifying the people whose citizenship and rights they are about to take away. For Richard, it happened in 1979—the year that St. Lucia followed in the footsteps of countries like Jamaica and Trinidad, declaring independence from the British Empire and silently shifting his status from a subject of the British Empire, with the rights of a citizen, to an immigrant who no longer had a right to live in the country without a visa. Leaving meant that he was now locked out of the country that was his home.

Sitting on the plane in 2018, Marissa wondered if her father's exile had anything to do with her deportation several decades later.

———

As soon as Marissa got home, she tried to move on.

"I had so much shame," she told me, remembering how she used to replay that night in Gatwick Airport over and over again. Some nights, she startled in the middle of the night—and while she tried to keep talking to Tony, as if nothing had happened, they were both processing their shock. "It was an emotional rollercoaster," she remembered. "We both had no idea what had just happened."

Three weeks later, she turned on the television, and a news anchor was announcing that thousands of people who had immigrated to the United

Kingdom from the Caribbean between 1948 and 1973 were being told that they had lost their status. Some were even being deported and separated from their families, and the reporter was calling it the Windrush scandal, after the name of the ship that had transported so many of the people who had first come to the United Kingdom from the Caribbean in 1948.

"My jaw just dropped," she told me. Suddenly, everything made sense: the obsession with her father's paperwork, the hushed whispers about travelers who were coming from the Caribbean. "It wasn't random," she said, remembering the moment that she started putting the pieces together. "We were victims. We were victims of a scandal."

Marissa knew that she had to call her father. Even though they rarely spoke to one another, it felt too coincidental not to reach out. "Have you been watching the news?" she asked, as images of the HMT *Windrush*—the first ship to bring emigrants from the West Indies to the United Kingdom—flashed across the screen. "They are looking for people who have been affected."

A few weeks later, Marissa and Richard were invited to share their story on live television—and as Richard began to tell his story for the first time, Marissa felt the ice between them beginning to thaw as she learned things about him that she had never known before. "I had always thought he was just a bitter man with a chip on his shoulder," she said, remembering the few interactions that she had with him as a child. "I thought he had chosen not to go back to the UK. But then I realized he was carrying all of this shame and embarrassment about why he couldn't go back." Now his pain and frustration felt so familiar that she was overwhelmed with a desire to understand him for who he was, not the absent father she had made him out to be.

————

You could say that the Windrush scandal first began when the Colonial Secretary in London caught wind of a ship carrying Black subjects of the British Empire, on its way to the Tilbury Docks in London.

"I regret to inform you that more than 350 troop deck passages by EMPIRE WINDRUSH have been booked by men who hope to find employment in the United Kingdom," read the telegram, sent by the British governor of Jamaica. "Most of them have no particular skill, and few will have more than a few pounds on their arrival."

Prime Minister Clemente Attlee went into a panic. At one point, he considered diverting the ship to Kenya, suggesting that the people on board be put to work picking peanuts. Up until that moment, he had always been in favor of open borders within the British Empire, as an essential aspect of free trade. He likely never imagined that Black subjects of the British Empire would benefit from freedom of movement as well.

As the HMT *Empire Windrush* got closer, some of the passengers on board started to get nervous that they wouldn't be allowed to dock. Many were former service members, who had fought for the British Empire during World War II. While they saw coming to the "Mother Country" as a homecoming, they were also accustomed to the colonial dynamics of the British Empire and didn't expect the country to take so kindly to them when they came on their own accord. Others were so eager to work that they had written their skills next to their names on the passenger lists—on the HMT *Empire Windrush*, alone, there were carpenters, tailors, engineers, wilders, a hatter, a potter, and two hair-dressers.

"We used to come over, two by two," Faye Smith, a retired NHS nurse with short, plaited silver hair told me over a cup of piping hot tea at the Whitgift Centre in South Croydon, London. Every other Thursday, Faye joins a few other Caribbean ladies—many of whom also came to Britain after the war to staff the recently established National Health Service—to drink tea and reminisce about old times, as a part of an ongoing exhibit on the Windrush generation. Sometimes, they answer questions from people who pass through the gallery—most of the time, they catch up with each other.

"Sometimes we broke the rules a little bit," Faye whispered to me, conspiratorially. During those times, Faye and the other nurses lived in a dormlike accommodation, which they shared with some of the Irish nurses. According to Faye, the Irish girls were always sneaking out, while the girls from the West Indies were unanimously well behaved.

"What did you do?" I asked her, eager to hear a bit of gossip, especially about a time I knew so little about in a country that I now called home. "We kept a hot plate in our room," she told me, her voice lowering. "Sometimes, we would sneak in spices and make a West Indian curry, even though we were supposed to eat in the mess hall—we would work so hard to hide the smell!"

I couldn't help smiling at Faye's version of a scandal—while it sounds as innocent as a college student making a packet of ramen in their dorm room, landlords were posting vacancies with the caveat, "No Blacks, No Irish, No dogs," and many of the West Indians and South Asians arriving had to help each other survive. Imagining a young Faye leaning over her hot plate, from which was wafting the delicious smell of Scotch bonnet and curry paste, surrounded by her colleagues and roommates, reminds me of Mona and the family, meeting every Saturday in the park in Frosinone, leaning on each other for the strength needed to persevere in the hostile world outside.

People like Faye paved the way for people like me and Salem to make our home in London years later, at a time when a West Indian curry is as ubiquitous as fish and chips. We might be from different parts of the world, but I can't help feeling like this generation made it easier for those who came afterward to nestle into the multicultural fabric that is the United Kingdom, and to feel at home in a place where our hodgepodge of nationalities and cultures makes us blend in more than it makes us stand out.

Those who ran the houses of Parliament during the 1950s and 1960s thought differently. Politicians, among them Winston Churchill, were actively trying to restrict freedom of movement from the West Indies and Southeast Asia. At one point, a working group was set up specifically to gather evidence that the Black British population caused a disproportionate amount of crime compared to the white population. (It failed to do so.) Unemployment offices across the country were instructed to surveil Black communities and report back on who was collecting benefits, and who appeared to be idle and unemployed—but again any actual evidence pointed toward the exact opposite: migration, particularly from the West Indies, was causing the economy to boom. As the British government tried to push the narrative that the Black population consisted of lazy outcasts, British institutions such as the National Health Service and British Rail were sending recruiters to Barbados and Grenada, placing job advertisements in the local papers, hoping to bring over more hardworking people like Faye and her friends.

Countries like Jamaica and Trinidad began their independence campaigns during the 1960s, giving Britain an excuse to cut off immigration from its former colonies with the 1971 Immigration Act, which made it so that no one could emigrate from the former colonies without an employment contract. However, the law included a clause stating the "right of abode," which allows any former colonial subjects to continue to come and go if they have a parent or grandparent born in the United Kingdom. Because of the timing of the waves of immigration from the colonies, very few of those former subjects had a parent or grandparent who was old enough to have been born in the UK. So, the law effectively facilitated emigration from only the descendants of British colonizers, in countries like Canada, Australia, and South Africa—who were, more often than not, white. Meanwhile, most descendants of the colonized in places like the West Indies and Southeast Asia did not have British parents or grandparents—and, more important, were not white.

Worse yet, this law made it so that anyone whose citizenship came into question would be responsible for proving their right to live in the country—which many people, like Richard, assumed would be evident from their family ties and near-lifelong residence in Britain.

A few years later, in 1981, Margaret Thatcher eliminated birthright citizenship—a policy change that would not only affect the Windrush generation, but their descendants. By the time that Theresa May rolled out the hostile environment in 2012—suddenly requiring people to present documents to rent an apartment or access healthcare—the collective force of these laws started to catch up to people. Suddenly, people who assumed they had always been British, including many who were born in the United Kingdom, were told that they did not have the rights of a British citizen. For many, being asked to present an identification document became existential; the country they thought they belonged to had decided that they didn't belong there after all.

As soon as Richard found out that he couldn't go back to the United Kingdom, it was only a matter of time before he started fighting with his wife.

"I was so angry—I was angry at myself and everyone around me," he said, remembering the way his experience with the Home Office, the British equivalent of the department of Homeland Security, began to sear itself into his marriage. At one point, his wife flew back to the United Kingdom, leaving him behind in Trinidad and announcing that they were over—a problem, given that he had been staying in her family's home until then. Suddenly, he was out on the street in a city that he had only ever visited as a tourist.

"I had nowhere to go, I had no money," he told me, remembering his first days being homeless. He started sleeping underneath the overpasses, with no way to get clean clothes or bathe. "You could smell me before you saw me," he said, cringing. During the summer months, he could pick mangoes from the trees and eat their fruit until the hunger pangs went away. Sometimes, families who saw him sleeping under the overpass invited him for cookouts. "Everyone is so friendly in the Caribbean, it makes it easier to be homeless," he told me, and I immediately recognized the perspective of a true survivor. But when he was truly hungry, he would plug his nose and eat from the garbage cans.

"I was destitute," he told me. "The only reason I was able to pull myself up was because a group of Christians decided to help me out—they gave me clean clothes, and a place to sleep in a shelter." Soon, Richard picked up work as a construction worker, and soon began to notice the unsafe conditions in some of the buildings. He became interested in safety inspections and started studying to get an OSHA certification.

"School was never easy for me," he said, remembering growing up poor, in underfunded schools in London. He always found reading difficult—and later learned that he was slightly dyslexic, which explained why the words sometimes swam together while he was trying to study. "I was really proud of myself that I passed."

Now he runs two businesses, each offering Health and Safety services across Trinidad and Tobago. "I will never forget the people that showed me kindness," he remembered, looking back on what he describes as being "dumped" in a country that was not his own. Now, Richard is a man with an overwhelmingly positive attitude; if you ask him if he has any regrets, he only has one.

"I wasn't able to be with my mother while she was sick, or be at her side when she died," he told me. Even though he applied for an emergency visa, it was rejected. "I will never forgive the Home Office for that."

———

One of the strangest things that I have ever learned about the UK immigration system is that the monarch does not need a passport. As all UK passports are issued in the name of His (or Her) Majesty, the logic follows that British monarchs do not need to issue their own travel documents— all travel documents refer back to them.

For the Windrush generation and their descendants, however, the Home Office pulled the rug out from underneath their entire community, potentially affecting an estimated 57,000 people from across the Commonwealth, including former territories in Africa as well as the Caribbean. "Many people have lost everything, they've lost members of their family, they've lost their employment, or their property," Garrick Prayogg, a Jamaican cultural ambassador at Rethink Mental Illness, told me when I met him outside the Royal Court of Justice, where we had both come to support a group of lawyers and advocates who were campaigning for the Windrush Act, a law that would grant amnesty to everyone affected by the scandal.

"Did you know it costs taxpayers fifty thousand pounds per head to put someone on a deportation flight to Jamaica?" he asked me, pointing out that over the past four years, the Home Office has deported hundreds of people on charter flights. While the Home Office argues that the people on board are criminals, lawyers and advocates are often able to stop these flights at the last minute, arguing that the people on board are either nonviolent offenders who have served their time in jail and don't deserve to be punished twice, or not even criminals at all, and likely should not have even been arrested and detained in the first place.

"What would it be like if they could give this money to people who have been wronged by the system instead?" Garrick continued, pointing out that the cost of deporting one person could easily pay the rent or mortgage of several people for months, or support someone while they looked for a job or took care of their mental health. While the UK government set up a compensation scheme for people affected by the Windrush Scandal in 2018, only 5 percent of the people who have applied since then have received any money. For those who have, it has been abysmal—Richard, for example, was awarded £10,000, which is barely £250 for every year of his life that he has spent in exile.

Regardless of compensation, there are layers of other effects on the communities pushed out of their homes, many that have yet to be studied, let alone addressed. Dozens of British institutions have funded research to analyze the psychological impact of Brexit on both the British and European communities living in the UK, but there are far fewer equivalent studies on the impact of the Windrush scandal on Black Britons, and as of this writing, no one has investigated the mental health impact of the hostile environment on the immigrant community as a whole.

"Black people have always dealt with racism," Garrick told me when I asked him about how it affects people's psychological well-being. "But on top of that, we have been excluded from certain services." Many mental health services, particularly with the NHS, offer what Garrick calls "a European-centric approach," ignoring culturally specific traumas such as structural racism or fear of the immigration system.

"If I walk into a clinic, and there isn't a darker-skinned person in sight, I am not going to feel comfortable opening up there," he continued. "So, I would just hold it in. And that's what a lot of people do, they just hold it in."

———

After more than forty years, Richard is still wrapping his head around the ripple effect that his prolonged exile has had on his family. "I was just twenty-nine years old when it happened," he remembered. "I didn't understand immigration law—I was just angry at myself and everyone around me."

Most of his family didn't understand either—his daughters in London grew up assuming that he had abandoned them. He was too ashamed to get to know Marissa while she was young, while he was homeless. "I didn't want her to see me like that," he said, softly. He doesn't know if his first marriage would have survived were it not for his experience with the Home Office—nevertheless, it undeniably created a kind of psychological turmoil that made a healthy relationship impossible.

"If you want to survive the Home Office, you have to be married to a psychologist," he laughed, when I asked him how he sees it, so many years later. "I felt so useless." He suddenly became serious. "I was totally emasculated as a man, completely out of control. My wife had every right to be frustrated with me."

After many years, Richard has found love again—another Trinidadian woman, named Cleopatra, whom he describes as patient and under-standing, an antidote to the years of chaos and confusion he spent wan-dering in a country that is not his own. "I even have a good relationship with my ex," he shared, proudly. But for me, the true love story here is about father-daughter love. Richard and Marissa, after years of being estranged, are now closer than they could have ever imagined, allies as they fight the Home Office together. Every other day, Marissa calls him, just to check in. "I know it isn't easy to go through this by yourself," she said, smiling. "So, I just like to make sure that he is doing alright and keeping himself busy."

Still, the Home Office has even put a strain on his relationship with Cleopatra—who he affectionately calls Cleo. A few months ago, Richard received correspondence from the Home Office that they would grant him a returning visitor's visa, but when Richard inquired whether or not Cleo would be able to join him, they went silent for several months. "If she cannot come with me, I will not be going back," he told me—he can't stand the thought of losing yet another relationship to the Home Office, especially not while Marissa is not yet allowed to enter the UK. Still, it is difficult to pass up the chance to finally get justice. "I'm caught between a rock and a hard place," he continued.

It isn't the only place where the Home Office created friction within his family. "Sometimes I feel like the Home Office is caring about his case and doesn't care about mine," Marissa told me, explaining that even though she also applied for compensation, she was told that she didn't qualify. "Having a relationship with the Home Office is like having a relationship with a man who will not stop beating you," she observed, pointing out that it feels like a form of gaslighting. If someone ends up on the wrong side of the immigration system, it is their fault for not having the right documents, or knowing the laws. It is never the system that is to blame for changing the laws at a moment's notice, catching ordinary people in its dragnet.

While Marissa's experience at the airport might have brought her closer to her father, it created distance between her and Tony. "I was so caught up in my emotions, that I didn't realize it was affecting him too," she told me, remembering how what was supposed to be the beginning of her love story turned into a reminder of the way that the Home Office could stop a relationship in its tracks. At first, Tony hoped that the media attention around the Windrush scandal might make it easier for Marissa to clear her case, and come back to the United Kingdom, as she had planned to do. But as time went on, it became clear that this was not going to happen, and they made the difficult decision to break up.

"I try to explain it to my family members, but it is so hard for them to understand," she said. Sometimes, she is jealous of her sisters, whose ties to the UK have never been questioned. Other times, she worries that her father will get a visa for his wife, and she will be left behind.

"What the Home Office does to families and relationships is morally wrong," she continued. With a deportation on her record, Marissa cannot travel to the UK at all—not even as a tourist. "It disconnects you from your family and leaves you feeling isolated."

Now, there was just one more thing that Salem and I had to do before applying for a spouse visa. We had to get married.

I always imagined weddings as big traditional affairs, but I knew that ours was going to have to be different—though how, I was not quite sure. At one point, I was visiting my mom in California, when she offered to plan our wedding. While I adored her for offering, I lovingly told her that it might be a little bit unconventional for her. We didn't even want to get married in a church.

"But won't it be weird for you not to get married in a church?" she asked me, as we caught up just the two of us, at a bar in downtown Berkeley. My parents actually met in a church—my mom was a twenty-two-year-old art student who was sick of living with her parents, going through (in her words) a "Jesus-freak hippie phase," while my dad was a quiet twenty-five-year old who had just come out of the seminary and was studying to be a priest. She thought he was cute, and asked him what brought him to the Bible study. He told her that he was studying to be a Catholic priest—which I think would have made most women give up. Not my mom. Her comeback? "No way. I'm studying to be a nun!"

My dad never became a priest.

"That would be weird for Salem, since it isn't his religion," I responded, imagining Salem's face if we exchanged vows at an actual altar. Turns out my mom was not picky about what kind of religious wedding, and was ready to switch teams at the drop of a hat. "Wouldn't he want an imam there?"

"Mom, that's not our religion either," I gently reminded her. She nodded thoughtfully. With both of our religions off the table, she had no choice but to turn to the last Abrahamic tradition that came to mind. "What do you think about a Jewish wedding?"—and we both fell over ourselves laughing at the idea that the only way to reconcile our different religious upbringings that was actually a shared ambivalence toward religion was to smash a glass and dance the hora.

Meanwhile, Salem was entirely unfussed—which was starting to drive me crazy. "I don't see why we have to do this," he said whenever I brought up wedding planning—a task that I refused to let be my mother's problem. "For me, the second you moved to Erbil, we were married."

As romantic as it was, the Home Office does not deal in emotional memories. It does not care about the moment that you stopped thinking about someone as a boyfriend and started thinking about them as a partner, or about the way that you combed through visa policies for various countries, trying to find a place where you might finally be able to live happily ever after. It cares about a marriage certificate, proof that you aren't trying to game the system. It cares about extorting you for immigration fees. It cares that you won't be a burden to the state.

"I suppose we could just sign the paper and be done with it," I mused aloud—but as soon as I heard the words come out of my mouth, it sounded wrong. The Home Office might have shotgunned our wedding, but we were getting married so that we could stay in the same country and never be afraid of being separated again. As far as I was concerned, that was the most romantic thing on earth.

First, we had to declare our intention to marry at Hackney Town Hall, where a ticker spat out number 434 at us, and a sign instructed us to have a seat. Next, we were taken into separate rooms to answer questions about one another, to prove that we were a legitimate couple.

"What does your partner do for work?" the registrar asked me.

"Cameraman," I wrote, on the piece of paper that she handed me.

"What city was he born in?"

"Idlib, Syria"—I was nailing this. Would she also like the story of how he was kicked out of Turkey, and I followed him to Iraq, and then followed him to London? Because I was ready to tell it.

Instead, she furrowed her brow.

"He wrote video journalist," she said, as if she knew that I was teetering on the edge of sanity, juggling wedding planning on top of a full-time course load and part-time job, and having a complete nervous breakdown over the possibility that the Home Office could fuck everything up.

"How do you think he makes the videos?" I asked, trying not to lose it.

If a government official thought that the difference between a video journalist and a cameraman was enough to raise suspicion that Salem and I were not a legitimate couple, immigration agents could show up to our home unannounced and rifle through our belongings, searching for evidence that we did not know each other at all. A few months ago, a couple had been told that their relationship was not genuine because they were wearing pajamas in bed and not naked. Another couple had recently been about to get married when immigration agents interrupted the ceremony, traumatizing all the guests.

Next, there was the issue of the wedding itself. While neither of us wanted a traditional or religious wedding—whether Christian, Muslim, or Jewish—there were traditions that did mean something to me, particularly the idea of bringing our families together.

I wondered how this would work when our families were separated across borders. Most of Salem's immediate family lives in southern Turkey, and getting his parents and all six of his siblings visas to come to the United Kingdom would be an Olympic feat. Salem obviously couldn't travel to Turkey now, and while my family could travel to London, my grandfather had recently developed dementia, and my mom felt a need to constantly be at his side.

It was starting to feel like it might be easier to just elope, but my mother had made it abundantly clear that she would like to meet Salem before we got married, so I convinced her to come—which she agreed to do, as long as my dad stayed in California with my grandfather. As much as I loved my parents' ability to unquestionably support one another—and hoped to someday mimic it in my own marriage—I had to accept that it meant that I would not be able to have both of them at my wedding. So, I flew to California to spend time with them both, hoping that I would at least feel like I had experienced part of this rite of passage with them.

"What do you mean your dad isn't going to your wedding?" my high school best friend Marie asked me, as soon as I saw her. Marie and I have known each other since we were twelve. Over the years, many things could have made us drift apart. I went to college on the other side of the country, while she stayed in California. While she was rushing sororities in Chico, I was covering the Occupy Wall Street protests in New York City. Marie spent our high school years crushing on jocks, her college years dating frat boys, and was now scouring the dating apps for a husband who would eventually mature into playing golf in the suburbs. I always fell for weirdos.

Nevertheless, whenever I visited my parents, Marie was always in their living room not long after I arrived, and we would chat for hours as if no time had passed at all. She might have not always understood my life choices, but she knew I wanted my dad at my wedding.

"You have to go to your daughter's wedding!" she said, the minute she saw my dad—who has always been like a second father to her. "Is that what you want?" he asked, turning to me, slightly perplexed.

To be fair, my dad assumed that I was planning to elope. Why wouldn't he? I had made it abundantly clear over the years that marriage was not a priority for me. I talked about how much I wanted to be a famous jour-nalist that traveled the world, turning up my nose at the idea of settling down and having children.

Most of my family probably assumed that I would be single and galli-vanting for the rest of my life, their first clue likely that when I was seven years old, I announced that I wanted to be a pilot, following in the foot-steps of Amelia Earhart, and then the next year switched my ambitions to essentially becoming Carmen Sandiego. It was slightly embarrassing that I was planning a wedding. Carmen would never.

Yet secretly, I had always dreamed about my wedding. I'm not sure if it's because I have been brainwashed by 1990s Hollywood rom-coms where leggy blondes end up with devastatingly chiseled men after an hour and twenty minutes of toxic manipulation, or if I'm genuinely such a hopeless romantic that I seem to have written an entire book about love, but I always imagined that my wedding day would be a festive occa-sion, surrounded by all the people that I cared about the most.

But this is a traditional celebration that works only for those whose families can travel freely, unencumbered by visa processing centers that do not care about a mother missing her son's wedding, or a sister who was always supposed to be the maid of honor. It felt unfair that my parents could come, while Salem's could not, but at the same time, it felt wrong to legally bind myself to someone without their support, their presence. On the one hand, it was just a piece of paper. On the other hand, it was the tentative celebration of the moment that we finally didn't have to worry about being separated, ever again.

So, when my dad asked me if I would like him to come, I sheepishly nodded—not because it was my wedding, but because I no longer wanted to take my loved ones for granted. After witnessing the ways that borders ruthlessly keep so many from being with their families, I felt so lucky to have the opportunity to be with mine.

"That's it!" he said, enthusiastically slamming the table. "I'm coming!"

A family friend eagerly offered to stay with my grandfather, assuring my mother that he would be fine. It was too short notice for Marie to make it to the wedding—but as far as I am concerned, she will always be my maid of honor.

As soon as I knew that both of my parents were coming to our wedding, I started feeling more like a bride and less like number 434, signing a paper out of convenience. Shuttling between work and my classes, I started daydreaming about what I was going to wear and inviting everyone that I ran into to the after-party. It might not be a traditional Arab wedding, but it was still an Arab wedding—and now that there was going to be a party, I would be a disgrace to our people if I didn't invite absolutely everyone that I had ever met.

A few weeks later, my parents were sitting at our kitchen table in Stepney Green, as if they had always come over for weekly dinners. "It smells delicious, Salem," Salem was making my mom his famous koosa meshi—a Syrian dish of zucchini and eggplant, cored and stuffed with rice and minced lamb before it's plunged into tomato sauce that is flavored with entire bulbs of garlic. It just so happens to be my mom's favorite dish—also a recipe passed down by my Lebanese family that she never has a chance to eat outside of family gatherings. If my mom ever had misgivings about Salem, they vanished the second she realized that she had just acquired a new family member that would make her meshi. "Salem, this is sensational," she said, taking another helping.

Now my biggest problem was that if we ever divorced, she would probably take his side.

Later that night, she beckoned me over and handed me a brown paper bag.

"I know you don't want to be traditional, but I wanted you to have this, just in case," she said, as I peered inside to see a beautiful ivory-colored crown, made entirely of beads, shaped into little flowers. I immediately recognized it from pictures of her on her wedding day—and my grandmother on hers.

At that moment, I felt like I finally had her blessing. We were finally doing the damn thing.

On the day of our wedding, I put on a long green dress that I'd bought from a street vendor in Istanbul during the days that our love story was just beginning, long before I knew where it would lead us. It seemed only right to wear something from the city where we first fell in love, and as I attempted to style my hair around the flower crown, I realized that in spite of this terribly untraditional wedding, I was actually bringing two traditions together. Looking at my reflection in the mirror, I saw my mother and my grandmother's face in my own and wondered what they thought about on their wedding days. Did they have doubts? My mother tells me stories about how my father was a terrible fiancé, which is only funny because he turned out to be a wonderful husband. My grandmother married at a time when women typically gave up their careers to start families. I wonder what she thought when she put on this flower crown, and if she was afraid of giving up a part of herself to be with the person that she loved.

I didn't have a doubt in my mind that I wanted to marry Salem, but I had wondered so many times if we would ever make it to this day. What if he had never gotten the UK visa, and we were still stuck in Erbil? Love is one thing, but a lucky break is something entirely different—and even though we fought so hard to be together, people all over the world fight equally hard, if not harder, but don't get there. I wished everyone could be as happy as I was, knowing my parents were sitting in my living room while I got ready to marry the love of my life.

"So, now that you're getting married, will you be able to come visit us more easily in California?" my dad asked Salem, furrowing his brow the way he always did when he was trying to wrap his head around something.

"No, Dad," I said, a reflex from being tired of constantly explaining that a US passport doesn't necessarily mean someone can do whatever they want. "We are getting married so that I can stay here—I'm marrying Salem for his papers." My dad let out a peal of laughter—when my dad laughs, it starts as a loud hoot and crescendos into a hoard of choking seals. When something is really funny, and he can no longer make any sound, he consistently slaps his knee, until, eventually, it subsides. I was so happy that this laugh was a part of my wedding day.

Once he recovered, he looked at us for confirmation. "She is marrying you for papers?"

"Yes," Salem said, gravely serious, as was so often his comedic style. "I have to warn all of my Syrian friends that the American girls are marrying us for our passports." I thought back to my indecent proposal, now almost four years ago. Somehow, Salem had pulled it off—and luckily for both of us, I had no problem marrying someone for papers. So, that day, surrounded by my family and our chosen family, we went to Hackney Town Hall to sign a stupid little miraculous paper that, in that moment, felt like armor against the world.

Afterward, we popped champagne in the park. As far as I was concerned, it was perfect.

13 | *The Green Card Marriage*

A few weeks after our wedding, I started gathering every document that I could possibly find that proved that Salem and I had a legitimate relationship into an expanding file folder for the Home Office.

Over the years, I had obsessively and meticulously saved every single piece of paper that could possibly tell the story of our relationship. A housing lease in Turkish, and the one that referred to me as "Salem Rizk's American wife," in Kurdish. Electricity bills from three different addresses in London, bank statements and tax returns that barely squeaked past the minimum income requirement. The successful asylum claim that changed everything, and of course, our marriage certificate. I learned that marrying someone for papers requires you to be both compulsively detail-oriented and a hoarder, organizing and reorganizing every single piece of evidence from your lives together, checking and double-checking the list of required documents until your head is spinning and you wish that you could just send a sex tape to erase any doubts that you are romantically entangled. Unfortunately, the Home Office does not accept digital files.

My folder formed a tome so thick that when I dropped it to the floor, it thumped. "This is not a manuscript," I wrote, posting it to my Instagram story. "This is what I have to submit in order to stay in the same country as my husband."

"I feel this on a molecular level," my friend Valentina wrote back to me, a few minutes later. "Have you seen this story?" she continued, attaching a link to an article about a couple in Maryland who thought that they were attending a United States Citizenship and Immigration Services interview to adjust their status after getting married, only to have ICE agents show up at the courthouse.

"So far, I've only seen this happening in Maryland," she added, as if trying to calm herself down. "But the possibility scares me so much."

Even though Valentina and I had never met in person, we had been in touch for years—she heard me on a podcast once and reached out, and even though she lives in Miami and I live in London, we have regularly chatted ever since, venting about the news cycle, and sharing ridiculous cat memes to get through the day. At one point, she told me that she was undocumented—and was scared that Trump might take away DACA, which had protected her for the last eight years. Now, she and her husband of almost two years, Lorenzo, were preparing for the infamous marriage interview—only to learn that ICE agents might surprise them partway through.

It is nauseating to imagine. Even before Trump took office, the marriage interview was notorious for trying to catch people who really were marrying for a green card in a lie, asking questions like "What side of the bed does your spouse sleep on" and "What color is their toothbrush?"

Love has shaped immigration policy ever since at least World War II, when it was American GIs who fell in love with Japanese women and wanted to bring them to the United States, only to realize the women were barred from the country under the 1924 immigration quotas. Several people in Congress took pity on the veterans and passed the War Brides Act of 1945, which, while flawed in that it prioritized the needs of US veterans over others, paved the way for family-based immigration. By 1952, undocumented immigrants could adjust their status through marriage,

and the Immigration and Nationality Act of 1965 made family reunification a priority.

In 1986—at the height of the War on Drugs and increased crim-
inalization of immigrants—Ronald Reagan passed the Immigration
Marriage Fraud Amendments Act to keep American women from being
"duped" into marriages with foreign men, making it so that anyone who
had been married for less than two years was a "conditional" immigrant. Since then, the idea of the fraudulent immigrant has occupied the
American imagination. First there was the plot of the 2009 rom-com *The
Proposal*, where Sandra Bullock marries a colleague that repulses her in
order to stay in the country, then came the popular reality TV show *90
Day Fiancé*, following US citizens bringing their foreign fiancés to the
United States for ninety days—the government-enforced deadline that a
couple has to get married—before their visa expires.

I must admit that the TV show is riveting. Many of the couples are
delightfully mismatched, and watching Russian dancers or Ukrainian
makeup artists try to adjust to life on a farm in Virginia or on a Louisiana
bayou provides a dopamine hit like no other. One of the stars even fell
in love with a Syrian guy who couldn't go to the United States because
of the Muslim ban—and for a split second, I wondered if pop culture
could put an end to Trump's draconian immigration policies. Instead,
the show focused on her converting to Islam so that she could get married in Lebanon.

While it accurately captures the way that some Americans assume
that all any foreigner wants in the world is to come to the United States,
it doesn't show how difficult it is for bona fide couples to prove their relationship to officers who are trained to catch them in a lie, or the heartbreak if they are denied the right to build a life together. It doesn't show
the beautiful moments of solidarity, where one person really can extend
the accidental privileges and real protections of citizenship to the person
that they love.

It doesn't show Valentina Aragundy and Lorenzo Acosta.

"Miami grows on you—you don't know if it is benign, or if it is a tumor, but it grows on you," Valentina told me, when I finally got to visit her for the first time. We embraced like old friends, because that is what we were, and she insisted on·giving me a tour, which was largely organized through food—including but not limited to: Colombian are-pas, Salvadoran pupusas, and Mexican paletas in flavors ranging from mango chili to café con leche. We snacked on them to cool off during a hot August day in the trendy, graffiti-covered Wynwood district in East Miami, which just happens to be the part of town where Valentina first laid eyes on Lorenzo, at an art show in April 2015.

"You have to understand, I did not go for the art," she told me. "I went for the food." Valentina is an enthusiastic vegan, which is particularly funny given that just that morning she had insisted on taking me to a Colombian breakfast, where the main event was a giant steak, served with a side of sausage and a cup of spicy beef broth. "There was a food truck, with vegan options, and I wanted to be there, because the food looked lit."

One thing that Valentina was not looking for was love. A few months before, she had broken up with her ex, after she discovered that he was not only cheating on her with more than fifty different women, but also embezzling money from the business that they had started together. "I was hating men," she groaned, remembering the feeling of putting her life back together after he had shattered it. "I thought men were the worst. As far as I was concerned, they ruined your life."

But the food was taking a while, so she wandered into the gallery and struck up a conversation with Lorenzo—a tall, soft-spoken man with the air of a gentle giant, possibly the least-threatening man on earth. When she found out that he was the artist, she gushed over pieces and imme-diately insisted on finding him on Instagram, and while Lorenzo would have ordinarily thought that she was just being polite, he could tell that her enthusiasm was real—and became a little bit more smitten with her every time she threw back her head and laughed in a way that made her long black hair shake from side to side like an ebony waterfall.

"I needed a way to talk to her," he remembered—shy and soft-spoken, Lorenzo's game is subtle but effective. "So, I decided to announce a raffle on Instagram." It was a genius plan—Valentina is the kind of overenthusiastic fan who reposts any article or enters any raffle if it means supporting an artist or journalist that she likes.

Naturally, she entered, and naturally, she won.

"It was rigged, wasn't it?" she shrieked, as he told the story, which she must have heard one hundred times by now. Lorenzo shrugged his shoulders, looking coyly in the other direction. Maybe we will never know, but it did give him an excuse to see her again—and they started going to the movies together and taking long drives. "We would just talk and talk for hours," Valentina remembered, smiling. "And that is when I realized he actually had a voice."

Valentina might make fun of Lorenzo—or, Zoe, as she was starting to call him at that point—for being so soft-spoken, but she loved listening to him talk about making art. It started when he was a little boy and saw a homeless man drawing characters at the park, sketching every day no matter what. Zoe picked up a pencil and started joining him. Soon, he was experimenting with different lines and shading techniques, trying to reproduce the long, graceful necks of the flamingos that roamed the mangrove swamps that he had grown up around in Miami. It became his signature character.

"Someday, I want to be able to just focus on my art," he confided to her—at the time he was working at a warehouse and only had time to draw on the weekends. "That's my long-term goal."

Meanwhile, Valentina shared how passionate she was about politics. She told him about how her obsession started while she was growing up in Colombia, but that she had really started discovering her political identity a few years ago, while she was working as a maid at an upscale clubhouse on the other side of town from where she lives—a job that meant waking up at a time when most of Miami was still out partying, and commuting almost three hours to get there, between three buses and a two-mile-long walk.

"I couldn't get a license and I couldn't afford a car," she remembered. "So that was the only way I could get to work." Without documents, she couldn't count on getting a job closer, so every day she woke up at two o'clock in the morning—and put on a podcast. It started with Rachel Maddow—a gateway drug to Democracy Now!, which lead her to independent podcasts like *Citizen Radio* and *BreakThrough Radio*'s *The Radio Dispatch*, which, coincidentally, is where she first found me— though I didn't know it at the time.

"I started to realize that everything is political," she continued. "It is the food we eat, the clothes we wear, where those are made, how they get here." Politics was the reason that she had to leave Colombia when she was young, and the reason she had to overstay her student visa to the United States, even though that was never a part of her plan. It was the reason that even though she attended a private Catholic high school in New Jersey, the minute that she graduated and her visa expired, she could only work jobs where she could be paid under the table—first at a bar, where she wore low-cut tops and caked on makeup in order to look old enough to drink with the customers, then at the clubhouse, where she cleaned up after rich ladies playing tennis and drinking cocktails with their friends, who made snide comments about her in English that they assumed she didn't understand. It was the reason that she couldn't go back to Colombia and that she hadn't seen her father in sixteen years.

"I find it funny when people say that they don't 'do' politics," she said, laughing. "Because honey, like it or not, politics are doing you."

But when they first started dating, Zoe was one of the people who didn't do politics, preferring to lose himself in apolitical jungle scenes of cartoonish flamingos and flamboyant toucans rather than connecting to the ugliness of a partisan shouting match. "I just don't think it will change anything," he said, shrugging his shoulders. He had his reasons for thinking this way—his own parents were from El Salvador, and he had watched them struggle in the United States, no matter who was in power.

But Valentina insisted that politics could change people's lives—for worse, and for better. While threats to her family from paramilitary groups like the FARC in Colombia forced her to move to the United States at a young age and to grow up far away from her family, US policies like DACA gave her the opportunity to explore new lines of work that would have been impossible without papers. She learned how to run a business and discovered that she had a knack for accounting and logistics, that she was organized in a way that could help small businesses become more successful. She could start saving her money and planning a future, and stop living paycheck to paycheck.

Realizing that Donald Trump could repeal DACA made her stomach turn. "It was slim pickings between Hillary and Trump," she continued, remembering the months leading up to the 2016 election, when she was falling in love with Zoe. Still, not being able to vote—particularly in a state like Florida—felt like a blow to immigrants like her, who couldn't vote in elections that would decide the politics that could shape the rest of their lives.

"You are my vote," Valentina told Zoe one day, hoping she could convince him to change his mind. Lately she had taken to registering everyone she knew to vote, even reaching out to strangers in other states over Instagram to make sure that their voice would be counted on Election Day. Maybe it was the immigrant in her, or maybe she was just hopeful—but she still believed that people had the power to change things.

"Would you do it—for me?"

Zoe reluctantly agreed.

On the day of the election, Valentina had a sick feeling in her stomach—as the results came in, all she could do was cry hysterically. Zoe sat on the couch next to her in silence.

"I had always felt American—I don't even know how to describe what that means, but I did," she told me remembering the morning after. "But when that happened, it very much reminded me that I was not."

Day by day, Zoe's art started becoming more political. First, there was a painting of a mosquito with Trump's face—a reference to the Zika virus, which was spreading like wildfire at the time, right next to his signature character holding a can of roach spray. While he kept painting the loud, pink flamingos with long, graceful necks and cartoonish eyes that he had always painted, he started experimenting with other birds—particularly the Salvadoran Torogoz, whose bright turquoise tail and rainbow of colors on its chest fit right into his style.

"It's political, because it is the national bird of El Salvador," Valentina told me, beaming with pride. "His family is from El Salvador, it is a nod to the fact that his people are immigrants." Seeing the ideas that were so important to her showing up in his artwork made her feel even closer to him than before, as if their passions were fusing together on the page, a love letter to how they opened each other's eyes to the worlds of beauty, on the one hand, and justice, on the other.

But politics didn't come knocking on their door until almost one year after Trump was elected, when Valentina came home to a letter from Immigration and Customs Enforcement (ICE) requesting that she come in for a "check-in." Her blood froze.

"It really might be a routine check-in," she reasoned, trying to remain calm. Still, she could just as easily disappear—over the past year, ICE had lured hundreds of people to similar "routine check-ins," only to arrest and detain them on the spot. She knew she had to talk to Zoe.

"We have to talk about what would happen, worst-case scenario," she told him, after he had a chance to sit down and process the information.

She had never seen him look so worried, his head in his hands as if he had the weight of the world on his shoulders.

"If I had to leave, would you come to Colombia with me?"

The last time she had been in Colombia, she was thirteen years old, and a strange man had tried to pick her up from school. She later realized that he was trying to show her family just how easy it would be to kidnap her. It was a common practice among both the paramilitary and the guerilla forces, which were vying for power and influence in her father's home state. "It put the fear of God in him," she told me, remembering the difficult decision to leave her family behind. "So, he just shipped me off here." It was years before she knew the full scale of the threats that were made against her and her family.

Now she hadn't seen him for sixteen years.

"No, Vale," Zoe said, quietly. "We aren't going to let that happen."

That day, Valentina and Lorenzo chose a date for their wedding. Sometimes, tradition is an unexpected weapon to smash the system.

"If someone needs help, you help them," Zoe said, when I asked him what it was like to start planning a wedding under these circumstances. "It is just what you do."

———

Every American who has ever fallen in love with a foreigner has been told to be careful that they aren't being swindled for a green card. Meanwhile, any immigrant who has ever fallen in love with an American has been forced to bend over backward to prove that they aren't swindling them— and while over the past twenty years marriage rates have declined in the United States to an all-time low, marriage remains one of the only ways that an undocumented person can adjust their status.

"I'm a millennial. I don't want to get married," Maria Lopez, a twenty-seven-year-old satirist and content creator who runs the Instagram page *ytienepapeles*—or, in English, "Does he have papers?"—told me, when we met up at a bubble tea shop in San Jose, California. "But these systems are forcing me!"

Even though Maria grew up in San Jose, she was born in Mexico City—and while she had been protected by DACA since the Obama administration, as soon as Trump was elected, she realized that DACA's days might be numbered. "We were high school sweethearts, so I hadn't really been thinking about my status, or anything like that," she told me, remembering the first time it came up in a relationship. But as soon as she shared her anxiety about protecting herself in the long term, her boyfriend told her that he was not interested in having those conversations.

"I thought I was never going to find love, because that just isn't real for immigrants," she continued, reminding me of my own realization that a wedding with everyone that I loved in the same room would be a fantasy. Maria started creating content to process her own frustration about dating as an undocumented woman—first poetry, and later, memes. "We aren't going to fix these systems by crying about them," she said, smiling. "So, I try to laugh at them instead." One of my favorite posts from her account shows a cartoon of three girls putting on makeup, but Maria has written over it: "My three personalities getting ready in the morning: wanting love, wanting dick, wanting papeles."

Little by little, more women started reaching out to her, telling her that the page made them laugh and feel like they weren't alone. "A lot of people ask me how long they should wait before they should tell someone about their status," she continued—and I am immediately curious about which date is the right date to have a conversation about papers.

"I ask them where they are writing me from," she told me, explaining that her answer might be different, depending on if they're in a state like Texas or Arizona, or a state like California. Safety always comes first, especially in a charged political environment; but even in a state like California, dating as an undocumented person can be a dangerous game. "I have definitely seen men who use status as a power play," Maria explained, saying that if one person has papers and another does not, it is easy for the former to threaten to call ICE or to take custody of the children, leaving their partner with no legal recourse. "A lot of the older women I talk to think that they are only being abused if someone is hitting them," she continued. "I try to tell them that this is abuse, too."

Meanwhile, popular culture, whether it is the producers on 90 *Day Fiancé* or the politicians who decide our laws, persistently cast immigrants in need of a green card as criminals. While marriage fraud undeniably exists, there are far fewer discussions about how papers are power, and an unequal power dynamic means that one person in a relationship will always be able to control the fate of the other. It forces people into commitments that they are not ready for, at best, and lays the foundation for an abusive marriage at worst.

Ironically, "undocu-cuties," as Maria lovingly calls them, often end up only falling in love with people who understand the struggle—people who are also undocumented. "Some of them say love is love," Maria reflected. "Others are optimistic that the government will do something for them." But in our millennial lifetimes, the only reprieve for undocumented people that has even come close to amnesty has been DACA, which even at its best only protects people who came to the United States as children and costs $495 to renew every two years. Originally, Obama introduced it as a stop-gap measure until there was a pathway to citizenship. Ten years after it was first introduced, there is still no path to citizenship, and DACA itself could be repealed at any time, depending on the political leadership in Congress and the White House.

"My advice? Don't romanticize the struggle," she continued. Maria understands the many reasons why people without papers might be drawn toward one another, beyond merely falling in love. Some are wary of the power dynamics of dating a citizen. Others prefer to be with someone who has stood in their shoes. Nevertheless, this isn't for Maria. "We grow up on telenovelas and assume that love has to be difficult in order for it to be real," she continued. "But you deserve to love and be protected."

Ordinarily, people think long and hard about marriage—so much so that more and more people are choosing to opt out of the institution altogether. However, when papers are a part of the decision, it can force your hand, putting unnecessary pressure on a relationship. Marrying a citizen doesn't always work, either. Karina has been married to Kevin for fourteen years and is still stateless. Ava and Cecilia are both US citizens, but it has not helped either of them get green cards for José and Hugo, who are each still waiting out their ten-year bans in Mexico. Mohammed had to fight the Muslim ban just to bring Amal to the United States. For a long time, I gave up on the idea of having a future with Salem in my country for the same reason. Even without Trump, sponsoring his green card from abroad could take longer than two years, with no guarantees.

"At the end of the day, marriage is a contract that can make your life easier," Maria continued, reminding me of the weeks when I contemplated eloping for the sake of an easy marriage certificate. "But you do kind of lose the romance." Filling out reams of paperwork, pulling a number at Hackney Town Hall, or turning over your most private communication to government authorities does make it feel as if these systems are trying to suck us dry, stealing any joy that we might have left. It is invasive and infuriating—especially when citizen friends around you are planning beautiful weddings without these anxieties, merely stressing over which family members can't be in the same room together or which florist is too expensive, rather than whether ICE, the Home Office, or any other immigration authority is going to stop their happily ever after in its tracks.

So maybe at some point we "accidentally" send a sex tape to the Home Office or shamelessly forward our entire texting history to the United States Citizenship and Immigration Services. We are fighting to be with the people that we love, and for this reason, an invasion of privacy for some is a grand romantic gesture for the rest of us. Bureaucracy—and the absurdity of the kinds of documents that are required to prove your love for one another—is demoralizing. But when those documents are the pages of your love story, assembling them in a file folder with color-coded descending tabs is the most romantic act in the world.

———

Valentina's ICE appointment turned out to be no more than a twenty-minute check-in—which she describes as "emotional terrorism" because of just how much it occupied her mind in the weeks leading up to it. Still, Valentina and Lorenzo knew that all they wanted was to be together, until death do them part, so, on a warm day in November, Valentina and Lorenzo gathered their friends and family together to exchange vows and affirm exactly that.

"I promise to always be faithful to you, unless Jason Momoa comes along," Valentina told him, trying to keep a straight face. He looked so handsome in a bright pink satin shirt that made his dark skin glow and his eyes twinkle as he giggled at her, responding with a vow of his own.

"I will go to the end of the earth for you," he promised. "Just don't make me dance or swim."

They had pupusas and arepas, and a cake shaped like a flamingo. Valentina wished that her dad and her family in Colombia could have been there, but that night she felt like she became part of a new family, too—Lorenzo's family, and the family that they were building together.

———

Two years later, after the required waiting period, it was time for Valentina's marriage interview. She woke up a full thirty minutes before her alarm, ready to put on her game face. "We are the first appointment, seven a.m. Miami time," she texted me. "Zoe has your number, just in case anything happens."

Five hours ahead of her in London, I tried to prepare for what I would do in case I didn't hear from her—as a journalist, I could write articles that would reach millions of people and raise hell on social media. I could tell her story and call in as many favors as I could with immigration lawyers. I could say I was writing a story and call ICE for comment—a technique that, I knew from previous experience, sometimes works as a scare tactic. While I felt a pressure to maintain personal and professional boundaries, that elusive "journalistic integrity," I often found that boundary blurring when the people that I cared about were actively experiencing the most gruesome aspects of the institutions that I wrote about.

Besides, Valentina might have found me through my journalism, but she wasn't a source—she was a friend. We were bonded by our twelve-pocket expandable folders documenting our marriages, our extensive online chats where we vented about how our future with our partners depended on someone else's opinion of how real our love was. "I think I've spent $100 on printing photos, alone" she wrote to me one day, just before her appointment. I wrote back: "I think the man who works at the copy shop downstairs thinks I'm unhinged."

We continued to chat throughout the day. "It isn't just about Trump," she reflected at one point. "It is about waiting for twenty years for this moment and everything hinging on someone else's opinion of my marriage."

What would happen if Valentina was detained? I could be as annoying as humanly possible, relentlessly calling government bureaucracies until they either released her to shut me up, or hung up on me. But at the end of the day, I couldn't control the US immigration system.

Meanwhile in Miami, Valentina and Lorenzo were pulling up to the US Citizenship and Immigration Services building. Valentina was already regretting her decision to wear a dark blue button-up shirt and black slacks, an outfit so different from the loud colors she normally wore that she felt alienated from herself as she checked her makeup in the rearview mirror one last time.

"I was trying so hard to be the opposite of who I am," she remembered. "No boobs, no neon nails"—ever since I've known her, Valentina has always sported statement nails, often loud, bright colors that I later learned were sometimes inspired by Zoe's art. That day, her only statement was respectability politics.

"My nails were powder pink, something like that," she said. "It was bullshit."

As soon as they walked through the turnstile, she looked over at Zoe. He was already sweating through his shirt, large puddles of perspiration slowly expanding from his armpits. Even if they had nothing to hide, the process made her feel like she was covering up a crime, although the very reason she was here was that she was trying to abide by the law.

"Where did you meet?" the USCIS officer asked, as if she were making small talk, like it wasn't her job to catch people in a lie. A simple-enough question, but where should she begin? Too many details would make it seem as if she was trying too hard, too few might seem like a half truth.

"We met at an art gallery in Wynwood." Valentina smiled, knowing there was more to the story. The USCIS officer didn't need to know that she had originally gone for the food, not the art. That Valentina hadn't realized Zoe was trying to flirt with her or that the raffle was most definitely rigged.

"What day did you get married?"

Again, an easy-enough question. But was it the twenty-fourth or twenty-fifth of November? This was not an interview for people who are notoriously bad with names, dates, and times.

"I kept racking my brain," she told me, remembering trying to maintain her cool. While she might not have remembered the date, she remembered the moment that Zoe's grandmother beckoned her over and handed her a shot glass filled to the brim with rum. "You're one of us now!" she gushed, squeezing her as they clinked glasses. While

Valentina often felt that Zoe's grandmother didn't exactly envision her grandson with someone as strong-willed and independent as she was, on that day Valentina felt like her second granddaughter, glowing in the warmth of her love and copious amounts of alcohol.

Meanwhile, Valentina's abuela had plans of her own—the minute she saw Valentina, she stole her away and presented a bottle of tequila. "Now we celebrate!" she shouted, popping open the bottle and drinking straight from it before instructing Valentina to do the same.

Valentina might not remember the exact date of her anniversary. But she knew that she could never smell tequila or rum without throwing up again. Wasn't that enough proof that she had gotten married?

"November twenty-four, 2017," she said, suddenly confident.

"Can we see your phone?" It felt like an invasion of privacy, but Valentina had long gotten her head around the fact that her entire life was up for inspection—from her bank statements and school enroll-ment forms that she had to submit to qualify for DACA, to her social media accounts. But what if they found something incriminating? As she punched in her passcode, she hoped that her political beliefs were not too obvious—at that moment, she realized that her passcode was Zoe's birth-day, her locked phone picture was of the two of them at the beach, hold-ing their little Chihuahua mutt, Chiki. Somehow, without even trying, they looked like the perfect little family. A few minutes later, Valentina and Zoe were free to leave.

"No news yet," she messaged me. "But I'm out."

A few days later, she received an email from USCIS: "Your Case Status: Card/Document Production." Valentina stopped short. Was this it, the email she had been waiting for for the past twenty years?

"Girl! This is not a drill," she wrote to me, with a screenshot of the email. It felt so nonchalant for something so life-changing—but emerg-ing from the shadows can be as simple as "document production," as complicated as twenty years of being separated from your father and not knowing your siblings.

"Is that it???" I wrote back, unable to believe how utterly boring bureaucracies can be—we expect fireworks but receive emails so formulaic in nature that it is a miracle they don't go straight to spam. We should be notified by flash mob performances and brass bands, instead.

But that same week, I received a similar template email from the UK Home Office. Somewhere amidst the case numbers and the long wait times, I had been approved—I had two and a half years during which I did not have to worry about being separated from Salem. After that, I could renew it until it was indefinite. "Look!" I messaged Valentina. "Us too."

A few months later, Valentina was hovering her mouse over two tickets to Bogotá. Even though it was only a two-hour flight from Miami, it always felt as if it were in another world, as if the deep emerald-green coffee fields that still lingered in her childhood memories were extraterrestrial, light-years and galaxies away. "It was surreal," she said, that she was finally planning the trip that she had dreamed about for so long. "Absolutely surreal."

Now, she was about to introduce Zoe to her family for the first time. Imagining the look on his face when he met all her aunts and uncles and cousins at once made her shake her head. Most of all, she couldn't wait to embrace her father for the first time in sixteen years.

"None of this would have been possible without Zoe," she told me. "He is absolutely making my dreams come true."

"Dad," she typed into her messages, "I'm coming to see you."

14 | *Breaking Borders*

I squeezed my eyes shut as the tattoo artist pricked my skin with his needle.

"What does it mean?" the artist asked me, as he started filling in the Arabic script on my arm in permanent ink, admiring the calligraphy that was expertly designed by my new sister-in-law, Nour. "It means fuck the border!" Salem whooped, enthusiastically. He was waiting to have his matching—albeit bigger—one filled in on his arm, as well.

"Actually, it says 'breaking borders,'" I corrected him, laughing. "It is kind of like our version of wedding rings."

Permanently etched into our skin, it reminds us of more than our commitment to one another. It is a chosen battle scar, a celebration of the love we fought for, a memory of what it felt like when we thought that borders might keep us apart, and a reminder to keep fighting for a world where no one experiences anything like that, ever again. Salem's on his left arm, mine on my right. When we hold hands, they touch.

As soon as I got my residency permit and we knew that we could both travel—at least to some places—without fear of not being allowed back into the country, we booked a belated honeymoon to Barcelona. Flying to a country that would previously have been unimaginable for us to visit together felt like more than a romantic vacation. It felt like we were levitating above the stratosphere and soaring through the clouds, suddenly limitless, as we took our first flight together in two years. I almost believed that our lives would soon be punctuated by trips around Europe, no longer missing weddings just because they were in countries that we couldn't go to, and finally exploring the world, the way that we had always dreamed of doing. Then, the COVID-19 pandemic happened.

First, it felt like a faraway problem. Live bats in Wuhan, a disease so exotic that, according to media reports, it could only be traced to strange foods and grotesque open-air markets. Soon, it reached more familiar locations: the Lombardy region of Italy, no longer the capital of La Dolce Vita as a virus ravaged through its neighborhoods. A cruise ship in Oakland, California, where everyone was quarantined in their cabins and the captain refused to dock. Suddenly we were furiously washing our hands in London, and I said goodbye to my colleagues, thinking that we would all see one another in two weeks. Later, we laughed at ourselves.

Salem and I had lived in war zones together, but we had never lived through anything quite like this. Bodily threats on a front line are tangible: a bullet whizzing dangerously close to your ear, a suicide bomber who explodes in flames. Now, the threat was invisible, harmless for some, deadly for others.

As borders began to close and international travel ground to a halt, I started to wonder if this would be the moment that people finally stopped taking their freedom of movement for granted. Suddenly, couples who had never felt the pressure of borders closing in around them before had to decide if they would spend the pandemic together or apart. Quarantining together became the ultimate expression of commitment. Would a couple grow closer together over lockdown, or would they crack under the pressure of having nowhere else to go?

Borders were no longer the boundaries of nation states, but of neighborhoods, delineating where it was permissible to travel and where was not. No one liked being told what to do, but some people took it better than others. As per usual, Salem had the perfect response. "Some people really need to experience jail," he said as we settled in for another quiet night of perplexedly watching the news, secretly entertained that suddenly everyone was experiencing the restrictions that we knew were familiar for so many.

The pandemic might have slowed the world down for a privileged few, but it did not stop wars from forcing people to flee their homes, or thugs shaking people down in their own countries. People living in refugee camps now had to worry about the ways that a virus could infect them in cramped living quarters. Anyone in a detention center was acutely aware that they were confined in a jail with an invisible threat that could kill them. Even immigrants in less dire circumstances were more likely to be frontline workers, facing the pandemic every day to keep food on their tables, and on the tables of more privileged families, as well. Others found that their work as housekeepers or restaurant workers dried up, and wondered how they were going to make ends meet. Those without papers were not eligible for the furlough schemes and stimulus packages that kept others afloat.

Limiting travel might have made sense to contain the pandemic, but it was also used as an excuse to crack down on people who needed to cross borders the most. In the United Kingdom, the Home Office slowed down processing of asylum claims, and the days of someone like Salem hearing positive news in only three months were over. Meanwhile in the United States, Trump invoked Title 42, an obscure provision, originally a part of the Public Health Service Act of 1944, that gives immigration authorities the power to expel asylum-seekers before they have even stated their case, out of concern for public health and contagious diseases. Even before the pandemic, anyone asking for asylum in the United States had to wait in Mexico until they could make their claim, leaving many stranded in shelters along the US–Mexico border. "We've been fighting all these extreme restrictions on the border under Trump," Julia Neusner, an associate attorney at the Refugee Protection office of Human Rights First, told me, when I asked her how the pandemic changed the border for good. "But this blatant ban on asylum, summarily turning people away and expelling them, not just to Mexico, but also to other countries that they fled, is such a blatant violation of US and international refugee protection law."

When it came to the border, Biden was not able to implement as much of a change from his predecessor as he had originally promised. While he made a dramatic show of overturning the Muslim ban on his first day in office and announced a Family Reunification Task Force to reunite families who had been torn apart by Trump's "zero tolerance" policy, he maintained the Title 42 expulsions, long after travel that had been suspended because of the pandemic had resumed. For a few months, he suspended Trump's "Remain in Mexico" policy, only for the court to reinstate it. During August 2021, I visited several migrant shelters in Juárez, Mexico, where some people had been told to wait because of one policy, others had been expelled because of another. Others had just arrived, fleeing gang violence in Honduras or cartels in Mexico. For them, it didn't matter whether Trump or Biden was president. They were still stuck in limbo, unable to continue their lives in the United States, and unable to go home.

Biden has also done nothing to address families who had been torn apart by ICE, or the systems that have been separating people from one another long before the Trump era. Even though he announced a symbolic hundred-day moratorium on deportations when he assumed office, it did not take long before his administration started deporting Haitian refugees in record numbers. Despite his pledges to protect DACA recipients, DACA has been challenged in court under his watch and, in October 2022, was ruled unlawful. For many, a path to citizenship is still a dream.

Other countries are no better. The United Kingdom's Hostile Environment continues to wrap itself around people's lives, from the Windrush generation to asylum-seekers. A privileged few are able to get visas and arrive by plane to claim asylum, the way Salem did. But the vast majority of applicants—more and more of whom are then taking matters into their own hands, hiring smugglers to take them across the choppy waters of the English Channel—are being turned away. In May of 2022, UK Home Secretary Priti Patel announced a new plan to deport asylum-seekers to Rwanda, as if this were a viable alternative to the United Kingdom. Even though she has since stepped down, the Home Office is still pushing for similar alternatives to crack down on migrants crossing the English Channel.

Sending asylum-seekers to Rwanda sounds absurd, but this strategy is copied and pasted from several other policies that have become popular in recent years. In 2016, the EU-Turkey deal intentionally left people stranded in Greece. A few years later, in 2018, Trump's "Remain in Mexico" policy mimicked this, leaving people waiting in camps along the US–Mexico border, often for months or sometimes years at a time. Now, the plan to send asylum-seekers—who have trekked across Africa or the Middle East, and then Europe, and across the choppy waters of the English Channel only to be deported to Rwanda, of all places—is only the most recent example of a wealthy nation treating migration as a problem to be outsourced.

Meanwhile, the European Union—now consciously uncoupled from the United Kingdom—has continued to try to discourage people from coming, sneakily creating policies that make their borders more and more difficult to cross, and life more and more difficult for people who cross them. Originally designed to keep families together, family reunification policies now often require years of processing, leaving people stranded across continents. Sometimes people hire smugglers, only to be pushed back at sea by the coast guard boats that once rescued them.

And then, in February 2022, Russian president Vladimir Putin invaded Ukraine, and we saw an alternative reality. As more than 2 million Ukrainians were forced to flee their homes in the first two months of the war alone, countries across Europe opened their arms to them, greeting people at the border with warm food and rides to nearby cities. Politicians did not mince their words while condemning Putin's actions and journalists eschewed any sense of objectivity, as they earnestly looked into the camera and told their viewers that these refugees were different. These refugees watched Netflix, and posted photos to Instagram. These refugees were just like us.

Watching these news reports made my blood boil. It was all too similar to the logic behind the 1924 immigration quotas that prioritized "Anglo-Saxon stock" or the carefully constructed UK immigration laws that lead to the Windrush scandal. What does it mean to be "just like us," and why are some people treated as such while others are not?

But if I look at it from another perspective, it is a glimpse into a vision of the way that the world could be. A little bit of compassion—whether it is as monumental as waiving a visa requirement or as simple as opening our homes to someone in need—can save people's lives. Shortly after the invasion began, the European Union announced that Ukrainians could stay for up to three years without seeking asylum, while people across the United Kingdom coordinated with refugees over Facebook to put them up in their homes as part of a government plan to extend solidarity. Even the United States agreed to take 100,000 Ukrainians and extended Temporary Protected Status to anyone already from that country, a designation that ordinarily takes years to get approved. A world without borders may seem like a far-off fantasy. I like to think that a world with more compassion is not.

Love stories are supposed to follow a narrative arc—two people drawn toward one another, often over or in spite of a conflict that nearly breaks them, dramatically coming together in a moment that smooths the bumpy ride with the promise of a happily-ever-after for the audience. But I found that love stories about borders rarely follow this formula. Borders provide so many obstacles that there is rarely room for the kind of intimate spats and lovers' quarrels that make us human. If we dare to let them in, even for a second, we may crack under the pressure. Limbo can be so prolonged and so painful that we have to forget our expectations for how our life together is supposed to look, and create new traditions, defined by patience and perseverance. A love across borders is most often defined not by soaring music and a dramatic chase scene, but by daring to believe that we can love whomever we choose, even in a world that is divided by passports and papers.

How do we break down these borders? Sometimes it is within our control. Other times, it is not. But we start chipping away at these borders the moment we take a chance on the people that we love. It is Wala'a stepping onto a rickety boat in the pitch-black night, Ava packing up her car and leaving behind everything that she knows. It is Amal sending Mohammed a friend request after twelve years of not speaking, and Mohammed fighting relentlessly until the day that they can finally be together. Even when our lives have not been dictated by passports and papers, love guides our movements, bringing us closer to where we need to be. We explore the world to go looking for new love, but sometimes end up closer to home craving something familiar. We take a chance on a new city to follow our heart, hoping that it won't end up shattered. We move home to take care of aging family members, holding on to as much time as we can have together.

Often, these decisions are difficult. Sometimes they are expensive or involve facing a fear of the unknown. We weigh the consequences of our actions and wish that we could be in multiple places at once, even when the borders that separate us are surmountable. What happens when they are not?

During the pandemic, the rest of the world got a small taste of what it feels like to have their freedom limited. Separated from our loved ones for months on end, we learned to create closeness over WhatsApp and Zoom, but quickly realized that the two-dimensional versions of our friends and family members were nothing compared to seeing them in real life. Barricaded indoors, we created new routines to stay safe, retreating from the outside world and turning to our imaginations to dream of a better tomorrow. We dreamed of a world where we no longer had to long for the people that we loved.

Now, we have learned to live with the virus, largely because we could not live without each other. We longed to be with our families during the holidays, and celebrate weddings, births, and baptisms together. Technology kept the world going at its barest minimum, and even allowed us to transcend some of these barriers, but we craved human touch. We wanted the electricity of a first kiss with someone new, and the deep warmth of an embrace from someone we have loved for a long time. We wanted to feel alive in a world without limits.

But for many, this remains a fantasy. International travel has resumed and even grown since the pandemic, but not for people whose passports do not allow them to board planes. According to the UNHCR, there are 89.3 million people around the world who have been forcibly displaced by war and conflict, and this does not count the number of people who are separated by immigration policies or mired in something like the Windrush scandal. Yet it seems like there is little political will to change their circumstances. Waiting on decisions from family reunification policies leaves families separated for years. People languish in camps, or take matters into their own hands. Sometimes they live with the consequences of their actions for the rest of their lives.

Over the next few years, we will need to reconsider these values. As the climate crisis amplifies, more people will be uprooted from their homes, and a world that polices where they can and cannot seek refuge will become unsustainable. Policies that differentiate between a migrant and a refugee will become irrelevant, and people who never imagined that they could be displaced might find themselves in need of refuge.

Sometimes the love that finds us is not a romance, but a friendship or community that we did not know we needed. Long conversations with old friends remind us of who we are, and creating our chosen family helps us support each other through difficult times, and celebrate when it passes. It is Mona and "the family" meeting every Sunday on a park bench in Frosinone, or Richard and Marissa realizing that it is not too late to lean on one another, even though they spent so many years estranged. Even our romantic love is nourished by the communities around us. It is Karina creating the community that she craved for so long, and nourishing it as it grows. It is Rayan and Samih paying tribute to the people who brought them together, and Cecilia fighting for families to be together even when hers is not. Our world has been built on policies that privilege some and exclude others. Love is the only antidote to a divided world.

Love means not giving up on one another. It is Valentina and Lorenzo getting married to live without fear of separation, Oscar and Darwin writing one another love letters even when they didn't know if they would see each other again. It is the feeling I had in a hotel room in the Kurdish mountains when I realized that the only way that Salem and I could be together would be if I took a chance and exchanged the life I thought we would have for the unknown, and the actions that give me strength as we navigate the highs and lows of a world that is still organized by passports and papers. As I gathered these stories, I realized that most of what we are fighting for is incredibly basic. It is the right to be together, to visit our loved ones and be with our families the way that we want to be. It is the right to have children without worrying about their papers, and to make sure that our children never have to worry about living without their parents. It is about the right to fall in love with whomever we choose and nourish that love wherever in the world we feel the most like ourselves.

It is so basic that it should be a universal human right, but unfortunately it is not. Until it is, our stories will be defined by how we love in the meantime, the way that we take care of ourselves through each other, as we brace for shipwrecks and storms, with hope that someday the clouds will part and the light will shine through, letting us bask in its warmth.

As long as we are fighting for the people we love, love is all around us.

NOTES ON SOURCES

Each of these stories was constructed through a series of interviews, often over the course of several months. Some were in person, others were over Zoom, and many helped me piece together their stories through their own records.

Along with these interviews, the work of people like Cecilia Garcia and Karina Ambartsaoumian-Clough, who run the organizations Family Reunification, Not Deportation and United Stateless, was enormously influential in constructing and supporting the arguments that run throughout the book. Organizations such as the Free Migration Project, Tsuru for Solidarity, Immigrant Families Together, and Migrants of the Mediterranean were also enormously helpful for my reporting and instrumental in the development of my ideas. If you are inspired to get involved after reading this book, I encourage you to check out their work.

Piecing together my own story presented its own challenges—memories are slippery, and creating a riveting narrative out of an otherwise ordinary life inevitably means prioritizing some details over others. Friends, and of course, Salem, helped confirm and jog my memories as I put pen to paper and tried to recreate the past five years. A number of diaries I kept sporadically helped, too.

I tried provide a comprehensive view into how borders—and the rules concerning passports and papers that control them—were created, but of course, a book has a finite amount of space, so, it is more of a sampling platter of the parts of these histories that I saw as most relevant to relationships, and to the love stories that they have shaped over time. For anyone curious to learn more, I encourage you to explore some of the texts, documentaries, and other resources that influenced me as I wrote, as well as the work of historians, scholars, and archivists who have made this their life's work. It is a fascinating, infuriating, and egregiously understudied aspect of our global history.

Be Brave:

Yassin-Kassab, Robin, and Leila Al-Shami. *Burning Country: Syrians in Revolution and War.* London: Pluto Press, 2016.

Torpey, John C. *The Invention of the Passport: Surveillance, Citizenship and the State.* Cambridge University Press, 2018.

Whitman, James Q. *Hitler's American Model: The United States and the Making of Nazi Race Law.* Princeton University Press, 2017.

US State Department, *The Legacy of the M.S. St. Louis.* September 24, 2012. https://2009-2017.state.gov/s/d/former/burns/remarks/2012/198190.htm

Your Relationship or Your Country?:

Al Ahmad, Safa. *Targeting Yemen: The Fight Against Al Qaeda.* BBC News, 2019. https://www.bbc.co.uk/programmes/b0c1x5dc

Bayoumi, Moustafa. *How Does It Feel To Be A Problem?: Being Young and Arab in America.* London: Penguin Books, 2009.

Emiko Omori. *Rabbit in the Moon.* Hohokus, NJ: New Day Films, 2004.

Tsuru For Solidarity: https://tsuruforsolidarity.org

Moench, Mallory. "US Citizen's Family Was Denied Visas Under Trump's Travel Ban. Then He Died by Suicide." *NBC News,* July 28, 2018. https://www.nbcnews.com/news/us-news/u-s-citizen-s-family-was-denied-visas-under-trump-n895381

Alobahy v. Trump: https://ccrjustice.org/alobahy

No Border Can Get in the Way of Your Love

Levario, Miguel. *Militarizing the Border: When Mexicans Became the Enemy.* College Station: Texas A&M University Press, 2015.

Rosas, Ana Elizabeth. *Abrazando el Espíritu: Bracero Families Confront the US-Mexico Border.* Oakland: California University Press, 2014.

Flores, Lori. *Grounds for Dreaming: Mexican Americans, Mexican Immigrants, and the California Farmworkers Movement.* New Haven: Yale University Press, 2016.

Goodman, Adam. *The Deportation Machine: America's Long History of Expelling Immigrants.* Princeton, NJ: Princeton University Press, 2020.

Coleman, Rev. Walter L., and Elvira Arellano. *Elvira's Faith: The Grassroots Struggle for the Rights of Undocumented Families.* Chicago: Wrightwood Press, 2017.

Cuauhtémoc, César and García Hernández. *Migrating to Prison: American's Obsession with Locking Up Immigrants.* New York: The New Press, 2019.

Das, Alina. *No Justice in the Shadows: How American Criminalizes Immigrants.* NY: PublicAffairs Books, 2020.

Dunbar-Oritz, Roxanne. *Not "A Nation of Immigrants": Settler Colonialism, White Supremacy, and a History of Erasure and Exclusion.* Boston: Beacon Press. 2021.

Lindskoog, Carl. *Detain and Punish: Haitian Refugees and the Rise of the World's Largest Immigrant Detention System.* Gainesville: University of Florida Press, 2018.

Family Reunification, Not Deportation http://www.familyreunificationnotdeportation.org

No Country to Call Home

Allan, Diana, ed. *Voices of the Nakba: A Living History of Palestine.* London: Pluto Press, 2021.

Samih & Rayan's videos: https://www.facebook.com/campji

Bernstein, Richard J. "Hannah Arendt on the Stateless." *Parallax*, 11:1 (2005): 46-60. https://doi.org/10.1080/1353464052000321092

Darwish, Mahmoud. *Mural.* London: Verso Books, 2000.

Siegelberg, Mira L. *Statelessness: A Modern History.* Boston: Harvard University Press, 2020.

Poladoghly, Joe. *When the Subaltern Speaks Online: Stateless Advocacy Through the Post-Pandemic Digital Space.* University of Melbourne, Aug. 2022. https://www.statelessness.eu/updates/blog/when-subaltern-speaks-online-stateless-advocacy-through-post-pandemic-digital-space

Ambartsoumian-Clough, Karina. *Stateless.* Ignite Philly 14, 2014. https://www.youtube.com/watch?v=BrQT6f7TXsg

United Stateless:https://www.unitedstateless.org

Migrant or Refugee?

Faloyin, Dipo. *Africa Is Not a Country: Notes on a Bright Continent*. NY: W. W. Norton & Co., 2022.

Bhambra, Gurminder K. *"Open Borders": A Postcolonial Critique, Spatial Transformations*. Abingdon: Routledge, 2021.

Hayden, Sally. *My Fourth Time, We Drowned: Seeking Refuge on the World's Deadliest Migration Route*. Brooklyn: Melville House, 2022.

Rodney, Walter. *How Europe Underdeveloped Africa*. London: Verso Books, 2018.

A Hostile Environment

Hargave, Russell. *Drawbridge Britain*. London: Eyewear Publishing, 2018

Goodfellow, Maya. *Hostile Environment: How Immigrants Became Scapegoats*. London: Verso Books, 2019.

Windrush Act Crusade: https://www.thewindrushact.com

The Green Card Marriage

Wang, Lee Ann S. *"Of the Law, But Not Its Spirit": Immigration Fraud as Legal Fiction and Violence Against Asian-American Women*. UC Irvine Law Review, 3:4 (2013). https://escholarship.org/uc/item/9b04k792

Maria Lopez's Instagram page: https://www.instagram.com/ytienepapeles/?hl=en

Lorenzo Acosta's artwork: https://www.instagram.com/_art_by_zoe/

Breaking Borders

Miller, Anna Lekas. The Invisible Lines that Break Our Hearts. *Newlines Magazine*, May 28, 2021. https://newlinesmag.com/essays/the-invisible-lines-that-break-our-hearts/

ACKNOWLEDGMENTS

First, this book would not exist without the people who opened their hearts and shared their stories with me. It also would not exist without the most brilliant editor and agent to shepherd it into the world. Madeline Jones, thank you for your thought-provoking, heartfelt edits that made this book into everything it could be. I can't imagine working with anyone else, and am constantly touched by how much you and everyone at Algonquin Books approach this book's journey with so much heart, care, and curiosity.

Rach Crawford, I couldn't ask for a better agent. You believed in this book from the very beginning and fought for it until the very end. I am so grateful to you for pushing me on the proposal while I was losing my mind in quarantine. I hope this is the first of many collaborations.

As I wrote this book, I leaned on so many brilliant minds to help guide its journey. Jamila Hammami and David Bennion, in particular—your tireless work advocating for free movement for all and belief in a world with open borders leaves me in endless awe. Tania Karas, Patrick Hilsman, Sara Yasin, Erika Sánchez, Emily Kinskey, Emily and Brandon Bailey—thank you for your hospitality while I traveled around gathering these stories. Our late-night chats are unforgettable, and the love and laughter in those moments flavor the pages of this book! Sarah Giaziri, Alice Martins, Cengiz Yar, Cathy Otten, thank you for always making

Salem and me feel like we were home, even when we were in the throes of our journey. Anna Day, thank you for introducing us.

I wouldn't be able to write the way I do without conversations with brilliant friends who lovingly and patiently discussed harebrained ideas with me. Molly Crabapple, Maya Gebeily, Katarina Montgomery, Lauren Bohn, Mati Milstein, Naziha Baasiri, Annia Cielzado, Ruth Michaelson, Jesse Rosenfeld, Jared Malsin, Sally Hayden, Dalila Mujagic, Zaina Erhaim, Allie Tempus, Teresa Cotsirillos, Yusuf Sawie, Afrah Al-Thaibani, Rebecca Smith, Sarah Samee, James Rippingale—you all mean the world to me. Pamela Kerpius, thank you for sharing your Italy with me. Sarah Jaffe, you have been everything from my boss, to my friend, to my mentor and my roommate. I am so grateful for the layers of our relationship, and love and support for each other over the years. Isabel Hunter, your apartment provided what I can only describe as a birthing pool for the second half of this book.

And of course, there are a few very, very special friends who must be acknowledged. Michael Oghia, thank you for calling me at five o'clock in the morning, screaming with excitement after reading the very first draft of the first few chapters of a much, much earlier version of this book. Every writer needs a friend like you. Valentina Aragundy, in addition to being *in* the book, your amazing friendship and endless support of my work for the past ten years and then some constantly buoys me forward, and always reminds me why journalism is important. Mahmoud Nowara, this book would not exist without you, or without us. I am forever grateful for our friendship. You are, and always will be, my weirdest shit.

My parents, Mark Miller and Tina Lekas Miller. You never questioned my wildest dreams to become a writer, and only slightly questioned my need to report from active conflict zones, which, in retrospect, was entirely appropriate. You are the kindest and most supportive people I know. Thank you for always being there for me and Salem, even when we live far away (for now).

Last but not least, Salem. I cannot imagine a more supportive partner. You have always been this book's most extreme, over-the-top, larger-than-life champion, even when being married to an author must have been an absolute pain in the ass. While I was tearing my hair out hyperventilating at my computer, you kept me fed and watered like a small and temperamental houseplant. You listened to me scream about borders and white supremacy, and then proceeded to scream at other people about borders and white supremacy, while telling them they should buy my book, even though it was half-written at the time. When I was off traveling, ironically spending time away from you to gather the stories of other people like us, you kept our little household going and became the greatest cat daddy ever in a way that I can only describe as making my ovaries pang.

Loving you has made me into the woman I am today, and the writer I have always dreamed of being. I am so grateful that I get to go through life with you at my side and cannot wait to see where our story takes us next.